CHESAPEAKE OUTDOORS

Tales of Fishing and Hunting on Maryland's Eastern Shore ...and Beyond

By
KEITH WALTERS

PUBLISHED BY:
AERIE HOUSE
P. O. BOX 279
BOZMAN, MD 21612-0279

BOOK DESIGN AND EDITING BY:
CAROLE WALTERS

CHESAPEAKE OUTDOORS

Tales of Fishing and Hunting on
Maryland's Eastern Shore and Beyond

Copyright© 2003 by Keith Walters

All rights reserved.
No part of this book may be reproduced in any form or by any electronic or mechanical means, including information and retrieval systems, without permission from the author or publisher, except by a reviewer who may quote brief passages in a review.

First Printing

Edited by Carole Walters

Published in the United States of America by
KEITH WALTERS LLC, AERIE HOUSE DIVISION,
P. O. Box 279, Bozman, Maryland 21612-0279.

Library of Congress Control Number 2003114300

ISBN 0-9627039-4-X

For my wife of 48 years,
Jean Carole Walters

For she is still,
And will ever be—

My ray of sunshine
On the cloudiest day,

My brightest beacon
In the darkest night.

ACKNOWLEDGEMENTS

First and foremost, credit for this book must go to my wife, Carole. She organized many years of projects and stacks of illegible field notes. She helped me gather and sift through hundreds of features and short stories to find the humor, adventure, and nostalgia we felt would complement the **Chesapeake Outdoors** title. Carole not only designed the layout of this book and edited my stories, but yanked me back on track whenever I went off on some tangent. She took care of all the business of producing a book while I did the writing. Without a partner like Carole, there would be no **Chesapeake Outdoors** book.

Second, there are so many people who helped me along the way by sharing fishing, hunting, and dog stories. I thank you for your help. If your name does not appear here, I thank you anyway. You will be in my next fishing opus, absolutely guaranteed.

Third, thanks to **Attraction, Bassin, Chesapeake Bay Magazine, Coastal Fisherman, Gun Dog, Maryland Magazine, The Fisherman, The Mariner, The Star Democrat, Salt Water Sportsman, and Wildfowl** for permission to use portions of material I originally wrote for them.

Last but not least, many thanks to the Fourth Estate—the press—most particularly the other outdoor writers who have helped me every step of the way. I hope that some day, in some way I can pay it all back.

TABLE OF CONTENTS

FISHING

HUNTING

INTRODUCTION —————————

Some of my favorite stories are included in this book. They have been edited and rewritten from past articles, columns, and experiences that we thought, for the most part, had a light side to them. I want to share the good times I've had on the Bay and afield, plus a few fun stories further afield.

Those who read our *Chesapeake Boogaloo: Fish Scales, Game Trails, and Puppy Dog Tales* book may find a few of our golden oldies, but that's it. The rest are new, and if I may say so, great stuff.

Hunting and fishing on the Delmarva Peninsula is about the best you'll find anywhere. Sometimes we have a busted trip or two, but the ambience and the experiences are important, too.

This may also be asked about fishing: "Is the kill the most imperative part of the hunt, or is the important part the hunt itself?" The answer is up to the hunter or angler, but the older I get, the less important is the game bag or creel. I love the chase and the outdoors, the rest is the icing on our outdoors cake. Or maybe a great game meal.

The purpose of this to me is to bring the reader into the story, to introduce some of my offbeat companions, and some sane ones, too. I want to share the good times and the off-the-wall adventures, both hunting and fishing this great island of ours, and hope you enjoy the reading as much as I enjoyed the writing and recalling.

Outdoors writing is a dirty, dangerous, minimum-wage job, but someone has to do it. Dodging flying sinkers and waving gun barrels, or dealing with Lab retrievers with an attitude is risky stuff. Avoid it if you can, but try to enjoy it if you can't.

Most of the material is factual, presented in an easy-to-read fictional style. There is also fiction presented as fact, something every angler understands. The reader can decide which is which.

Enjoy!!!

—

SHARPENING PENCILS ────────

Several years ago, humor writer Art Buchwald gave a motivational talk to our local writers club, something he says he normally "gets big money to do." However, his sister-in-law was a club member, and she told him "If you don't give the talk, you'll find a dead horse in your bed."

Buchwald didn't give away his secrets about writing his style of humor, because there is only room enough for one Art Buchwald in this world. He talked about all the things we writers do to keep from writing—he called these non-productive peripheral activities "Sharpening Pencils." He said the thing to do is sit down and write something, anything, just to get the juices flowing.

Writers know what he means. I asked another writer at a recent party, "How's the book coming?" "That DAMN BOOK," he said with some additional emphasis on the DAMN. It turns out that he and a good friend agreed to do a fishing book together, and it required an awesome amount of travel and research. Somewhere in mid-stream they both ran out of steam, and the thing wasn't fun any more. They were fished out.

Me too. I've been working on a major article for about a year and a half. Every time I got near the end, some new crisis occurred in the subject material and I had to wait another month or two for it to be resolved. It got so I hated that %#$@ article, having to re-interview the people repeatedly, and even the &^$# keyboard kept sneering at me and accusing me of sloth. I finally finished the piece, and called my editor, who said he'd take a look at it, but he didn't have room for it for a while, anyway. At least the DAMN thing is DONE. But, I was burned out.

So, to take Buchwald's advice and get some productive juices flowing again, I put some thoughts on paper about the difficulty of man/woman communications. At times I think we're from different planets, and how that would be a good title for a book.

"Bring up the square pillow from the sofa in the rec room," Carole called down to me in the Dungeon (where I write). Carole was recovering from some surgery and wanted a pillow to sit on for a long ride somewhere.

"You sure you don't want the bigger one, the one we use in the boat?" I answered.

"No, I want the square one."

"You sure it's big enough?" Oh, crap, I thought. She may misinterpret that, being she's a woman and all.

"That's enough out of you, MISTER!" she hollered. I'm rarely respectfully called "mister," so I thought I had shown proper concern and said something good, right?

 Wrong. Icicle City.

"What's the matter?" I innocently asked later. Icy stare.

"You know."

"Don't know, unless you thought I insinuated that your posterior was too large for that square pillow, and that wasn't the case, anyway. I did not mean that your behind was too large for the pillow, but that the pillow was much too small, and I was concerned that you'd slide off."

Icy stare. Wrong again?

I felt like the chap who said something in the woods where no woman heard him. Was he still wrong?

•••••••••••

Later, after the dust cleared and my wounds healed, I was whacking away at the keyboard again.

"What are you doing down there?" Carole called through the bars on my cell.

"Sharpening pencils" I replied.

FISHING AND MARRIAGE

Carole and Keith celebrate their 48th wedding anniversary.

It may have been a harbinger of good fishing things to come: After Carole and I married years ago in a small church in Glen Burnie, our first night was spent in the Rod and Reel Motel on Kent Island. Our first dinner as a married couple was at the Fisherman's Inn. So, guess what's coming here.

Carole and I went together for about six months when, one February 14, (Valentine's Day) we had a date. It was snowing hard. We went out anyway. I was following a snowplow in my old 1950 Pontiac when I told her I had a present for her in the glove compartment. She took out the box and opened it. It was an engagement ring. We set the date, June 17. Ever since, we've celebrated two anniversaries, engagement and marriage, some of which I've missed because I absolutely had to go fishing. Why?

Because soon after our nuptials, Carole's cousin, Jimmy Tracey, took me fishing. Wow! What fun! I fished a lot after that. So much that Carole and I had some long and serious discussions about why anyone who fished as much as I did should be married.

We spent our honeymoon at the old Snow Hill Inn in Snow Hill which was owned by her aunt and uncle, Edee and Erf Barnes. We spent a lot of time crabbing with hand lines from the pier at Public Landing on Chincoteague Bay. Uncle Erf, an avid bass fisherman, took me fishing on the Pocomoke River which is still one of the prettiest and bassiest tributaries of Chesapeake Bay. By then, I was hooked in more ways than one—on Carole, and on fishing, in that order. In over four decades, that has not changed.

Some newlyweds may question why and how I was able to go fishing on so many anniversaries.

First, Carole likes to fish. We've spent many vacations that revolved around stories I read about great fishing in remote places like Marco Island, Florida. Long ago, Marco Island was a marsh on the edge of the Everglades with a fish camp perched on a tidal river. One fishing guide worked the waters with great success. I got a flu bug and didn't get to wield a rod on that trip. Now, Marco Island has been developed beyond belief, with beautiful homes on canals and shopping centers. It can still be good fishing, but the competition is fierce.

Our first home was on the Little Magothy River in Cape St. Claire, because we wanted to be on the water (read good fishing). I fished two or three evenings a week and once or twice on weekends. Saturday mornings I played a game: Snuggling up to Carole, I gave her a big toothy smile.

"Why don't you go fishing?" She'd say. "Really?" "Geddoutdahere!" It took me three minutes flat to get my gear and jump in the boat.

After work on one anniversary, I noticed the tide was high and the wind was minimal. Rockfish had been hitting popping plugs along the shoreline and live eels at the Bay Bridge (one bridge then). OK, guys, now comes some advice.

THE LAB RETRIEVER PLOY

Ever notice a Labrador retriever when it's really sad? Tail down, ears down, eyes sad. Copy that. Look wistfully at your boat. Drool.

SHOCK AND AWE

Shock: "Why don't you go fishing? It's really pretty out there."

"Aw, really?" Two minutes later you can be in the boat.

S and A takes practice, but once perfected, it works every time. See, men are naturally good actors, and women are always concerned about our welfare.

THE BUDDY ON THE PHONE BIT

Phone rings. "Yeah, Harry, what's happening? You say the fishing is great at Harker's Island? Big king mackerel? Wow! You say you usually go down to North Carolina for about a week? When? Oh, oh, Harry, I can't go THAT day—it's our (your numbers here) anniversary. Too bad. Wait—why don't we take our wives?"

Some mumbling from the kitchen.

"Not a bad idea, huh? Rats? What rats? In the room? Wow! That big, eh?"

From the kitchen: "Why don't YOU go, honey? I'll pack for you!"

The really fun part is when you return home with a half-dozen king mackerel to prepare for the freezer (read "deer, rabbits, Canada geese," etc.).

"Look what I caught, honey! Enough king mackerel and cobia to last the rest of the year. It'll only take us four or five hours and we'll have it all packaged."

"WE! What WE?" There might be some discussion about the division of duties, like, "You caught the %$^#@ things, you clean 'em." This situation takes tact and diplomacy, since it's already about midnight when you got home (had to stop for supper, you know), and sleepy to boot.

"But, think about all the money we'll save on food. And, you LIKE fish." No use mentioning the trip set you (and her if she knew it) back about a grand, which would buy a lot of chow, even in a gourmet restaurant.

NEW TOYS

Low-key subterfuge and duplicity come in handy to justify (or sneak in) that new shotgun or fishing reel, too. One chap I knew overimbibed at a fund-raising dinner and wound up with a high-end engraved over and under 12 gauge shotgun. He wasn't so plastered that he stalked right into the house and showed honeypie his new collectible fowling piece. Oh, no. He wrapped it in a tarp and hid it in the wood pile. There are better times to approach the subject about needing a new shotgun than when you stay out half the night and come home snockered.

CEREBRAL ATROPHY

Temporary amnesia can help when it comes to that special hunting or fishing trip that (unfortunately) falls on an anniversary.

"What are you doing?"

"Getting some big game tackle together."

"Why?"

"Harry's going to Costa Rica for sailfish."

"You're loaning him some tackle? How nice."

"Well, not exactly. I have to take my own gear. I'm going, too."

"I didn't know about this trip."

"Oh, I must have forgotten to tell you. I leave tomorrow at 5 a.m."

"Do you know what tomorrow is?"

"Um, let me think – Thursday?"

"Our ANNIVERSARY!"

"Really? I must have forgotten about that. I'll stay home, but I'll lose my deposit."

Women can say things in a way that could freeze boiling water when they're upset. Try to ignore her snarl and clenched teeth when she says, "Go ahead! Go fishing. I have plenty of housework to do here. Yard to mow, six kids to feed and diaper. I'll have a LOT of fun."

"Gee, I'm really happy that you'll have a good time while I'm gone."

LOSE ONE OCCASIONALLY

"Who was that on the phone?"

"Jim Price wants me to go to the Power Plant tomorrow for some catch and release rockfishing. Gonna be a pretty day, warm, not much wind."

"You know we're having company for dinner tomorrow! And I need your help."

"Oh, yeah. I forgot." (Reread the amnesia part, above).

Some heavy-duty pouting here. Lots of icy silence.

"Oh, heck, I'll call him and beg off. Doesn't mean anything to me, anyway. I have lots of chances to go FISHING."

"OKAY."

So, I called Jim and rescheduled for the day after. No problem. On the scale of smoochie points, I scored 100. I even peeled potatoes the next day, did KP, and ran all sorts of errands. I'm a really good guy, you know.

Like the old song about poker says, "You gotta know when to hold 'em, and know when to fold 'em."

Carole and I just celebrated our 48th wedding anniversary.

The bottom line for you newlywed guys? If you want longevity in marriage, fish a lot. Take it from an old-timer.

● ● ● ● ● ● ● ● ● ● ● ● ● ● ● ● ●

A wealthy man of my acquaintance decorates his flounder-fishing rigs with real pearls. "Does Amanda (not her real name to prevent lawsuits) know you're using her good pearls?" I asked.

"Not her GOOD ones. I got these at the Jackie Onassis auction." my friend said. "Only cost me $475." Lucky flounder!

SPORTSMAN'S PARADISE

Those of us who live here know we're lucky. The Eastern Shore (always capitalized), when compared to the western shore (never capitalized), is a Sportsman's Paradise.

Every year, folks from the western shore (ws) come here to the Eastern Shore (ES) to attend The Waterfowl Festival®, and every year some who have seen the beauty and outdoorsy potential of the place, vow to come back. Some never leave. That's what happened to this writer. When I started to grow webbed feet from hunting in the swamps, I knew I had to return.

Carole and I came to the ES to visit with her aunt and uncle, the late Edee and Erf Barnes, who, in the 1960s, managed the Miles River Yacht Club. Edee and Erf were gregarious folks, and by the time we'd made a few visits to them, the Barnes had introduced us to a lot of locals. We already knew about the hunting, fishing, and beautiful ambience, and we vowed to return upon retirement. We did that in 1979, and built a new home here on Broad Creek in 1981. By all local standards, we are still, even now, considered "come-heres" as the late Bill Perry frequently called us. He was joking, of course. I think.

Waterfowl Festival past presidents, Bill Perry and Lou Satchell.

The late Bill Perry, Festival Co-Founder, got me involved in The Waterfowl Festival back then. I had retired from NASA as a photo supervisor, and the Festival suddenly needed a coordinator for the photography exhibit. One evening, after a Festival Board meeting, he called me and said, "You're on the Festival Board, what do you think of them apples?" I was taken aback slightly, not knowing what he/they wanted me to do. Well, then-President Scott Beatty said he'd like to make the Festival's Photography Exhibit more national in nature (bad pun). So, Carole and I recruited nationally-known outdoors photographers like George Harrison, Gary Zahm, Scott Nielsen, and many others of national stature.

It was a fun job, and in my naivete, I didn't know then that Festival Board membership is a job many "come-heres' would kill for. The Festival has over 1000 volunteers, and the job-advancement ladder is short and steep. Two years in my photo-exhibit job was labor-intensive, so please respect and honor those who fill board positions—and the volunteers! A board job is almost a full-time position. It was for me. But, we made wonderful friends by doing that job.

●●●●●●●●●●●●●●●

To carry on the thought about being a Sportsman's Paradise, I'd like to explain a few of the outdoors opportunities that exist here. First, come-heres (like me) must accept the premise that the ES is an island. Think about it; we are completely surrounded by water. With the Chesapeake Bay, Delaware Bay, and Atlantic Ocean bounding us on several sides, we are only connected to what some call "civilization" by bridges: the Chesapeake Bay Bridge Tunnel (CBBT) to the south, two Chesapeake Bay Bridges to the west, and a bridge across the C&D Canal at Chesapeake City on the north. We actually live on an island, and are damn happy about that. Our rustic environment separates us from urban noise, pollution, heavy traffic (except for the %&$#@ "Reach the Beach" bunch in the summer), and stress. Have you ever seen a stressed-out waterman? Or find a Type A personality in someone who has retired here?

We have some of the best fishing, hunting, and also some of the greatest non-consumptive outdoors activities one could want. First, the fishing. Look at the map. We are completely surrounded by water. We have ocean angling for tuna, king mackerel, white marlin, black sea bass, ling, and the list goes on.

Down Virginia way, we have huge striped bass around the CBBT right now (on light tackle), cobia, red and black drum of prodigious proportions, and smaller gamefish like yellowfin trout, summer flounder, spotted seatrout, humongous bluefish, Spanish mackerel, and smaller game like white and yellow perch, all in narrow creeks so pristine you'd think the original Indians had just left the place without a trace.

Within a short run from local rivers here on the ES of Maryland, all the fish mentioned above for Virginia are available, plus a few that show up here every year like sheepshead and other salty dwellers from down south. A 35-pound female mahi-mahi was caught in a pound net off Tilghman Island in mid-summer, sparking the speculation that one could troll weed lines off that same ES island and catch ocean-running gamesters.

Chris Knauss, Chuck Prahl, and Captain Mike Murphy
with their catch: Trout, bluefish, and stripers.

Light tackle anglers catch stripers and bluefish here on spinning, levelwind, and fly-fishing gear right here in local rivers all summer. Structure is important, and rocky shorelines are best. We have both. Shallow-running lures like the Red Fin are re-rigged with two single hooks instead of two trebles, and most fish are released. Who needs more than two stripers a day to eat, anyway?

In autumn, outdoorsy shoreline property owners have big decisions to make! Should I go fishing for big stripers on light tackle, or should I brush my duck or goose blind? What about muzzleloader deer? Or bow hunting for the same over-abundant species? Small game hunters have a choice of 20-gauge targets like mourning doves, squirrels, rabbits, and some even save up their Hevi-Shot 20-gauge loads for ducks and geese. Sea duck hunting, combined with a light-tackle, deep-jigging trip for late fall stripers, is called "Cast and Blast."

If shooting from a boat in the Bay that is rolling, pitching, and yawing at the same time, hitting a feathered buzz bomb of a sea duck is not all that easy. Once, when seaducking with Captain Norm Haddaway, I hit the third seaduck in a string. "Nice shot, Keith," he hollered over the noise of a 20-knot wind. "Nothing to it," I replied, but I didn't tell Norm I was leading the FIRST bird in the string an ES mile!

Hunting farms have been at a premium. Several of my friends have places that hold ducks, Canada geese, deer, doves, and a lot of small game. One farm was configured for hunting before my friend bought it, with ponds and irrigation systems already in place. Many of the best places have been divided for waterfront lots. Our place was part of a large farm, and our piece of it is almost nine acres. I have a hedgerow blind for geese, a dock out front for my boat and two summertime crab pots. Deer overrun the place, drinking from our pond at dusk, and making our farmer miserable when they crop off soybean plants only an inch high.

If one wants to see pristine waterfront up close, rent a canoe or kayak. They can be found through local kayak retailers. In Talbot

County, you can paddle along waterfront that is much the same as the American Indians left it. In Dorchester County, the MD-DNR has dedicated water trails through the marsh where one can see all manner of waterfowl, eagles and hawks, up close and personal. Bird watchers love these trips.

There is a lot to be said for the ES ambience. There is so much to do and see here, one can't live long enough to do it all.

We heard that Eastern Shoremen were clannish and wouldn't accept us. Not so. I think it's all in the way you approach the locals—as equals. My first experience was when the late Poodle McQuay approached me at the Bozman Store years ago, held out a hand as big as a ham, and said, "Hi, I'm Poodle McQuay, and I have a boat just like that." He was talking about the 20-foot Mako I had on a trailer as I gassed up at the store. He later went fishing with me, and showed me "ups and downs" (uneven bottom) where fish could be caught.

Captain Mike Haddaway, a retired State Trooper and charterboat captain, marked charts for me showing the best places in Broad Creek to catch rockfish. Captain Henry Gootee of Golden Hill in south Dorchester, marked charts for a group of interested anglers at a fishing club meeting. See if THAT would happen on the ws!

The Waterfowl Festival in Talbot County and the Grand National Waterfowl Association in Dorchester County south of here, are great events that draw many outdoors folks to the area. They are in the phone book if visitors want to know more. But, they are both wonderful places to meet locals and come-heres alike, and find out why this place can be called a "Sportsman's Paradise."

I know Carole and I will always be "come-heres," but I'm really thankful that we "came here!"

• • • • • • • • • • • • • • • • • • •

TRUCK FISHING

On these first pretty spring days before the boat is overboard, the fishing itch begins its incessant agitation. Jim Walker and I have a way of getting out fishing with a minimum of effort. We call it "truck fishing."

We load a pickup or Suburban with some light spinning gear and perch-type rigs, lunch (naturally, anyone who is as concerned as we are about keeping our stomachs happy considers this first), and stop for bloodworms or minnows for bait, and head for lower Dorchester County.

When we stopped at Tommy's Sporting goods in Cambridge for some skinny minnies (they are better for perch than big, fat ones), Chuck Prahl told us he was on his way back from a successful outing at the Power Plant on the western shore, heading toward the Taylor's Island Campground launch ramp when he saw huge stripers breaking in mid-Bay under a flock of frantic gannets. "We caught [and released] rock from 5 to 8 pounds all morning," he said. "But the breaking fish were much bigger. We caught them up to 30 pounds on bucktails and jigs."

While Jim and I digested this information, we were heading down Aireys Road toward Drawbridge. But, it was exposed to a 20-knot north wind, which lowered the comfort level of the clear 57-degree day quite a bit. We didn't stop at Drawbridge, but turned off on Griffith Neck Road for a quarter mile or so to the "pipes." Here, twin culverts carry tidal water under the road, and we have done well here before.

As soon as we were set up with minnows suspended about 30 inches under our bobbers, I caught two keeper white perch in a row. We thought we were in high cotton, that we had come to the right place first. The wind was at our backs, the fish were biting. Well, that was the last fish we caught. Jim had a lot of bites on his minnow, but couldn't set the hook. He even examined his hook closely, but it was OK.

Jim lost a nice largemouth bass when it broke his line right near the bank. How big was it? It can be as big as he wants, since no one saw it. I'd guess 5 pounds, but he'd say bigger, much bigger. He scrambled down the bank to get his loose bobber, which had slipped off his line, and which the wind thoughtfully brought to shore.

On the way to our next "hot spot" Jim told me about the summer he spent between his junior and senior high school years, scraping crabs with Bobby Ewell, Jr. of Smith Island. Bobby had broken his arm and needed help winding in [by hand] the crab scrape. Now they have hydraulic winches to do that job. "I'll give you three weeks until you get used to it," Ewell told Jim. He slowed the boat for that length of time. Jim stayed with Bobby's parents, Robert Ewell, Sr., and his wife Ann, who's table was set with all manner of chow. By the time Jim went home, he had gained weight and built a lot of arm muscle.

They caught hard, soft, and peeler crabs, and Jim says they didn't harm the abundant grasses because the scrape had skids to hold it off the bottom several inches. "We'd stay out of that area for two weeks and when we came back the grass had grown back. The water was clear then."

Jim fell asleep during a church sermon one Sunday. The preacher said, "I guess he went to Crisfield drinking with the boys last night." Everyone laughed.

We went back up Steels Neck Road to New Bridge on the "Chick," or Chicamacomico River. Jim caught several fish from the bridge, his partner caught naught. We met Bob Fagan of Arbutus, who had his new 16-foot War Eagle aluminum hull in tow, powered by a shiny new 15 hp Mercury outboard. He had really rigged out his new boat for one-man small river fishing. A bracket on the bow held an electric motor. His van was outfitted inside for one-man camping, though he usually stays with a friend in Cambridge on his fishing forays. He wasn't about to put his boat overboard in that high wind. I told Bob I had fished the Chick with Jerry Gore who had a fish camp on the river. We caught some really nice bass on Minus-1 plugs that run shallow over the grass. Bob showed Jim and I photographs of bass up to 8 pounds that he caught in the Chick. He was a bit fuzzy about exactly where they were caught. He releases everything after a photo session. His favorite lure is a $1.79 chartreuse spinnerbait.

That's the thing about Dorchester bridge fishing. If the fish aren't biting, it becomes a social event, with each angler's stories topping the last one.

At our next stop, another set of pipes, I heard Jim crashing through the reeds. "$%$#@ cable," he said poetically. Then, "&^&%$ reeds!" "What are you doing?" I asked. "Cussing my way through the reeds" he said. It worked. He made it.

"Can I use your fishing towel in the truck?" I asked. I had some fish slime on my hands from all the crappie I'd been catching.

"Sure, that's what it's for," Jim answered.

"Well," I ventured, it doesn't look like YOU'RE going to use it anytime soon."

"I use my trousers," bachelor Jim answered.

And that's how it goes on an average trip of the Eternal Optimists Fishing Club.

Jim Walker unhooks a yellow perch in the reeds.

FISHINGUS INTERRUPTUS

Oh, yes, my spell-checker had conniptions over that title. It was meant to convey to the angling literati that the contemplative and intentionally solitary sport of angling can often be interrupted by sometimes well-meaning, but incredibly stupid people wielding big and/or unyielding watercraft. Let me illustrate:

I'd like to go back 35 or 40 years to a time before the DNR, watermen, and legislators began actively managing rockfish (actually, when stripers were incredibly abundant).

Carole and I enjoyed quietly fishing along the shorelines of Gibson Island and other spots within easy reach of our home on the Little Magothy River in Cape St. Claire on the western shore. Our method of catching stripers was to drift quietly along on shallow water near the shore and cast surface popping plugs in hopes rockfish up to 25 pounds or so would pounce on our lures, and that happened more often than not. Smaller rock in the 3 to 5-pound range were everywhere we fished back then.

One morning we happened to see a friend, Jimmy Tracey, in his boat anchored near a favorite hot spot. He was catching rockfish on poppers. We laid off a bit away and watched. He waved us in, and we anchored not far from him. He pointed to the productive spot, which was no bigger than a bathtub. It was actually a sandstone outcropping that was only a foot or so above the sandy bottom, but that small structure held numerous stripers.

We'd usually stop casting when another boat came past, headed to the Bay Bridge (one bridge back then). Unfortunately, Carole had a fish on when one angler roared past, and he spun around on a dime and came closer to us than we considered polite. He started casting to what he thought was the hot spot. We stopped fishing and watched, albeit with some evident hostility.

Finally, Jimmy had enough of this chap's lack of consideration. He hollered, "Why doncha go down to the Bay Bridge with all them other nuts?" The interloper jammed his throttle to the firewall and roared around in a circle in our hot spot and left—for the Bay Bridge, naturally.

We went back to casting and, miraculously, caught a few more fish. Amazing. The fish had enough couth to stay put, in spite of the inconsiderate actions of the interloper.

Another event of that era was explained to me by a co-worker. He was anchored not far from the shoreline in a quiet cove off the Severn River near Annapolis, fishing with a bobber and minnows for yellow and white perch when a couple of hoodlums water-skied between him and the bank. So, he hollered at them. That was the invitation they needed to come back and do it again, but this time he tossed an oar between the ski boat and the skier, which caused some skinned shins, and raised the possibility that the next pass might cause some real damage. They left.

When bluefish were abundant in local Eastern Shore rivers a few years ago, Mark Galasso and I were fishing with Jack Wiley on his boat in the Miles River near St. Michaels, and lost the school of fish. At that time, we trolled surface popping plugs to re-locate the fish. This time they were near buoy #2 at the entrance to St. Michaels Harbor. Near the buoy, we stopped to cast our plugs. The problem was that every sailboat coming out of the harbor needed to come so close to that buoy they could read its serial number, or leave some buoy paint on their hull, so we had to move frequently. Finally, we gave up.

Sailboaters are not the only species that love to interrupt people fishing. Powerboats the size of the state's research vessel, Aquarius, have changed our angling plans many times. Hey, a dipstick is a dipstick, no matter what he drives. It's often road rage transferred to the water, and seemingly, the more horsepower they have the less sense.

Carole and I were drifting for flounder on Cook Point Bar in our 22-foot walkaround cuddy, certainly a large enough boat to be seen miles away on a clear day, when we noticed a large state vessel approaching at a speed unhelpful to anglers drifting along and not under power. Jim Walker was drifting nearby in his boat.

It was obvious the large vessel was not changing course for buoy #10 in the mouth of the Choptank River, even to politely give a wide berth to drifting fishing boats. It was probably on autopilot. I saw someone on the bridge who could have steered the boat around us.

As the boat came closer, Carole got nervous and jumped for our helm, started the engine, and jammed it into gear to avoid the unrelenting vessel. I told her I thought he was going to miss us, thinking no one in his right mind would want to be responsible for crashing through a drifting fishing boat. Wrong! In retrospect, he would have hit us amidships. Walker was about 50 yards away. He agreed. Carole and I, and Walker, rode out the huge wake he caused. I wrote a letter to the boat's manager, who wrote back saying he was aboard and never saw the event I described. That unfeeling and unapologetic replay made him - in my mind - as stupid and loutish as the boat's captain. Better to run over someone than take the boat out of autopilot and avoid fishing boats. Incredible.

Recently, Jim Walker and I were again drifting for flounder in about the same location. (I'll never learn). The wind and current were moving in the same direction, so we had a good drift. We noticed a Chinese junk-looking sailboat with square red sails coming right at us, but it was at least a couple of miles away, and we figured its captain could certainly change course slightly and sail aft of us. Wrong. Our drift put us in his unrelenting path. He periodically peeked around some junk on the junk to see where he was going. Jim was getting nervous: "That somebitch is gonna hit us!"

I jumped to the wheel, started the engine (good thing it started), and quickly moved off 50 feet or so. He went past just off our stern. I managed to get a photograph or two. He would have cut us in two.

Jim and I used our most colorful language to describe his idiocy, and I politely asked him if he'd lost his %$#@% steering. He said, "No," and went past in serene, but I think, stupid, bliss.

"That somebitch woulda hit us," Jim explained. He was preaching to the choir. I knew it. The junk continued toward the spot-fishing fleet, and we kept an eye on him in case we needed to radio those anglers to be on the lookout.

I'm really not picking on sailboaters, honest. I remember having trollers come through our chum lines - right off our stern - on the dumping grounds in the 1960s. And, just recently, we were (again) flounder drifting near Buoy #9 in the False Channel that leads out of the Choptank when a go-boat came roaring past so close I could see the driver's sneer. That buoy is thought to be the "turn buoy" for boaters heading up the bay. We waved at him in a fashion that didn't show all our fingers. He waved back as he charged through a thick field of crab pot buoys.

I don't know why, but anglers seem to attract all the nutty boat drivers, sort of like moths to a flame. A friend was anchored over a pile of rocks locally called "The Icebreaker" when an arrogant sailboater wanted him to move. My friend tried to explain about the rockpile, but the captain wasn't having any of this dumb angler's explanation. "I see that buoy," he said, "It marks the channel, and I want you to move so I can get through." So my buddy upped anchor and moved, whereupon the captain ran up on the rocks. Then, he asked my buddy to pull him off. What would you do in a case like that? That's what he did.

Most recently, I was a guest on Buddy and Bud Harrison's charterboat out of Tilghman Island. We already had our limit of rockfish and the pair of captains decided to try for some hardheads on "France" in the Choptank River.

We were drifting along, motors off, having a great time talking to honored guest, Brooks Robinson, after whom the boat, "Brooks Hooks," and Bud's son, Brooks, were named. You know what happened next; a sailboat, no one at the helm, was headed right at us, most likely on autopilot. It was some distance away, but its course was not changing enough to miss us. After all, a 48x15 charterboat is hard to miss seeing, if you're at the wheel and paying attention. We started yelling and the sailor came up out of the cabin and said, "Oh, I didn't see you." Unbelievable.

Sailboat off the stern of the "Brooks Hooks."

Unfortunately, the sailboat passed 10 feet off our stern at the same time someone tossed unused half-rotten menhaden chum overboard.

It has been suggested, not by me of course, that if anglers were required to carry paintball guns, we might get a bit more space to fish uninterrupted. But, heck, I replied, that would most likely be illegal, right?

● ● ● ● ● ● ● ● ● ● ● ● ● ● ● ● ● ●

THE IDES OF MARCH

The temperature was 37 degrees on the car's thermometer as Gordon Ries and I drove to meet Chuck at the Federalsburg launch ramp.

"We must be crazy," I muttered to my companions as we sped down the Marshyhope River in Chuck Prahl's 17-foot Lund aluminum hull.

Now, Chuck's boat, groaningly on plane because his 50 hp Suzuki four-cycle outboard motor was really mad that it had to lift 600 pounds of anglers and 100 pounds of lunch, plus fishing gear up on top of the water, was now making maybe 25 knots. So, the wind chill was enough to make me glad I'd worn my waterfowling parka and insulated deerskin mittens. Gordon wore a windbreaker jacket over a plaid shirt and insulated underwear, but no gloves. He had turned an interesting shade of blue right up until we stopped. Chuck wore waterfowling gear plus a hood and gloves. "I knew it was going to be a cold run," he said. He faced into the wind, but Gordon and I faced the back of the boat.

Slightly before the Ides of March, local anglers get the twitchies to get out and catch something. Doesn't matter much what it is, and we don't keep much anyway, but a weatherman's promise of a nice day stirs up all kinds of phone calls, plus fishing license and bait purchases.

As we ran down the Marshyhope, we commented on the lack of faith in weather predictions. I, as a former NASA employee, noted that we've had four decades of weather satellites, and we still don't know if it's going to rain tomorrow. This day's forecast was for sun and 67 degree temps—it was 37 degrees and a low cloud hung over us most of the morning, sort of like a fog we thought would "burn off" later. Uh-uh. Didn't do that.

As we passed slowly to one side of two anglers anchored in mid-channel, Chuck asked if they had any good news. No, they answered in thick Baltimorese, all they had was some bluegills, no perch. It's easy to tell Balmer diction from Shore-talk. Them people don't say "Haven't caught neither one." (Neitherone is one word, quickly pronounced neethrwun").

About six miles from the ramp, we pulled up on a favorite edge. Chuck's Lowrance depthsounder had showed us some fish in a 20-foot hole, but we were headed to the traditional spot, whether the fish were there or not. Chuck had caught 10 perch there several days before, a harbinger of great catches to come soon.

We anchored in about 14 feet of water, between a six-foot deep flat near shore and the 20-foot deep channel. Perfect, Chuck said. This was the place.

"It'll take a few minutes to get them feeding," Chuck said. Bait fishing is somewhat like chumming, in that our three bloodworm baits emitted great odors into the moving water (if you're a fish), and gathered up a school in short order. Gordon and Chuck caught the first several fish. Chuck doesn't usually eat fish, and I had plenty of frozen filets of flounder, rockfish, and perch at home, but Gordon wanted a few fresh fish for dinner.

Chuck showed us a new landing net with a brace near the end of its handle. "It gives you more leverage when you want to net a big rockfish by yourself," Chuck explained.

"Yes," I replied, "but you don't catch any big rockfish."

"I know, but my arm isn't that strong, either," Chuck chuckled.

We baited up with small pieces of bloodworm on number 2 hooks. I used small baitholder hooks, and Chuck used gold longshank hooks made of light wire, which are easily bent and easier to extract from a perch's mouth if deeply embedded. I told Chuck all I had handy when I tied up my bottom rig was 40-pound test Stren, and asked if that would be strong enough for the fish we planned to catch.

Chuck held up a new closed-face spinning reel intended for crappie fishing. "This is my cobia rod," he said.

"Do cobia ever come up here in the Marshyhope?" I asked.

"No, but if they ever do, I'm ready for them," he replied.

One might detect that there is a good deal of jocularity between us anglers on these trips. Oh, yes. Sometimes there are long periods of inactivity before the fish finally find us. Kidding around breaks the monotony, unless some of us might get a bit testy after several hours of boredom - then the jocularity takes on an acrimonious edge.

When the perch first showed up, Gordon and Chuck started bailing them with great glee. The larger ones went on ice, but most went back overboard.

I needed the others to catch two big perch so I could make a photograph. Gordon caught a big perch at the same time Chuck was into a big fish. It was a channel catfish, and some discussion centered on their eating qualities. Chuck doesn't eat fish, and I'd never tried channel cat. Chuck said he likes the catfish they serve in some Florida restaurants. Gordon said he likes channel catfish. Chuck asked if Gordon wanted this one.

"NO!" Gordon exclaimed. Perch would be just fine, but keep only the big ones for him.

Gordon Ries and Chuck Prahl

The photograph of both anglers, each with a big perch, required some discussion. Chuck said, "Now, Gordon, you catch a big one so we can get our picture taken," as he held up a nice "picture fish."

I said, "Yeah, like it's no problem for Chuck to catch a big one." Gordon used his pliers to help get a hook out of Chuck's fish and asked if Chuck had a pair of pliers. "Yes, I do have a new pair here," patting the holster on his belt, "but they're new and I didn't want to get them dirty."I gave my rod a twitch or two, but the perch let go. I managed to get the hook away from him, I admitted to my companions.

Chuck once wrote a newspaper outdoors column, but the editor wouldn't run his picture with it. "It was scaring little children," Chuck said as he brought in a double header of perch. I commented on his perching prowess. "There is no limit to my resourcefulness," he said. "There is no limit to the damage you can do to the resource," I corrected him.

About noon, hunger pangs slowed our fishing. Rods hung over the side with baits out of the water as we munched on sandwiches and chips. We had been catching perch steadily for about two hours, and had kept enough big ones for Gordon's dinner and several of his friends' dinners as well. The sun had emerged from its hiding place behind the clouds. It was tolerably warm.

As we ran back to the launch ramp, Chuck spotted two friends in a 16-foot Apache center console hull with a 25 hp Suzuki four-stroke outboard motor, anchored near the shoreline. Mike Germany and Lenny Hyre of Cambridge caught stripers, white perch, yellow perch, bluegills, pumpkinseeds, and catfish in this spot, plus a golden shiner. The previous day, they caught crappies up to 15 inches, Lenny said. They were using two-hook bottom rigs with number 4 Aberdeen hooks dressed with 2-inch yellow Twisters. Sinkers appeared to be about an ounce. Cast them out and jig them a bit seemed to be the drill.

Back at the ramp, Gordon sacked his 18 big white perch. We guesstimated we caught about 60 or 70 perch that morning, plus a channel catfish and a mud catfish. Not a bad morning, even if it was a bit chilly.

STRIPERS ON THE FLATS

The first thing you notice as you enter Herb's Tackle Shop in North East, Maryland is a sticker that says, "Rockfish/Gamefish." That sets the tone, for this is sportfishing territory, big time.

The second thing you notice upon entering is the friendly ambiance, sort of like the warm glow emanating from a log cabin's fireplace. Tackle is Eleanore Benjamin's domain, and her use of space to display tackle is legendary, like a bobber "tree" that extends from floor to ceiling. "Good use of vertical space," she says.

An open door on your right leads to the adjoining Herb's Hair Depot, where Eleanore's husband, Herb, leads the discussion of friendly customers waiting to get clipped.

I was there to fish the Susquehanna Flats with Captain Mike Benjamin, Herb and Eleanore's son, who also cuts hair. In the tackle shop, I found a jig mold I had to have, then I wandered into the barbershop to wait for Mike and Herb to finish work.

As Herb cut a teen-ager's hair I said, "I see crew cuts are coming back. I used to have one 40 years ago." "I had one too," Herb replied, "But Eleanore said it didn't look good for a barber to have such a simple haircut. I haven't had one since."

A chap stuck his head through the door and addressed Herb: "I saw you on TV," he said. "Oh yeah," Herb said, "I'm on there all the time." Seems that the Sunpapers did a story about locals carrying dogs, mostly Lab retrievers, around in the back of their pickup trucks. A local group wants to pass an ordinance forbidding it. Then, Channel 13 called about doing a story on the situation, but Herb couldn't find anyone who would put a Lab in a pickup truck for filming.

"I had to call all around," Herb laughed, "couldn't find anyone in North East. A friend finally said he'd do it, but they only interviewed me and Mike, never asked him anything."

Our vet, the late Dr. Ed Hahn of Centreville said, "If you'd see all the injured dogs I see, you would realize it's a serious matter. I get 25 or 30 a year all busted up." Queen Anne County has an ordinance about dogs in the back of trucks, "But it isn't enforced," Dr. Hahn said. "My girls (technicians) hate it. Here, talk to Sue."

"I want to choke them," Sue said, "One guy brought in a Lab with a broken leg and we fixed it. Three months later, he brought it in again with a broken leg." "Same dog?" I asked. "Same dog." "Same leg?" "Same leg," she said.

In the barber shop, there was a bit of joshing about the way some outdoor writers embellish the truth. "Well," I replied, "Outdoor writers only need to catch one fish. We pass it around so every writer gets a picture. Then, we release it so we don't have to clean it, and adjourn to a local bar so we can make up a story to go with the pictures."

"That's about right," Herb Benjamin said, "one writer called me 'Benjamin Herbicide.'"

"Pull down the shades," Mike told Herb, "As soon as we clean up this backlog, we're going fishing!" Eleanore had a bag of lures ready for her husband and son as they went out the door.

We launched at Charlestown. Mike has the procedure down pat, and we were soon motoring down the Northeast River toward Carpenter Point in Mike's 23-foot C-Hawk center console hull powered by a 115 Evinrude. Mike had moved the console off-center for more fishing room.

There were only four boats on the Susquehanna Flats between Carpenter Point and Stump Point, and they were widely scattered. Some predictors of doom and gloom said there would be mass murder of rockfish on the Flats when several hundred boats gathered there to catch and release striped bass in this first experimental season. Last year's controlled DNR study showed a minimal mortality of stripers, nowhere near the waste Mike Benjamin once photographed: hundreds of dead and rotting rockfish in a pound net.

"It really burned me up," Mike said, "all those people down the Bay that didn't want this fishery. They didn't understand it. But, go down the Bay in mid-summer when 500 boats are chumming and dead fish are floating all over."

Big male stripers stay on the Susquehanna Flats to feed on herring, according to the biologists. When the females come up the deeper main channel off Turkey Point, the males go out and spawn with them. Then they go back on the Flats again to feed some more. "Just like a man," says my wife, Carole.

"Some of the old-time netters say that's where they always caught big cows in the spring," Herb said, "out in the deeper water, not here on the Flats." The major concern about this spring catch-and-release sport fishery was that anglers might be killing spawning cow fish, but the DNR study had disproved that. Spawning areas have current flow, the Flats has almost no current.

"Look out there," Mike said, "where are all the boats? We had more boats when this fishing was illegal!" This was a Saturday, and the "Pennsylvania Navy," so called by locals who benefit from the business brought in by Pennsylvania's trailer-boating anglers, was pretty much absent, perhaps due to dire weather predictions.

Mike caught the first striper, about a three pounder, on a 3/4-oz. shadhead jig with a barbless hook, decorated with a 7-inch Bass Assassin in Glass Shad, a rainbow color. "That's why I'm paid the big bucks," he chuckled.

I didn't get a strike on my favorite white bucktail with a 6-inch white grub, a great combination in my home river, the Choptank. I hinted around for one of Mike's lures, so he rigged me one at the end of a 30-pound test leader. Herb had some hits but hadn't scored yet.

"I'm watching him," Herb said looking at me, "What are you doing?" "Well," I said, "I'm not from around here—these fish don't know me. You guys are out here every day, and they're tired of looking at you."

Mike commented that the lack of boats that day was good for our fishing. "Too many boats scatter the fish in this shallow water," he said. "Stripers that feed here on the Flats on herring have all been males," Mike said. He checks them by gently squeezing their stomach near the vent. Males usually squirt milt, or sperm. Cow stripers will eject eggs.

Mike's ancient Browning spinning reel gave him a fit when fighting a big striper. He had to hold the bail closed to keep it from releasing line. "I only paid $15 for it on a close out," Mike said. Here we have a tackle shop and a charterboat, and I'm using an old $15 reel!" He had better reels on the boat, but never used one.

"They're for clients."

Herb caught a 41-inch striper, estimated about 30 pounds. It was fat! "That's the biggest rockfish I ever caught," said 66-year-old Herb, who has fished this area all his life. "Usually, they're not half this big," he said, "normally about 5 or 6 pounds."

After eight drifts, the fish were still hitting our lures. It was cold, and the wind had picked up considerably as the sun ducked behind the clouds. A rain storm was just off to our east. Dark clouds were trailing thin tendrils toward the ground, like a

Mike & Herb Benjamin with Herb's striper.

giant blue jellyfish. Someone was getting wet over there.

"Well, maybe another drift," Mike suggested. With fishing this good, even though rain threatened, there was no disagreement. Another drift or two and this writer could begin his two-hour trip home.

To those who might oppose this spring catch-and-release fishery, I have to reply that the DNR estimates a 50-percent bykill (my word) from summer chumming, due to stressed fish, high water temperatures, and low dissolved oxygen. I've seen a lot of undersized released "floaters" down-current of the chumming fleet. And, when I think about the netter who brought in a 10,000-pound catch (allowed less than 1,000 a day, even with several licenses aboard), using anchored (illegal) gill nets anchored overnight (illegal), then the catch-and-release spring fishery on the Flats, with its tiny mortality, pales by comparison.

• •

SPRING FLING

"You only brought one rod?" Jim Walker asked me as we loaded gear into his van.

"Yup."

"Suppose you break it."

"Not gonna break it," I replied, "Besides, you have three rods, if mine breaks, I'll use one of yours."

And so began the non-stop interpersonal teasing on our annual spring fishing fling on the Marshyhope River near Federalsburg, MD.

Our third angler, Ned McCall, was probably thinking this would have been a good day to stay home.

"Ever fished the Marshyhope before?" I asked Ned, who wanted some white perch for dinner.

"No, why?" He replied.

"Because, until you master the Marshyhope Touch you won't catch much," I answered, "But don't worry, Walker and I will catch you some big ones."

"Yeah, right."

We stopped for some humungous hoagies. Geezers like Walker and I can't fish when our stomach gauge nears "empty."

"Got plenty of gas?" I asked Walker as he prepared to launch his 16-foot Carolina Skiff.

He shook the tank and allowed as he had plenty, which brought to mind a story: As we motored about nine miles down the Marshyhope, we reminisced about Walker's fishing trip with a friend, a Bay Pilot, who ran out of gas in his personal boat while fishing near Cook Point one night. I got a call about 10 p.m. asking if I could bring them a can of gas. My boat was in the hospital, so I called a neighbor, Mike Haddaway, and volunteered to ride along. This, I didn't want to miss.

Mike had just refilled his portable gas cans, so we got underway in his 25-foot C-Hawk with his teen-age daughter, Kathy, riding shotgun. We saw the gasless Bay Pilot's boat on Mike's radar and pulled alongside to render assistance, and a lot of lip.

"When you're piloting those big ships up and down the bay, don't you ever look at the gas gauge?" I joshed.

"Not my responsibility," the Bay Pilot mumbled as he dumped gas in his tank. He was not in the mood for a lot of lip. He explained the gas gauge in his new boat must be stuck, and that he thought he was getting a lot better mileage than he really was.

As the three of us motored down the Marshyhope, Walker picked up his gas tank and jiggled it again, "Just checking," he laughed.

"We'll stop here at the Barking Dog Hole on the way back," Walker said. It has been a yellow perch hot spot in past years, but we don't keep spring yellow neds, anyway. Let the troubled species spawn, we say.

When we reached our annual perching hot spot, we found Chuck Prahl and Tommy Hooper of Cambridge anchored there in Chuck's 16-foot Lund aluminum hull. There was a shiny new Suzuki 50-horse 4-cycle motor on the transom. There was some discussion about how lucrative it must be to work part time at Tommy's Sporting Goods. Chuck chuckled.

We anchored up-current from Chuck and Tommy, and tied on our standard two-hook bottom rigs with one-ounce sinkers and numbers 4 or 6 hooks. For baits we had minnows, bloodworms, and nightcrawlers.

When you first get your baits down, it takes a while to attract fish. It has to do with the scent of the bait wafting off down-current, and giving the fish time to swim up, nuzzle the goodies, and decide whether to have lunch.

Ned started a scientific discussion about how to get nightcrawlers to come up out of the ground at night so you can harvest them for bait. Some people use a battery attached to a steel rod jammed in the ground. Others, Walker said, bang on the ground with a shovel. Ned insisted the best way was to drive a dowel into the ground and rub the top of it with a stick, "It's the vibration that brings them up," he said.

Ned hung bottom. "Look, it's moving," he said. His line appeared to be moving to one side. Perhaps it was something really big, since he couldn't stop it.

"The boat's swinging at anchor," I announced, stopping all speculation about the critter's size. "You've hung a big log on the bottom."

Ned slowly moved the boat ahead by pulling the anchor line until he could get his log-finder rig loose.

We started to catch perch, small ones at first, but a few bigger ones mixed in. I began a ritual that may have irritated Ned, but he didn't show it. "Want this one?" I asked him as I brought each one aboard. If it was big enough to join Ned and his family for dinner, he nodded. Otherwise it went back overboard. Walker kept no fish.

Chuck and Tommy were bailing white perch two at a time, and releasing most of them. "They were really biting earlier," Tommy Hooper said, in reference to our late arrival. "Bigger ones, too," he added.

Walker had a "great bite from a great white," but it got off. "It can be as big as I want it to be, since it got away," he said. "I say it weighed 10 pounds."

Walker used a two-hook rig with a spinner at each hook. Ned used a two-hook rig with beads and spinners and number 4 hooks. I used a home-tied monofilament rig with two number 6 hooks and a one-ounce sinker. The greatest number of bites seemed to come on my monofilament rig, which gave me many chances to ask, "Want this one, Ned?"

Ned's rig seemed to have an affinity for logs and tree limbs, though he caught some perch, too.

Ned's ability to spot and identify birds at great distance amazed me. He'd say, "Look at the black ducks," and point to two black dots on the horizon. He duck hunts a lot, and his talent must be valuable in the blind.

During lulls in the fishing, we saw mallards, wood ducks, an immature bald eagle, woodpeckers, greenwing teal, buzzards, crows, osprey, turtles on a log, and several Canada geese, all pointed out by eagle-eye Ned.

I had trouble making field notes of all the action, due to the patchy ink lines laid down by the ball point pen I borrowed from Walker, and I said so. "Nervy $&%#," Walker said, "Borrow somebody's pen, then bitch about it!"

"Yeah," I countered, "But, suppose you had a contract ready to ink, and all you had was this lousy &%$#@ pen" (Walker sells skylights whenever he's not fishing).

After one move, Ned didn't let the anchor go in time to suit captain Walker, who hollered, "I thought you were going to let the %&*$# anchor go."

Ned, a bit nettled, said, "Don't sugar coat it, tell me what you really think!"

By the time Walker and I had fed eight big white perch into Ned's cooler, the weather had cooled and fishing was uncomfortable. Meanwhile, Ned's log-finder rig had located a few more sticks and a perch or three.

"O.K.," Walker said, "let's try Barking Dog Hole (BDH), then give it up." The score at the BDH was no fish, one (incessantly) barking dog.

Off a big blown-down tree that jutted into the narrow waterway, we found a deep hole. I caught and released a small yellow perch, Ned caught a possible world-record tree limb. We called it quits.

"Want to fish tomorrow?" Walker asked. I had writing to do. Ned said he had to cut wood.

"If you'd kept all the wood you caught today, you wouldn't have to cut wood tomorrow," I needled our good friend, the Bay Pilot.

Ned McCall with his "world record tree limb."

• • • • • • • • • • • • • • • • •

MARSHYHOPE MEMORIES

Later, I recalled watching a squirrel crawling slowly down a tree limb over the water while fishing the Marshyhope recently. The farther out on the limb he went, the lower it dropped toward the water. He was after a hickory nut lodged in the fork of the limb. Suddenly, a big bass jumped up and grabbed the squirrel. It was touch-and-go for a bit.

We waited to see if the squirrel would get away. When the water calmed a bit, we were amazed to see the bass come up out of the water and gently deposit another hickory nut on the tree limb!

WATERS AND WOODS BALL

"Barbara, grab that rod!" Buddy Harrison yelled at Senator Barbara Mikulski, as a fish began to take out line. Dr. Stanley Minken ran over to assist Barbara. As Barbara began to wind in the rockfish, Stan helped raise the rod, then as he lowered it, Barbara cranked the reel as fast as she could.

"Short women, like us," Sunpapers reporter Candus "Candy" Thomson, said, "lack the leverage needed to crank in a big fish."

As Barbara's fish neared the transom of the "Buddy Plan," Buddy told his mate, "Rodney, grab that net off the cabin roof." Rodney handed the huge net to Buddy, who dipped the striper and swung the 31-inch, 8-pound fish around for all to see.

"Exactly six minutes since all the rods were set," Bill Burton said. "That's a new Waters & Woods record!"

Senator Barbara Mikulski and Buddy Harrison with Barbara's striper.

As photos were taken, nothing new to a polished politician, Barbara jibed, "It's like People Magazine," she said, "It's taking longer to get the pictures than it took to catch the fish!"

This was the 47th year Waters & Woods Ball (WWB) has been held at Buddy Harrison's Chesapeake House. Bill and Buddy met shortly after Bill was hired as the Baltimore Sunpapers outdoors columnist. Burton was writing about freshwater fishing, since he came to Maryland from Vermont, where freshwater fishing reigns. Buddy asked Bill why he didn't write anything about Chesapeake Bay fishing, and Bill jumped at the opportunity to go fishing with Buddy. It was Kismet that these two met, since they were both in the fishing business, or as it's called here on the 'Shore, "bidness."

The first WWB named after Burton's column, "Waters and Woods," included three people, all friends of Bill Burton and Buddy (FOBBB), but now about 100 show up for the pre-fishing party the evening before, and about 60 people actually fish on Buddy's boats the next day. The WWB is always held on the last weekend of April, with the party on Friday evening and the fishing on Saturday.

On Friday evening, Senator Barbara Mikulski; my wife, Carole; Candy Thomson; The Mariner Editor, Chris Knauss; and I shared a table in Buddy's Bar at Chesapeake House. A buffet including chicken, oysters, and other goodies was set up after the cocktail hour.

Barbara told us she lives in East Baltimore, and attended Hausner's Restaurant's historic closing where she ate the last crab cake ever served there. She even ducked into their famous stag bar, where huge fine-art paintings of naked ladies hung for many years. They were understandably reluctant to let women into the bar, perhaps thinking the ladies would not appreciate good art. She lamented she missed the last two WWBs due to senatorial duties.

Heading out of Dogwood Harbor the next morning, Burton turned to Buddy and said, "Well, Buddy, we made it another year."

"Yes," Buddy replied, "But we still have to make it back in!"

On board Buddy's boat, the Buddy Plan, the first order of bidness is to draw numbers for the fishing rotation. Barbara always draws number 1, because if there is only one fish caught, the reporters get photos of the most visible and famous person aboard, and everyone goes away happy. The famous get publicity, the reporters get a story, and Buddy's bidness gets a little ink, too.

After the picture session with Barbara's fish, which was caught on an umbrella rig trailing a bucktail dressed with a chartreuse sassy shad, things settled down a bit.

I asked the mate, Rodney Crooks, where he was from. He had a slight accent. He's from Trinidad, and fishes there on a "smaller scale." He's slated to return home soon.

We were fishing near Buoy Number 2, at the end of the False Channel. The LNG docks, called the "Gas Docks" locally, and the Calvert Cliffs Nuclear Power Plant were off to our west. Senator Mikulski had some real concerns about these two facilities being so close together—particularly after 9-11. First, she expressed concern that the LNG facility would be supplied from Algiers, and that between 200 and 300 LNG ships would visit there annually. She has been a major researcher for knowledge about the problems that could occur in that area, calling various agencies for reports and information.

Conversation turned to beauty, for some reason that can be quickly discarded. "Beautiful people are not the norm," Dr. Minken, a student of such matters, said. He believes that average-looking people are the norm, and that beautiful people—perfectly formed ladies come to mind—are really not the norm.

"You mean they're anomalies?" I asked.

"What's an anomaly?"

"Well, remember the news commentators remarks when a NASA rocket blew up all over the sky on TV? The announcer would say, 'We have a slight anomaly here.' I remember the late Ed Mason, a NASA PR chief named his rickety, raggedy old work boat 'Anomaly' right before it sank.' That's what it means."

"Well, there are only two things you can't avoid in this life," Dr. Minken said.

"Death and taxes?"

"No, time and your genes."

Candy Thomson regaled us with her stories about covering the last Olympics. "It was cold, she said, super-cold. As she approached the security gate (secured by National Guardsmen), she had to open her coat (body bombs, you know), and it was cold! She cut the amount of gear she carried to a camera and a laptop computer, making it easier to pass through security."

A pelican flew past the boat's transom, a sure sign fish were present. They make their living on knowing where to fish. We had one pull, but the fish got off when everyone got real polite about who was next to reel it in. It was an Alphonse and Gaston routine, "After you." "No, I insist, after you." The fish got bored - and got off.

After a day on the Bay that included stimulating conversation, and a good deal of hard work by Buddy and mate Rodney changing rigs and trying new ones, we headed for the barn. At Buddy's dock, everyone had fish to take home.

As Barbara, a very sharp Democrat U. S. Senator, walked up the dock, someone called to her, "You're pretty lucky to catch that big fish, you know."

"Why?"

"Talbot County is Republican, you know."

"I know, I know." She slumped her shoulders and walked away.

• • • • • • • • • • • • • • • • • •

DR. STRANGELURE

Many anglers operate under the premise that there is no lure too weird to show to a fish. I say let the fish decide what they like. That type of thinking leads some of us, perhaps me more than most, to fashion fishing baits that border on strange - maybe even weird.

Fishing historians tell us that the whole fishing lure thing began back in the late 1800s when Jim Heddon sat whittling a stick on a river bank. He tossed the stick in the water, and a big bass hit it, which spawned an entire fishing plug industry that fed Heddon, his family, and legions of PR guys for generations.

Of course, Eskimos and Polynesians have used bone and fur fishing lures for centuries, and there was mention of fly fishing in Cleopatra's day, but facts like that could ruin this story.

So, I try to defeat the midwinter blahs by combining hooks, wire, chunks of lead, blades, beads, and miscellaneous car parts to fashion ever-stranger fish-foolers.

One might think fame and riches are my goals, but such is not the case. If one of my creations, born at the stroke of midnight on the workbench amid sweat and no small amount of blood, catches a fish, it was all worth it.

One of my heroes in the experimental lure field is Jack Stovall. He spends cold winter days hunkered over a wood lathe and artist's air brush turning out beautiful wood lures, then painting them so beautifully I'm afraid to use them. Jack and I were plugging the shallows around James Island one May when a mean old striper took a 50-hours-of-labor plug of Jack's and wrapped it around a stump. He repeated that action two more times, and lost two more work-of-art plugs, in less time than it takes to tell about it. Jack started rooting around in his tackle box.

"Whatcha lookin' for?"

"Something cheaper," he answered.

One of Stovall's brightest adaptations was a big aluminum buzz bait spinner and some beads above a flounder hook. It had more drag in the water than a small helicopter, and I imagined it sounded like an atomic sub to a flounder—but it caught flatties! Big flatties. He was out-floundering me five to one.

"Got any more of those rigs?" "Yeah, but they're five bucks each," Jack kidded, handing me one.

Another trip it was pay-back time. Jack and I were tossing jigs with 4-inch grubs for spotted seatrout (specs) near Cook Point at the Choptank River's mouth. No luck. I impaled a colossal 10 inch pearl plastic worm on my 1/4-oz. jighead and cast it out. Jack asked why I hadn't thrown those silly worms away years ago. Never catch anything on that, he said. As I picked out a backlash on my reel (my boat's name is "Backlash"), I mentioned that silly stuff often catches fish. Meanwhile, my jig/worm had found bottom. When I tried to reel in, I met with resistance. "Hung bottom," I said. Bottom started moving away, picking up speed.

After a tugging match, Jack netted a four-pound spec for me. Please understand, Jack loves specs. Mention "spec," and he begins to salivate. "Got any more of those silly worms?" he asked.

"Yeah, but all the $5 ones are gone. All I have left are the $15 ones," I said. That was the last fish we caught, anyway, but it proved the point: Silly's not silly if silly catches.

While fish have been caught on lures made from all sorts of strange stuff including 1/4-inch diameter chrome pipe, knife handles, fountain pens, beer cans, wine corks (these last two are fun-makers), and tampon applicators (honest), most of us only adapt factory lures for some specific reason.

In recent years we have adopted a conservation ethic on the Bay. We release undersized or over-the-limit fish. Historically, surface popping plugs like the Atom plug come from the factory with two treble hooks. In recent years, we have replaced the belly treble with a small lead weight in the plug's gut for balance and exchanged the tail treble hook with a single, barbless one. This allows us to release fish easier, and avoid getting an important body part impaled with a second treble swung by a flopping fish. Our experimentation with single-hooked plugs paid off. Now, you can buy some lures with a single hook.

I asked the PR guy for a major lure maker why his company didn't sell baits with a single hook. It would be a lot easier on the fish, I said. "Fish don't buy lures," he said. In side-by-side tests on tackle store walls, all the treble-hooked plugs sold out before even one single-hooked lure moved. Anglers perceive the more treble hooks that hang on a lure, the better their chances of hooking Bubba Bass.

Bait fishermen will quickly scan this piece and determine there is no innovation or information they can take to the Bay. Not so.

A few years back, huge trout infested the waters off Hooper Island in June. We caught weakfish up to 14 pounds on a lure/bait combo devised by Bill Cannon. It was efficient and productive. And BIG. I called it the "Cannon Ball."

We started with a 1/2-oz. shadhead jig, added a six-inch chartreuse, silver flecked sassy shad and a Tony Acetta yellow-feathered replacement hook as a second "stinger" hook. Next, a jumbo Gulf shrimp was impaled on the stinger hook, and a 4 inch purple worm was added to the jig's hook. Don't laugh. The Cannon Ball caught trout.

From the trout's point of view, Cannon Ball colors were wild enough to make any stomach gurgle. The combo was bigger than your average lunch, but smaller than a farm hand's supper. A humungous Gulf shrimp for the gourmet. And, what anti-bait purist can resist adding a pinch of meat when a horde of 14-pound trout under the boat get lockjaw? It's funny, but many people mess around with their boats, experimenting with different electronics, rigging, and so on.

Cannonball lure.

But, not many folks mess with fishing lures, assuming bait makers know best. They're missing the best part of fishing.

Picture this: One winter, after a late night lure-making stint in what I lovingly call the "dungeon," I show my wife, Carole, my latest piscatorial seducement. She looks up from her embroidery, peeks over her glasses at my concoction, then squints at me.

"Yeah," she sighs, "the full moon brings them all out."

● ● ● ● ● ● ● ● ● ● ● ● ● ● ● ● ●

FISHING GUIDE STORIES

What do fishing guides talk about when they get together? Why, fishing, of course. At a local get-together of the Chesapeake Guides Association (CGA), a light-tackle group, fishing fiction flew like mush in a kid's food fight.

Mark Galasso, Association Vice-President, was the host, Prospect Bay was the place, and roast pig was the main invited guest. Beer and soft drinks flowed like the water over Conowingo Dam during Hurricane Agnes. Two writers showed up to partake of the hospitality, Ed Russell and I, plus my wife, Carole, and Ed's wife, Doris. Doris is the lady I've often mentioned who talks to a worm when she puts it on a hook: "I'm sorry, little worm, really sorry," she says.

One of the more interesting stories came from CGA member Tom Cross, who told about fishing off Ocean City, Maryland before the recent White Marlin Open Tournament. They had 10 lines set, four off the gunwale holders, four off the outriggers, and two off the flying bridge. Some were for tuna, others baited for white marlin. When they trolled beside a line of lobster pot buoys, this array of lures and baits attracted a dolphinfish and two white marlin, which caused pandemonium aboard. Tackle was strewn all over the rear cockpit after the fish were photographed, measured, and released.

Tom happened to be looking over the transom and saw a marlin tail free-swimming, finning along under the boat. He did the expected thing—he yelled to the captain to "cut the engines, don't ask why, just do it!" Then he grabbed the small marlin by the tail and hauled it aboard. It had run its bill into one engine's exhaust. It's a wonder that engine didn't overheat. Tom said the fish was in bad shape, "with 250 degree water in its face for quite a while," and it was measured and released, but not photographed.

There was a lot of talk among the guides about where the fish were biting. Most guides trailer their 20- to 25-foot center console outboard-powered boats so they can move around the Bay for the best fishing. In the spring, Susquehanna Flats are the hot spot for catch-and-release striper fishing. They move down the Bay as the fishing heats up in other areas.

Writer Ed Russell said he and Bill May were about to finish a book about light tackle fishing around Chesapeake Bay. The pair had been "working" on this book, doing a lot of "research" for about two years. Ed's partner, Bill, called it "That Damned Book," because it took so long and made them do so much fishing and other labor-intensive research. The book has been published and is called *"Fly Fisher's Guide to the Chesapeake Bay—Includes Light Tackle."*

The pig-pickin' was fun. Several guides' wives brought covered dishes of baked beans and salads. Again, fishing stories were–well –mostly believable.

● ● ● ● ● ● ● ● ● ● ● ● ● ● ● ● ●

BLESSING THE RODS

I saw this ceremony several years ago, but haven't needed it since, so I had completely forgotten about it until recently when we were almost skunked. Here's how the ceremony bailed us out:

On Buddy Harrison's "Buddy Plan," a 46-foot charterboat with a 14-foot beam. The day was rainy-misty, with a 15-knot wind out of the northeast.

As we left Harrison's Country Inn on Tilghman Island, I counted noses. We had seven anglers, one writer, a mate, and our captain, Buddy Harrison, who wears enough gold and diamonds to uphold his reputation as a really-really-rich guy: "It ain't easy being me" is Buddy's motto.

Our mate was David MacElree, a neat guy from Pennsylvania who I'd met before. Anglers included Bill Burton, who was the Outdoors Editor for the Baltimore Sunpapers for 32 years and now writes an outdoors column for the Annapolis Capital; Dave Dudley, Joe Gaul, Steve Snizek, Jen Lyon, Johnny Marple and his wife, Elaine. Three were Burton's grandchildren, Jen, Dave, and Steve. The Marples had recently retired and sold Johnny's Bait Shop on Deep Creek Lake in western Maryland. Johnny was called the "Worm King" for the 50 years the Marples ran the shop.

Buddy's twin-Diesel charterboat picked up speed after we cleared Knapp's Narrows, the channel that separates Tilghman Island from the mainland. We were headed for Buoy 82 across the Bay in search of rockfish over the 28-inch minimum.

On the way, Burton wrote some numbers on a sheet of paper and tore it into separate pieces with a number on each. He then had each angler draw a number, that would be their fishing rotation. The writer never takes a turn; he's there to work. Pity him. No one else does.

Arriving at Buddy's hot spot as his Furuno GPS indicated, Buddy and mate David began to set out the 14 rods they use only on striped bass trolling trips. Several rods got umbrella rigs; others were fitted out with dual bucktail rigs, essentially a Gypsy rig with two, 6-ounce spearpoint bucktails decorated with 6-inch sassy shads. Chartreuse was the primary color.

Before all the lures were out, we had a strike. Steve had number one, so he grabbed the badly-bent rod out of its holder and began to crank. The fish gave him quite a tussle. Meanwhile the mate went for the huge net. Buddy left the cabin and ran back to the rear steering station. As the snap swivel that connects to the leader neared Steve's tiptop on his rod, Buddy grabbed the 100-pound test leader and walked back from the transom, bringing the fish closer. David netted the fish and brought it aboard. It was measured immediately, since it looked to be so close to the minimum 28 inches, and it had to be released if it didn't meet the minimum. It was 29 inches, and went into the 50-gallon cooler. Yep, you read right —50 gallons! It doesn't take many big spring stripers to fill that box.

We seemed to be rocking in the waves since we traveled mostly east and west in a northerly wind. Joe bowed his head and sat down on an engine box. He had turned an interesting shade of green, and looked miserable. Steve went over and talked to Joe, then shook his head. Joe was seasick. We all knew how he felt. Had Joe stared at the horizon, he might have escaped what happened next; he was at the rail hanging overboard talking to "Raaalph." Been there, done that, everyone thought.

The fish-catching almost came to a halt. We didn't have a bite for two hours. Buddy was constantly on the VHF radio or his cell phone talking to nine other captains in his fleet. The news that fish were biting several miles down the Bay put Buddy in a quandary; stay here and tough it out, or pull in all 14 lines, plus a dummy line, and run south. That takes up valuable fishing time. Lures in the boat don't catch fish.

Box lunches came out while Buddy studied the problem. If you fish the "Buddy Plan," Buddy's answer to filling out fishing parties with odd numbers of anglers, you get a piece of fried chicken, a sandwich, a bag of chips, an apple, and a brownie. Enough food to fill the void for everyone, but Joe. Drinks in the cooler included beer and sodas. Joe, for some reason, declined all the goodies, although he seemed to think he might live, after all. He had turned a lighter shade of green. Some varieties of seasickness make you feel like you'll have to die to get better—that's the type Joe had.

Buddy decided to run south. All hands pitched in to wind 'em in. Lures and umbrella rigs were separated on the ample 14-foot wide deck, and rods were secured in holders. Buddy hit the throttles, and we moved out at 16 knots, not bad for a boat of this size.

At the Gooses not far from the False Channel that leads to the Choptank River, we helped Buddy and David put out all the lines. Another hour went by with no hits.

Joe was looking pretty perky by now. "Joe," David the mate asked, "Do you drink beer?" Joe answered in the affirmative.

"Do you believe in the Fish Gods?"

"If they'll help us catch fish."

"Come with me. Face the transom," David instructed. Now say with me, 'Fish Gods, Bless these Rods." Joe did as told.

"Now, open that can of beer and take a sip." Joe did. Lite beer doesn't work, David said, only the real stuff.

"Now, pour a little beer on each rod, then take a final sip." Joe did.

Joe blesses the rods.

David guided Joe back to the transom and told him to face aft, and he did. Joe followed David's instructions to hold his hands in the air and wave them around, again calling on the Fish Gods to "Bless these Rods!" This ceremony includes elements of religion and paganism, but practitioners claim excellent results.

"Somebody grab that rod!" Buddy yelled. "And that one, too!"

Suddenly, four rods were bouncing, bent, and pulsing, indicating interested fish. It was bedlam! Writers are no longer allowed to insult ethnic groups, but you know what kind of a fire drill it was. Nets flying everywhere, lines getting tangled, two leaders at a time being walked back into the boat, and Buddy yelling to "Get that %^$# net over here!" Anyway, it was a lot of fun, though short-lived.

When it was all over, four more keeper rockfish were in the cooler, all large enough that they didn't have to be measured. Lines and rigs were strewn all over the rear deck. MacElree sighed and went to work with our crew members to untangle the mess. That was the last bite, though we dragged our lures until 4:00 p.m. that evening.

Now, tell me something, readers. Did the Rod Blessing Ritual turn the tide for us? I'm no expert in arcane matters, but I've seen it work twice, and I believe! Hey, and the sip of beer settled Joe's stomach. Can that be all bad?

•••••••••••••••••

DOUBLEHEADS

Chuck Prahl and I were on our way to Cook Point when we stopped to check out one of my hot spots for white perch. We caught a few perch next to an old rock jetty when someone in a boat not far away hailed me by name.

"Who's that?"

"Dick Clayton," came the answer.

"Catching anything?"

"We're fishing for doubleheads," he replied.

Now, no one actually fishes for a doublehead, better known in polite society as a cownose ray. People catch them by mistake when fishing for something else. Scientists call the huge critter a *Rhinoptera bonasus*, but anglers who are often light tackle fishing for smaller edibles like trout and stripers when they hook a 40-pound doublehead – call it something unprintable.

Chesapeake's doubleheads weigh from 20 to 40 pounds or so and fight like tigers, but as an example of their low esteem in sportfishing circles, I could find no mention of them in the IGFA (International Game Fish Association) record book. Even in the saltwater fly fishing records category!

The cownose ray's snout is deeply indented to form two lobes says McClane's Fishing Encyclopedia, which description was far behind that of the good 'ol boys on the Eastern Shore, who described the critter as a "doublehead" before the beginning of time. These fish can attain a width of 7 feet and weigh up to 100 pounds, which indicates why they have become the proud owners of a lot of fishing tackle.

Doubleheads eat crabs, lobster, oysters, and razor clams by crushing them with their concrete-like grinders.

Cownose rays bear live young as do sharks. But their look-alikes, the skates, lay eggs in little sacks that wash up on the beach. Confusion arises since both are considered edible (by some people). Their relative edibility depends on what country you came from. More on that later.

"Got one on," Dick Clayton hollered. He was using medium spinning gear with 17-pound test line and peeler crab for bait. "Fought one for 45 minutes yesterday evening," he added.

John Clayton and Dick Clayton on the "Reel Time."

Since I wanted some boatside photos of Dick conquering his doublehead, we decided to hang around, though we were losing a lot of rockfishing time. To understand how important rockfishing is to Chuck and I, go back 40 years, when Chuck weighed a 32-1/2 pound striper for me that won the striped bass category of the then-new Maryland Sportfishing Tournament. We have fished together, off-and-on, for over four decades. When I reminded him he weighed my big rockfish so long ago, he said, "I must have been about 10 years old." Yeah, right.

Chuck had fished the Choptank River that morning at daybreak for stripers. When I invited him to go shallow-water casting with me that evening he didn't hesitate.

"Isn't it kinda hard on your 'ol geezer body to fish for rock twice a day," I asked. He just look at me and smiled. Hoo-ha.

Meanwhile, I circled Dick Clayton's boat, waiting for the doublehead to tire. Ha! Also meanwhile, Dick's nephew, John, hooked into another doublehead, so I had two lines to dodge with my boat as the duo fought their fish around their boat.

After about 30 minutes with no sign any doublehead was going to show itself at boatside, Chuck and I went rockfishing. We caught about 10 stripers by casting bucktail jigs and sassy shads over some near-shore rock piles. Actually, I caught two on my homemade white 1-oz. bucktail decorated with a 6-inch white swimmertail grub; Chuck caught 8 stripers on his 5-inch chartreuse sassy shad. There's a message there - somehow that needs more study. Only one rockfish was a keeper at 19 inches - Chuck's.

Dick Clayton called me that night. His wife, Ann, had told an Irish lady friend, Colette, about Dick's bout with doubleheads. By this time he'd looked up the fish on the Internet and found it was a cownose ray, and the lady wanted to cook some of it. Well, they do look like skates, which are popular fare in Erin, where they consider it a delicacy. Dick's son-in-law is from Indonesia and Holland: "It's a delicacy there, too" Dick said.

Dick was concerned about the buildup of uric acid or something else nasty in the fish's flesh from a prolonged fight, and the way it might flavor the flesh. The fish I saw him fighting didn't let him get his hook back for 1 hour and 25 minutes! I suggested heavier tackle if he was going back for more (he'd released the others they caught). I suggested he shoot the critter in the water. Some people lip gaff them and whack them between the eyes with a pacifier where the brains are supposed to be, before boating them. I like the idea of shooting them first, since that is quicker and more humane to both fish and angler. "There's no place to club it. It's an amorphous mass, sort of like a stealth bomber," retired aerospace engineer Dick said.

If you've ever seen the fight a doublehead can put up at boatside, you'd immediately conclude you don't want a 40-pound "green" fish slashing around inside the transom whaling away with his barbed tail at your tackle and valuable body parts. If you are impaled by a barb, seek immediate medical attention! Like any other bacteria-bearing fish spine puncture wound, it must be cleansed and treated by trained personnel.

The next night, the Claytons were back at it with 30-pound test line and heavy boat rods, convinced that Colette had a good recipe, and some gourmet friends should be invited to share the repast. They called me about 11:00 p.m. to see if I wanted pictures of the carnage as they filleted two 30-pound critter's wings. I declined.

Like sharks, cownose rays are cartilaginous, no bones. The intrepid anglers filleted both top and bottom sides of the wings. The old myth about using a cookie cutter to stomp out scallop-like portions of wing applies to barndoor rays, a different fish, another story.

"The skin has no scales," Dick said, "slick as glass. The meat was white, marbled with dark streaks. It didn't have much flavor, sort of like squid. If it had any flavor, it was like black drum, which tastes a little like pork."

"But, everyone ate it," Dick reported. "Six people, no one hesitated." Dick's wife, Ann, and her friend, Colette, had prepared the fish several ways.

"The meat was not white like skate," Ann Clayton told my wife, Carole, "It was gray. It was pretty good. The texture was lobster-like. My Irish friend came over and we marinated some pieces in a teriyaki sauce and broiled it. Other pieces we put in beaten egg and rolled in cracker crumbs and fried. That was the best. The lower wing pieces were not as tender as the upper wing pieces."

"Ann didn't sound anxious to try it again," Carole reported. "She wanted to know if we have skate here. That's the species they use for cookie-cutter 'scallops.'"

So, what are the fishing secrets of the top cownose ray specialists who pursue the sporty and scrumptious doubleheads?

"I think you should use 30-pound test tackle instead of light tackle if the fish are going home for dinner," says the deadly doublehead bait dunker Dick Clayton. "That doesn't let the uric acid buildup taint the fish's flesh. If you are going to release them, use medium spinning gear, or like my nephew, John, use a baitcasting outfit."

And, prepare for an hour or two hassle, I say. Doubleheads can really put up a fight.

• • • • • • • • • • • • • • • • •

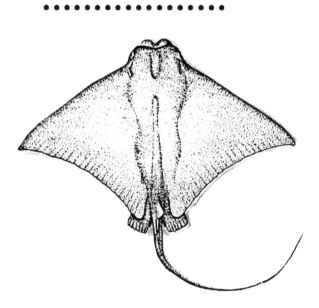

FURTIVE FISHING

We were introduced to the deceptive art of Furtive Fishing in the 1960s on the Dumping Ground. On the fishing chart, the Dumping Ground lies in 30 to 40 feet of water just north of the Bay Bridges off Kent Island.

In the hearts and minds of most upper Bay rockfish, it was a great place to mingle and munch mashed Manninose clams supplied by willing anglers above. To anglers with clam-baited hooks waiting for rockfish to nibble their bait, it was a feeling contest. (Whoever feels the best, wins).

Thousands of boats anchored daily on the Dumping Ground, many catching up to 100 rockfish a day. Newcomers arriving outside the fleet would cruise around, waiting for someone to catch a fish, then anchor as close as possible to the lucky angler's boat, sometimes too close.

The unwritten rule that latecomers should respect a certain amount of elbow room around an anchored boat catching rockfish was seldom followed. Normal people, when closely hunkered over rockfish, went nuts. They acted like people in a midsummer traffic jam—except that angries in automobiles don't have heavy lead sinkers to toss at nearby windshields. On the Dumping Ground as on the road, communication consisted of snarling and various hand signals.

My wife, Carole, and I had more reclusive fishing habits. We avoided crowds whenever possible. To delay a dreaded morning trip to the crowded Dumping Ground, we often dawdled along the shoreline between our home on the Little Magothy River and Sandy Point State Park, tossing surface lures at the occasional striper.

Chumming for rockfish was fun fishing, if one could avoid the crowds. A bushel of Manninose clams, some spinning rods and 1/0 hooks, and you were in business. A handful of clams were mashed in a bucket with a ball bat, then ladled overboard to attract and hold huge schools of rockfish. Rock came so close to the transom you could see them. It was like fishing in an aquarium. Carole and

I anchored well outside the crowd on the Dumping Ground. Not as many fish, perhaps, but a lot less hassle. The closest boat was 100 feet away. Its lone fisherman looked bored. I began to watch him out of the corner of my eye. Bored, hail! He was bailing rockfish, but the casual observer wouldn't notice it. He fought his fish with his rod tip underwater. His reel clicker was disabled. He didn't wave a net in the air, but simply slid his fish in over the low transom, all the while looking relaxed, sometimes even while sipping coffee.

"Howcome you do that?" I asked, "sneak your fish aboard?"

"See all those boats over there?" he replied.

I looked over at the main fleet. Cuss words and flying sinkers filled the air. Hostility was rampant. I imagined the names on their boat transoms: "Take No Prisoners," "Slam Dunk," "Pit Bull," "Ram 'Em," and "No Mercy."

"Yup, I see them," I answered.

"Want them over here?"

"No!" If we stood in the boat and waved a net in the air we would have soon been the epicenter of the City of Hostility. We formulated the basic rules of Furtive Fishing right then and there.

Clickers were removed from all our reels. Near crowds in daylight hours, we fought our fish with the rod tip under water and never waved a net (or gaff) in the air. We began to fish more at night. Under cover of darkness we could fish next to the Bay Bridge pilings or rock piles without showing others why we were successful. Plugging or bucktailing the rock piles at the edge of dark was productive too, but we rarely did it if other boats were nearby.

Furtive Fishing in the 60s and 70s, I feel, was necessary not because rockfish were in short supply. They were plentiful. But, in crowds, courtesy was in short supply. Problems arose from aggression or maybe ignorance (some anglers felt they could anchor right in your chum line and you'd be happy to see them!).

My boss, Pat Kelly, and I accidentally found a deceptive ploy that raised our Furtive Fishing to an art form. We left my Little Magothy River dock one morning with rockfish on the mind and a peck of clams for bait. A huge fleet of boats was anchored off

Podickory Point, where every boat in Anne Arundel County was hunkered over a big school of rockfish. I dreaded getting into the fray. Luckily, I found some fish on the depthfinder just off the Little Magothy, and we anchored over them. We were alone, and I wanted to keep it that way, so I began schooling Pat in the intricacies of Furtive Fishing. A natural-born actor, he was a quick study, though he might have overdone it just a bit.

Since we were anchored halfway between the mouth of the big Magothy River and the fleet off Podickory Point, every boat coming out of the Magothy just had to slow down and give us the once-over before joining the main fleet. We did our best to look bored, sipped coffee, and gave passersby the universal palms-up signal for "Nothing doing." Most went on to the fleet.

But, some anglers are just naturally suspicious. While I always believe anything another fisherman tells me, not everyone is that trusting. One boat slowed, and circled us so close I could see the captain's unbelieving sneer. The boat was BIG. Painted black. Menacing. The mate stood on the bow, anchor in hand, ready to sling it at our boat if one of our rods so much as twitched with a rockfish bite. Pat and I were prepared. We had reeled up our clam baits so near the surface that only a truly suicidal striper could get at them and betray us.

They circled us like buzzards, closer and closer, near enough to hear rockfish thumping around in our cooler. I stage-whispered to Pat that an angler in the fleet off Podickory was standing at the transom, rod bent, drag screaming. His buddy waved a huge net in the air, a welcome sign to every angler in sight. Other boaters were already tossing anchors next to them, close enough to shake hands.

Pat, a masterful and enthusiastic actor, whispered, "Watch this." He stood up in our boat with all the stage presence a 250-pound Irishman can muster and pointed at the hapless, about-to-be-surrounded angler.

"FAITH AND BEJESUS," Pat roared, "LOOKIT THE BIG ROCKFISH THAT GUY JUST NETTED!!"

Breakneck head-swiveling on the black boat told us they hadn't missed Pat's theatrics. The captain jammed both throttles to the bulkhead, nearly tossing his anchor and mate through the windshield. Black Boat disappeared in a cloud of blue smoke, off to make new friends among the fleet.

Pat and I smiled and lowered our clam baits to the waiting rockfish. Furtive Fishing had saved us again. The sun was bright. The fish were biting. Life was good.

• • • • • • • • • • • • • • • •

ON THE FLY: BOYD AND LEFTY

One of the neat things about being an outdoor writer is that you get to hunt and fish with others of that persuasion. Outdoor writers have found a way to hunt and fish their whole lives and get paid for it. Basically, they have never matured.

Two of my favorite outdoor scribes, C.Boyd Pfeiffer and Bernard "Lefty" Kreh fly-fished with me on my boat awhile back. They are both fly-fishing experts. An expert I am not, so I hid under the Bimini top where I was safe from flying fly lines, ran the boat, and observed.

Boyd (in his 50s) and Lefty (70s) have been full-time outdoor writers and good friends since time began. I am 72 today, but they are my boyhood heroes. They have both written dozens of books and thousands of magazine articles, acted in and produced videos, and given hundreds of talks about fishing. Knock off 95 percent of that and you have an output I am trying to achieve.

Boyd is quiet, and once taught anatomy to medical students—until the cadavers started to talk to him as he ate his lunch.

Lefty is ebullient, talkative, and remembers thousands of jokes, though his wife, Evvy, says he can't remember two or three items to buy from the store.

"Know what food completely turns off a woman's sex drive?" Lefty asked my wife, Carole. She already knew the answer: "Wedding Cake."

Carole quoted mutual friend and Louisiana outdoor writer, Bob Dennie, who said when he was first married they had a mirror over the bed, but now that they are older, he moved the mirror over the dining room table so they could watch each other eat.

"That's a good one all right," Lefty said, "let's go fishing."

Fly-fishing the shallows at mid-day for stripers at low water with no moving current is not productive, at least in the Choptank River. Dawn and dusk at high water are best for actually catching fish, but we were fishing, which is something else entirely. Like one friend says, "It's the ambience that counts, the comraderie, and watching the poetry of fly casting. Bringing smelly fish aboard only stinks up the boat, and cleaning them delays the cocktail hour."

As I maneuvered my outboard-powered 22-foot walkaround cuddy cabin hull along the shoreline, Boyd cast from the bow. Lefty occupied the relatively open rear area. I watched in awe as Lefty placed one of his famous Lefty's Deceiver flies 75 feet away under a dock and right next to a piling. Sure, six decades with a fly rod in hand can increase accuracy and distance, but this was still a really neat feat. The fact that no fish were there to appreciate the cast didn't lessen its awe-factor.

Lefty and Boyd talk fly tackle.

"You don't want to false-cast a sinking line," Lefty said, "you use a water haul to load the rod." Water haul is a term for letting the line rest in the water momentarily; as you pick it up the friction bends, or "loads" the rod. "If you change direction quickly, you tie knots. And, there is no such thing as a 'wind knot.' The wind doesn't tie knots."

Lefty works for Sage, so he naturally uses their rods. "There are three stages in an outdoor writer's career," he says. "First, we get into it so we can buy stuff at a discount. Then, they give you the stuff so you'll use it. Then, they PAY you to use it." Lefty is at stage three. Boyd admits he's not quite there yet, and I only get a discount if I cry a lot.

"Actually," Lefty says, "any [fly] rod over $150 is good, and if you can't cast it, it ain't the rod."

Boyd and Lefty both recommend Scientific Anglers® fly lines, and have so many rods, reels, and other tackle of various makes they both made out what Boyd calls a "death list" so their expensive stuff wouldn't go at yard sale prices when they flop over on their side. Not a bad idea for any outdoors folks, but the name of the list is a bit chilling.

"A guy from California called and asked me to talk to their fishing club sometime between old age and death," Lefty said. "I gotta get out there and see what those people look like."

Boyd caught several small blues and rock on a "no-name" fly, basically a hook dressed with several strands of bucktail hair. Lefty caught a really small striper and turned his back to release it so I couldn't get a picture to embarrass him with later.

"Our guide in Alaska showed us some really big brown trout caught on a Lawyer Fly," Lefty said. "What's a Lawyer Fly?" The guide said, "We used to call it an Egg-Sucking-Leach Fly."

"Tide moves bait," Lefty said, and we had no tidal current. He jerked his rod suddenly. "Little suckers, blues. But, I got it away from them."

Lefty and Boyd compared rigging. Boyd likes loop-to-loop connections between fly line and leader. Lefty doesn't: "All loops do is hang in the guides." Lefty was using one of the new large arbor Tibor fly reels that let you take in more line at a time. He had helped design the reel. Boyd was impressed, and particularly liked the "click stops" on the reel's drag knob like those on a camera lens.

I mentioned that Atom plug-maker Bob Pond was fishing with Jim Price. "Golly, is Bob still around," Lefty asked. "Yep, he's 80 now," I said. "Bob took us out on Chesapeake Bay in the 1950s," Lefty said. "He showed us rockfish would take popping plugs on spinning gear. I had been catching a lot of smallmouth and largemouth bass on fly rod poppers; then we found that rock would take them, too."

By this time we had fished the lower Choptank River's shoreline pretty thoroughly and caught no fish big enough to impress people in photographs. We headed for the open Bay to look for breaking fish with birds over them. Boyd took a nap on the rear deck, shunning the comfortable bunk in the cabin. Since Lefty had missed his nap this day, he said he'd take two tomorrow.

We stopped at a rockpile off Cook Point and caught several small blues and rock. No keepers.

Lefty kept a running patter of observations and jokes. "Saw a bumper sticker: Grandchildren are the reward for not having killed your children."

Lefty travels to fish or give talks almost constantly. "If I'm home more than a week, Evvy says 'Don't you have a trip to take somewhere?'"

No birds were out on the Bay marking breaking fish for us. We decided to call it a day. No "picture fish" meant a wasted day for Boyd and Lefty, both big-time, full-time, hard-working outdoor writers who need good photos to illustrate their stories.

I didn't fish at all, all day. Good thing. I mighta jinxed 'em.

● ● ● ● ● ● ● ● ● ● ● ● ● ● ● ● ● ● ●

SECRET LUMP

"Should we blindfold him now?" Jim Uphoff asked our host, Jim Price. Price just pulled into the launch ramp at Bellevue on the Tred Avon River to pick me up in his 20-foot Mako center console boat. Price promised to take me to a productive lump in the Bay he has been fishing for over 20 years.

"We caught several red drum there the other evening, between five and eight pounds," Price told me, "and I'll take you there, but I might have to blindfold you so you won't know where you are. I don't want the word to get out about my secret lump."

"I've never given away the other good spots you told me about," I reassured him.

Price is so protective of his lumps, he even stops fishing there when other boats come near. The best action on the lump is between sunset and dark, when big stripers roll on the surface. But, I didn't need striper pictures. Red drum are another story.

The drought in the summer of 2002 caused more saline waters to move way up the Chesapeake Bay. Someone reportedly caught a tarpon near Baltimore, and stories about other ocean-running fish like cobia and tautog being caught off Tilghman Island were making the rounds. One chap caught sheepshead and tautog on the Icebreaker about a mile south of Sharps Island Light. Higher salinities had allowed these salty species further up the Bay than normal. I thought it might make a good story.

"What did you catch the drum on?" I asked Price.

"Jackey Jigs," he said. I'd never heard of them, but Price said they were like Stingsilvers, only better. Uphoff had lost all his Jackey Jigs to fish on a previous trip. All he had left were the old standard deep jigs like Crippled Herring, Strata Spoons, and other solid spoons that resemble a knife handle. I had a selection of similar lures, including a number that were home-made from flattened and painted inline sinkers. This evening would be a test—factory made lures versus my homemades.

We left Bellevue and motored down the Choptank River, pushed along by Price's 175-horse Evinrude. I bought a similar

175 in 1992, but on the strength of positive ads in all the fishing magazines, I bought a 175 Johnson FICHT in 1998. Price said he would wait until they had the bugs worked out before buying a motor like mine. I agreed, though OMC has furnished three upgrades to my motor in the last two years. My FICHT, I told Price, barely sips gas, doesn't smoke, but it is noisier. His 175 conventionally-carbureted model purred like a kitten. We could even hear each other talk.

Exiting the Choptank, Price turned south as I tried to keep track of buoys as we passed them. No such luck. He was running far from the buoys to keep me "in the dark." His old, dependable Apelco 6000 Loran unit was set to a way point, but the TDs didn't show on the screen. No help there, and I needed lat/lon numbers for my GPS, anyway. I scanned the skyline, trying to line up marks like buoys and shoreline features that would give me his "secret lump" location.

In about 20 minutes, Price slowed the boat. "Sometimes I have trouble finding the lump," he said. "It's not very big."

When his Loran indicated we were at the spot, Price tossed over a plastic jug attached to a heavy lead weight. Then, we began to circle the buoy, looking for a depth change on the fishfinder that would indicate the "secret lump."

"I notice your jug is gray," I asked Price. "Is that on purpose?" "No, I was just looking for a jug that would fit under the gunwale," he said. "But, actually, the gray jug is hard to see from a distance. Anyone else would have trouble finding it." Another way of keeping the place secret.

"There it is," Price said. The depth had changed from 27 to 20 feet, a substantial change. But, it was not a very large area. No fish showed on the old Lowrance 2030 model flasher depthfinder. An expert like Price, who has spotted fish with the old-style flashers for decades can tell hard bottom from soft, and even detect fish that are hugging bottom. That's where you find the largest stripers, right on the bottom. Price's lump was about 50 feet east of his jug. Pretty close.

We started a drift upwind and upcurrent from the jug in about 27 feet of water. The drill is to let your heavy metal jig drop to the bottom, raise it a foot or two, then slowly raise and lower it against a taut line. Most fish will hit the lure on the drop. Some jigs have a single hook, but the ones we used had a single treble hook. To make it easier to disgorge a hook from a struggling fish, we clip one of the tines off the treble hook. Be careful if you do this; aim the part to be clipped away from yourself, it comes off like a bullet.

Uphoff used a Crippled Herring jig, Price cast a Jackey Jig, and the writer stubbornly used a home-brew molded lead flat jig with large doll eyes glued to each side near the hook. Eyes indicate the direction the baitfish is traveling, and gamefish key on the eyes, most of the time taking the baitfish head on, right where I had a hook.

As we drifted up the side of the lump, Price caught a striper. On a succeeding drift, Uphoff caught a keeper, too. I had a touch, but no taker.

Between drifts, I looked around the horizon, trying to find any two things that lined up. "Is that number six?" I asked Price, pointing to a buoy.

"No, that's number three," he said. No help there.

At the edge of dark, fish started to roll on the surface. Big stripers after baitfish.

We all had several hits. Some fish got off, what is politely called a "long-line release." Time was running out. Dusk is the magic hour, and a 20-minute window was all we had before dark.

Price and Uphoff each caught another fish, which filled their limit of stripers. All of the fish were about 24 inches. The writer caught naught. He was only there to do a story, remember? But, the red drum didn't show. Since this trip was just after Hurricane Floyd, I speculated that the influx of fresh water brought to us by Floyd had chased the saltiest fish back down the Bay.

Price ran east for a mile or so before turning north, probably so I couldn't read the back course on his compass. Tricky! Ha, ha, but I still had some buoys to check out on the way home. The half moon's-light would help, I thought. Wrong.

"I always pass 12B close on the way home," Price said.

Now, with all the clues I had "gathered," I thought I had the position pretty well defined. Ha! Now to get out a chart and put it all together. Chuckle. I had it all figured out.

A big chart and a T-square, plus parallel rules helped me zero in on the elusive target, the "secret lump." In an hour or so I had so many light pencil lines across the chart, I was getting confused. The intersections of all of the lines were all across lumps! The area is a veritable "Lump City!"

The next day, I told a mutual friend of Price and mine about the trip. "He even wanted to blindfold me!" I told Fred Friendly.

"I know where that lump is," Friendly said, "I even have the numbers on it. All you have to do is line up Buoy Eleventeen with a big clump of trees across the way, and line up Buoy 000 with Dilbert Island, and you're right on it." Turns out the friend regularly catches nice stripers there.

Some "Secret Lump!" Only the entire angling population of Talbot County (minus me) knew about it.

● ● ● ● ● ● ● ● ● ● ● ● ● ● ● ● ●

DR. DIMENTIO

Dr. Dimentio, CollegeEnglish Professor, Sam Blate, proposes a 47-weight fly-fishing outfit to try for the 143-foot long concrete muskellunge that decorates the mall at the National Fresh Water Fishing Hall of Fame in Hayward, Wisconsin.

While most of us fly fish with 8-or 9-weight gear, Dr. Dimentio figures his 47-weight fly tackle would be sporting for such a large quarry. His Dimentio Deceiver fly is on a 98/0 barbless hook (he is, after all, a sportsman) using the tail feathers from 23 peacocks. His 27-foot fly rod will be adorned with a telephone cable reel holding 4,000 feet of backing. "Think BIG," says Dr. Dimentio.

No, we don't know what he smokes.

THE AIRPLANE WRECK

The "Airplane Wreck" near the mouth of Maryland's Choptank River is a fishing hot spot for locals who want to catch bottom fish like weakfish (trout), croaker, and spot.

Somewhat hard to find, even if one has the LORAN-C numbers (27496.0 x 42481.9), Captain Mike Murphy of the Tiderunner has perhaps the best method of finding the "Wreck." Murphy motors to the spot where his LORAN-C says the wreck is located and tosses a buoy. Then he circles his buoy until he sees the wreck on his depthsounder, and prepares to anchor. His large buoy has a short line attached between the large buoy and a smaller plastic bottle; after settling down, the small jug points downtide and downwind to tell him how his boat will lie at anchor.

"Funny," Captain Murphy says, "people come in and anchor all around my buoy, which can be 100 feet from the wreck." Does he tell them? Nah. Who knows? They might catch fish over there.

Murphy said there are times when a boat on one side of the wreck will catch fish for 30 minutes, then the fish will move to the other side and try a different angler's hooks, alternating every half-hour. Who can figure fish? "If the tide is strong, and the wind calm," Captain Murphy adds, "you can see a third rip downtide of the wreck. That's where the fish will be."

The "Airplane Wreck" is a Navy PBM3s flying boat that crashed and sank in the Choptank River at 2:30 p.m. on January 2, 1944.

"I was the instructor for a series of takeoffs and landings," Commander Jack Chase, USNR (Retired) later wrote about the crash. "The student pilot [an Ensign] apparently got vertigo, and while we were on the step, at near takeoff speed, turned the wheel sharply left. The left float dipped with such force it was torn off; with the sudden release of that drag, the right wing went under and the plane cartwheeled. Fortunately, after the flips (2 or 3), we came to rest upright."

No injuries were reported, but the main cargo door was open. Water was pouring in with such force they couldn't close it. Three officers and three enlisted men watched from two rafts as the plane sank in about five minutes. With an air temperature of 35 degrees F and water temperature at 38 degrees F, the soaked airmen paddled to shore and built a fire. Aircraft Commander Chase walked to a nearby farmhouse and telephoned the Officer of the Day at Patuxent River Naval Air Station, who sent another PBM to pick up the crew.

Dick Moale, an amateur diver of Woodsboro, Maryland has done a considerable amount of research on the wreck and provided Aircraft Commander Chase's account. "We dove on the wreck for years," Moale said. "It used to be covered with humungous oysters. They even had blue paint on them."

Moale and his Maryland Hydronaut diver buddies hired Captain Donnie Gowe of Tilghman Island, MD to take them to the wreck. On December 15, 1973, Captain Gowe found the wreck using "marks" on land. He stopped where the water "looked right." When Gowe anchored, they were directly over the unbuoyed wreck in the middle of the Choptank River, a navigation feat that always amazed the divers.

Following the boat's anchor line down, Moale's divers had exceptionally good visibility, six feet at slack water. After Moale had stuffed his "goodie bag" with fat oysters, he had a look around. Through an open port on the side of the fuselage, he saw a tangle of wires, pipes, and fishing lines. It was too dangerous to swim inside. He found the pilot's yoke (steering wheel), but couldn't tug it loose. His air was low. He was tired and cold. Moale's diving buddy, Ron Baker, was rested and warm topside, so Baker dove to get the pilot's yoke. The other yoke was later cleared of silt with a pump and recovered.

The divers agreed the pilot's yoke should go to the pilot of the aircraft when it crashed, then Lt.(j.g.), Jack B. Chase. They found that Chase was working as a news anchor at WBZ-TV 4 in Boston, Massachusetts in 1974, and surprised him with his plane's yoke on live TV on the 30th anniversary of the crash.

"The wreck lies on her side at about 45 degree angle," according to a 1975 Navy Wreck Report, "One wing missing, part of the one wing intact. Hull partially demolished. Tail section separated. Mud bottom. Visibility usually 1 foot or less during tides; 4 feet during slack tide."

Decades later ....

When I took cousins David and Shannon Wright to dive on the wreck we were met there by divers Kenny Doyle, Kenny Walton, and Jack Garvey in another boat. The divers were practicing as part of their volunteer efforts in the Mid-Shore Underwater Recovery Team based in Caroline County. David's brother, Danny Wright, was "anchor man" in my 22-foot outboard boat.

As I searched for the wreck, consulting my LORAN-C, I spotted a stack of fish downtide of the plane on the depthfinder, exactly where you'd expect to find them. Unfortunately, we had no fishing tackle with us to check out these fish, since my boat was already crowded with dive gear and air tanks.

We marked the area with dive buoys for safety. I anchored uptide of the wreck so we could drift back over its main part. The divers used my anchor line as a path to the plane.

Danny Wright and I watched as a trail of bubbles on the calm surface marked the diver's travels. They swam almost 100 feet in one direction, following the fuselage. On a second dive, they worked off at 90 degrees for 30 or 40 feet. The plane is now in three parts, according to Captain Allan Faulkner, who also dives on the wreck when there is good visibility.

Unfortunately, on that day the visibility was only about three feet. The wreck is dangerous to dive on. The divers worked in pairs, loosely bound together at the wrist for safety. Clams and oysters grow out 6 inches from the skin, Shannon said. They constantly met big oyster toadfish face-to-face, who seemed as surprised as the divers.

"I saw a big 'ol toadfish face to face," said Kenny Boyle. "It startled me. I thought about stabbing it, but Kenny [Walton] came into view."

"If there's a hole in your suit," David Wright kidded Walton, "Doyle thinks you're a toadfish." The Airplane Wreck is "Snag City," an economic boon to local tackle shops.

Anchors, fish hooks, and mono line were everywhere, Shannon said. Divers must be wary not to tangle in webs of monofilament line. Also, they don't want to impale themselves on fish hooks with wire leaders, since they would then be attached to the plane, and cutting a hard-to-reach wire would give them big problems.

"There are big holes in its side," said David Wright. "Big sections are rolled back like there was an explosion. It was so dark near the bottom we used flashlights, but about 15 feet up on the wreck it gets a little lighter. Wires and cables are everywhere."

The extra drag of divers hanging on a rope bridle attached between my boat and the diver's boat caused my Danforth anchor to slide along bottom and toggle into a hole in the plane. On their last dive, the divers thoughtfully brought my anchor up with them.

They also brought up several parts that were covered with mud and barnacles. One electronic panel looked antique by today's standards.

The divers did not enter the body of the plane. Too dangerous. Not only were wires and pipes hanging everywhere, but "You can't tell whether part of it is at the point of collapse," said David Wright.

There are many local stories about the Airplane Wreck. One story published in The Star-Democrat of Easton, Maryland on August 11, 1944 stated: "Vernon Howard was fishing the Choptank River in his new cabin cruiser. After a successful catch, he and his guests began the trip home after dark."

"Suddenly, in the dark, there was a crash. The wooden canopy came down, windows were broken, and the entire cabin was raised slightly from its base. No one was injured seriously, but there were numerous cuts and bruises among the passengers and the boat looked rather sad. It seems there was no light on the airplane wing which juts above the surface of the water there to a considerable height, and in the darkness, Mr. Howard just didn't see it."

The Airplane Wreck wing in 1945.

Photo courtesy of Ridge Cecil.

"The wing stuck up for years," Captain "Buddy" Harrison of Tilghman Island said, "we've caught a lot of fish there." Over the years, some of the local good 'ol boys (under cover of darkness) added a few items to the Airplane Wreck to insure its continuance as a fish-gatherer: Car bodies, refrigerators, tires, plus many other items too large to cart to the county dump. Today, Bay lovers would have hissy fits about unclean items dumped in Bay waters.

Frank Hurley of Neavitt, Maryland suggested that the MD DNR establish the Airplane Wreck as an official fishing reef, since "It's been one so long, anyway."

If Captain Mike Haddaway of Bozman, MD and Captain Mike Murphy were limited to one place in the world to fish, you'd find them hunkered over the Airplane Wreck dunking peeler crab baits for white perch, rockfish, croaker, weakfish, bluefish, etc.

Local anglers use many different anchoring schemes at the wreck. Captain Haddaway uses a grappling anchor with a ring on its base for an extra trip line in case he gets hung in the wreck. Special wreck anchors can be made from rebar or aluminum rod that will bend easily and free themselves, and can be rebent for the next trip.

Don't even think about diving on the wreck, even to recover an expensive anchor. It's much too dangerous.

And, anglers should keep an eye on the weather when toggled into the wreck. Cut loose before a gale hits. The wreck is way too big to drag back to your home port when you're running ahead of a storm!

SHAD RECOVERY

American "white" shad, an important sport and commercial fish whose estimated Chesapeake Bay spawning stock fell from 1.4 million in 1965 to roughly 26,000 in 1989 is making a significant recovery according to Maryland Department of Natural Resources biologist, Dale Weinrich.

Four dams on the Susquehanna blocked the fish from spawning for years, and low populations of shad caused the DNR to declare a moratorium on them. Two $12 million fish lifts were in place at Conowingo Dam to capture spawning shad, which are then transported upriver in tank trucks past the last dam at York Haven, PA, so they can spawn as far north as Binghamton, NY.

While current Maryland regulations do not permit the possession of American or hickory shad, I had an opportunity to fish for them with Weinrich in his hook-and-line survey just below Conowingo Dam.

I hadn't fished for shad since 1960, when at least 50 anglers stood shoulder-to-shoulder casting shad darts into murky Pocomoke River waters from the old wooden Porter's Crossing bridge above Snow Hill. I remembered that the silvery rascals could fight in the poky Pocomoke, but on my that Conowingo trip a rapid current of 10 knots or better dampened the fish's enthusiasm to jump.

Weinrich explained some of the shad studies in progress at that time as Joe Townsend of Rock Run Landing at Port Deposit and I put our fishing tackle aboard a 16-foot aluminum outboard boat.

During the upper Bay pound net season, Weinrich counts and tags shad released from the nets. Every pound net fish was not tagged: "Too many to tag and release as healthy fish."

Later, he fished with two hook-and-line anglers from his boat below the dam, measuring and tagging everything they caught. When a lot of shad were present, and two anglers are bailing in fish, Weinrich was one busy biologist. Blood is taken from sample fish to determine hook-and-release stress. Tag returns and the catch-per-unit-of-effort (CPUE) enable biologists to estimate total numbers of fish. Tag recaptures at the fish lifts reinforce the data.

When we first anchored about halfway between the dam and Rowland Island just downstream, only two small turbines were open. Water velocity didn't suit Weinrich or Townsend. "Wait until they open the big ones (turbines)," they said.

Dale Weinrich releasing a shad at Conowingo.

Townsend and I were using 8-pound test spinning gear with two small shad darts on leaders of unequal length, called a "gypsy rig." With the boat anchored in a swift current, all we had to do was cast out and hang on. The lures "trolled" themselves in the current. There was no trick to hooking a fish.

Strangely, we caught only two small rockfish, yet schools of five- to 10-pound stripers came right next to the boat chasing gizzard shad possibly stunned by a trip through dam turbines, busting them right on the surface. They were feeding in a fast-moving "chum line." In all my years of rockfishing, that was the greatest thrill, to see six big stripers busting a 12-inch shad at arm's length.

I caught the first white shad, about a three-pounder. Weinrich measured it, took a scale sample, determined its sex, planted T-bar anchor tag #5816 in its back, and released the fish in no more time than it takes to tell about it. We caught about three more shad before enough gates were opened (7 small turbines, 4 big ones) to suit my companions. "Shad are current-specific," Weinrich said, as we re-anchored the boat on the edge of a current so swift the water made a roaring sound and miniature whitecaps covered the water's surface.

Something big grabbed Townsend's rig and ripped off a lot of line before breaking off. "A ten-pounder?" I asked. "At least 12 pounds," he laughed. When you lose a fish, it can be as big as you want.

While 6- to 6-1/2-pound shad were about the biggest Weinrich caught when the run was at peak, the farther north you go up the coast, the bigger the fish. "A 10-pound shad in the Hudson is not unusual," said Weinrich. The Maryland record American shad, caught in the Wicomico River by Vance Carter in 1975, was 8 pounds, 2 oz. The hickory shad record at that time was 4 pounds, caught in the Susquehanna by John E. Schaeffer, Jr. in 1972.

Chesapeake Bay American shad re-enter their natal rivers to spawn in the spring, then leave for the ocean, migrating as far north as the Bay of Fundy. In the fall, they head south to winter off the mid-Atlantic area. Starting in February, they begin their long trek back to their natal rivers to repeat the process.

Townsend hooked a shad that began to jump like a tarpon. "Don't make too much commotion," Townsend warned the shad, "A big rock will get ya!" His shad measured 490 mm to Weinrich—19+ inches to the rest of us.

In 1999, the tail-race population was an estimated 580,000. The next year it peaked at 960,000, then fell back in the 500,000 range for three more years, "Not unusual," Weinrich said recently, "there is a normal fluctuation in the wild population. Interestingly, the percentage of hatchery shad in the wild population has decreased from 86 percent in 1996 to 67 percent in 2001, a good sign.

Would Weinrich be happy to see the shad fishery open? "That's my goal," he says, "I'd like to see it reopened before I retire."

•••••••••••••••••••

BROOKS ROBINSON – A BIG HIT

Captain Jo-Jo met me on the dock and said, "I've been offered $20 to throw you overboard."

"Is that all I'm worth?" I asked. I momentarily mulled over the offer, assuming it came from a charter captain who gill nets in the winter, and may have objected to my striped bass - gamefish stance. This needed more study.

We left the Chesapeake House docks at 7 a.m. on the 42-passenger, 48-foot x16-foot "Brooks Hooks," Captain Bud Harrison at the wheel. Three generations of the Harrison family were aboard, two of them charterboat captains, and one who was studying to be one, 8-year old Brooks Harrison.

There were enough anglers aboard to allow us a 40-fish limit of stripers. Chumming at the Gooses would be the order of the day, Buddy said. His boats have been limiting out every day with rockfish from 18 to 30 inches long.

The "Brooks Hooks," a Chesapeake 48 with two 3208 Caterpillar diesel engines, made good time from Tilghman Island as the anglers got to know each other. Bud's boat is named after his son, Brooks, who is in turn named after Brooks Robinson, of the Baseball Hall of fame. That's quite a series.

Brooks Robinson was aboard as part of a charity event to benefit the St. Johns Chapel at Tilghman. Every year in February, Buddy holds a dinner and auction. The main item to be auctioned is a fishing trip with Brooks Robinson. Phil Price has won the bidding for the last three years. Phil then gets to invite his friends, who help him a bit with the cost. Phil is the owner of the Charlestown Marina up the Bay. Several of Phil's guests were also his employees, and often join him in Costa Rica for some winter sailfishing.

By 9 a.m. Bud was backing the "Brooks Hooks" down after releasing his plow anchor at the Gooses. He picked a position behind and between Captain Jeff Shores' "Hard Ball" and Mike Keene's "Dog House." Bud called out that we were over a school of fish.

"Start tossing chum," Bud told his son, Brooks (Bud calls him "Brooksie" when Brooks is aboard. Two mates also helped with

Buddy & Bud Harrison and Brooks Robinson with Brooks' striper.

disbursing the ground menhaden chum. Whole menhaden were cut up and used for bait. There were 15 other boats anchored around us, every one tossing chum over. Quite an attraction for gathering up rockfish.

"Choose your weapons!" Bud called to the anglers, who grabbed the rigged and baited rods and lowered their 2-ounce sinkers to the bottom. The rail would only accommodate so many anglers, so some sat back and grabbed a Bud Light. On board was Bird Dog Wheeler, who works for Budweiser, and whose job aboard seemed to be keeping cans of beer buried in the ice for maximum cool.

"Where'd you get that name?" I asked Bird Dog, who has a well-known local band, "Bird Dog and the Road Kings."

"My dad and I both had 'Bird' in our names. So did my uncle and a nephew. So we're all called 'Bird Dog'. The whole county is full of 'em," Birdie joked as he picked up a can and shook it. Everyone close ducked because he might open it and squirt it at someone. After a good shake, he slowly rotated the can end-for-end and chanted "B-U-D." When he popped the tab, only a bit of foam escaped. Do not try this at home - at least in the house. Bird Dog is an expert with a long history in beerology.

"Does that work with sodas, too?" someone asked Bird Dog.

"I don't know, I've never had a soda," he replied.

"Fish on!" hollered Brooks Robinson. His rod was bent and line was disappearing at an alarming rate. This was a good fish.

Chris Haddaway said "He'll never get it in." I asked why. "Because I'll cut the line."

One of the mates, Jo-Jo's son, grabbed a net and brought Brooks' striper aboard. It measured 31-1/2 inches. Buddy said 'That's the biggest one I've seen for a while, chumming." That started the rumor that Buddy had hired a diver to put that fish on Brooks' rod. It was to be the biggest rock of the day.

From then on, little Brooks netted most of the fish. At age 8, it is tough to lean over far enough to get a net under a fish, so when he leaned way over, his body suspended like an upside down "U" over the rail. Buddy ran over and grabbed his feet, afraid he'd lose a grandson overboard.

Wilson Daffin called out, "Mark's got a marlin on," joking about Mark's bent rod and a great deal of fish resistance.

I asked Bud why black drum hadn't shown up at the Stone Rock on June 14 as they've done most every year. He speculated that they passed the Stone Rock because all the oysters there are dead. "Patent tongers pulled up nothing but dead ones last year. Not a one was alive," Bud said. Bud was one of the biggest oyster buyers in the area.

"Melvin's got one," became the battle cry of the day. Mel Stevenson works for Phil at the marina. Phil ran over and cut Melvin's line with a well-honed filet knife.

Someone put Buddy's new audio tape on the player. One song, the "Buddy Plan" refers to the plan where Buddy puts a group together to make up a party of six for a "six-pack" charterboat licensed to carry up to six anglers. In between the background singers, Buddy croaked, "It ain't easy bein' me." And, it ain't— Buddy wears enough gold and diamonds to weigh down most people, says it keeps him in shape to "Carry a pocket full of Viagra," another one of the songs on his tape. He's sold 400 copies by word of mouth so far.

As I chatted with Bill Burton, thankfully upwind of that boiler he calls a pipe, I mentioned that Jo-Jo had an offer of $20 to toss me overboard. "I know," Burton said, "That was MY offer." So that's why Jo-Jo's son kept asking Burton all day, "Is it still $20?"

Brooks recounted some of his baseball stories. "Lee Anderson made me famous," Brooks said. "He said, 'You could pitch Robinson a peanut butter and jelly sandwich, and he'd turn it into a double play!'"

I asked Brooks if he remembered the time on a local farm when his deer ran over me after he shot it? "Oh, yes," he said, "I remember THAT!" I had ducked into a ditch as Brooks' wounded deer headed straight for me. I shielded my Nikon under me. The buck stumbled and hit me full force, tumbled onto the ground, and lay there, kicking. I administered the coup de grace. There was blood all over the back of my jacket, and I asked Brooks if there were any puncture wounds in the back of my head, which was numbed by

Brooks Robinson with his deer.

the impact of the dear, but luckily, no injuries. The Nikon was still operable, and I took photos of Brooks and his deer. "I don't hunt any more," Brooks said when I recalled he frequently hunted geese with the late Bill Perry.

By 9:45 a.m. we had limited out with 20 keeper rockfish. Brooks flopped down beside me in a deck chair. Teased about his big rock, he joked, "There's nothing like getting a lot of runs in the first inning."

Bud said we'd run to a place locals call "France" and catch called that ever since he could remember. A friend he grew up with, Barry Schweitzer, "Was so madly in love he promised his girl, 'Marry me and I'll take you to France.'" Bud said. "He took her fishing in a skipjack right here at France!"

A sailboat came directly toward us. There was no one at the wheel! We were yelling, and finally someone came up out of the cabin. "Oh, I didn't see you," the guy said. His boat came within 10 feet of our stern at the same time one of our anglers was tossing old menhaden baits overboard. Unfortunately, one smelly fish lit in his cockpit, another stuck to his sail. He may remember that he could have caused a really bad accident by not being at his helm— at just about the same time those menhaden ripen in the sun.

Brooks left his rod in a holder and walked away. The rod developed a definite bend, and little Brooks saw it; he ran over and wound in a big hardhead. Brooksie reeled in big Brooks' fish. A fitting end to this fishy "series."

● ● ● ● ● ● ● ● ● ● ● ● ● ● ● ● ●

CAPITAL CITY BASS

The Potomac looks like any other good bass river in the early morning, when mist shrouds the shoreline and blots out all traces of civilization. But now, it's just you and the bass in the quiet of dawn. And bass are there, too, aplenty. It is not unusual for three anglers in a bass boat to catch 40 largemouths a day, with a few striped bass thrown in, according to master bass fishing guide Ken Penrod—and the catch could be as high as 150 a day on certain spring or fall days.

On this foggy morning, Penrod operated the bow-mounted electric motor on his 20-foot bass boat and cast his Fire Tiger 7A Bomber with the constant cast-and-reel of a seasoned pro, hour after hour. His passenger tried a chartreuse Deep Wee-R, having often heard about tidal water bass fishing: "If it ain't chartreuse, it ain't no use."

Above the morning fog, the jet engines of airliners in-bound for Reagan International Airport whined as pilots eased back on their throttles on the landing approach. "One plane a minute," Penrod said. The huge airliners were out of sight above, but not out of hearing.

As much as the anglers would have liked to be left in peace along their wooded bank, the fog soon lifted and the Nation's Capital materialized out of the mist. The wooded Maryland shoreline was replaced by downtown District of Columbia cityscape as the anglers moved upriver.

"This point is always good for a few fish," said Penrod, as the boat moved under the Woodrow Wilson Bridge. "And, don't be surprised if you hook a big striper here," he added. The point was lacking in willing bass or stripers that morning. Two other bass boats ahead had already worked the shoreline with worms and crankbaits.

The Potomac River cleanup started in the mid-1960's, Penrod explained. When President Lyndon B. Johnson announced a nationwide clean water program, reporters reminded—and embarrassed—him about the hometown river, the Potomac. Since that time there has been a gradual clean-up of the river, and aquatic vegetation has returned. Penrod said bass were reproducing naturally in the Potomac now: "The hydrilla provides cover and oxygen, and it's also a good channel marker, because it grows in relatively shallow water." By avoiding the grassy areas, you can generally stay in the channel, but newcomers should use navigation charts to avoid problems.

The cleanup and the return of largemouth and striped bass to the upper Potomac was good for the recreational fishing business, too. Penrod has built a sizeable following of clients for his guide business because of the plentiful supply of fish. His guides take 1,000 parties a year fishing, mostly on the Potomac. If parties can catch 40 fish a day here, why would they want to fish other rivers and lakes where the average is 15 or less bass per day?

Several bass boat anglers were casting to the rotted pilings of an old ferry dock that juts several hundred feet into the Potomac. Some of the fishermen worked hard at it, but others were just out for a relaxing morning in the sun. Penrod pointed out: "Those (relaxed) fellows are on the wrong side. Uptide. And they are bound to get hung up in the submerged pilings." They did, constantly. "That guy knows what he's doing," Penrod said about a wormer who cast from the downtide side of the pilings. He had several hits, but didn't connect. In Penrod's boat, his angler fished a yellowish Hawg Boss Super Toad past a piling, retrieving it downtide. Three feet from the piling, a bass slammed the tiny crankbait. Ten-pound test line and a lightly set drag made for a longer fight than competition anglers might tolerate, but this was fun fishing. The bass was 14 inches long, about the size of most of the fish caught that day, although four- to seven-pounders are not unusual.

All of the piers along the Potomac are bass habitat said Penrod as we motored past the Naval Research Station and Bolling Air Force Base. Farther upriver, the three bridges that cross the Potomac near the Pentagon hold stripers next to their pilings, where bucktail jigs decorated with pork rind will take both bass and stripers.

The scenic George Washington Memorial Parkway winds along the Potomac through Virginia in a parklike setting for several miles, passing over a picturesque stone bridge near the Pentagon.

Ken Penrod catches stripers and largemouth bass
within sight of the Washington Monument.

Commuters on the parkway above often see bass boats fishing the lagoon below. The lagoon is not only scenic from the water, it is bassy looking, too. Both shorelines are rip-rapped with stone. A great spot to cast crankbaits or work a plastic worm. Pier pilings inside the lagoon at the Pentagon Marina hold bass for worm fishermen. This part of the river alone would take weeks to fish properly, even if the angler could ignore the scenic beauty of the place. Coming out of the Lagoon, the Jefferson Memorial and the Washington Monument across the Potomac are framed by the same arched stone bridge.

Tidal water extends upriver to the Key Bridge, but Penrod headed downriver past the peninsula that forms East Potomac Park and around Hains Point to check out the Washington Channel. Joggers in the park sometimes walk-troll crankbaits along the seawall as they get their exercise and fishing done at the same time. They catch both stripers and bass.

We trolled up the Washington Channel along the Fort McNair seawall with the same crankbait that he had been casting all morning. Stripers showed on the chart recorder, stacked up like cordwood over deep holes and bottom lumps. No strikes from the unpredictable stripers disturbed the anglers' quiet, scenic journey.

Penrod changed to a rigged worm. It is amazing to watch this pro toss a lure and control it perfectly. Underhand or overhand casts, no matter. They are all accurate. He is able to stop the bait precisely over his target and have it drop alongside a piling or pier. Cast and retrieve, no waste motion. Every second the lure is out of the water, it is not in front of a fish.

It was time to release the fish in the livewell. Penrod's anglers understand that they will not keep fish unless they catch a trophy, or absolutely insist on taking home a limit of five bass. "Think about it," Penrod said, "Our guides make a total of 1,000 trips a year. With two anglers and a guide in each boat, and a five fish limit, that's 15 fish per trip, or 15,000 bass removed from this part of the Potomac each year. The fish won't stand that kind of pressure. If all of the guides here release their fish, we can maintain a quality fishery for tomorrow."

It would take a lot of tomorrows to fish every bit of this scenic river. The number of pilings, rip-rap seawalls, submerged trees, points, grass beds, and drop-offs that hold bass and stripers are mind-boggling, and each one must be fished differently. Although challenging to the angler, there is a world of fun in the trying.

See your Nation's Capital from the river, just once. You'll never forget it. And, fish capital city bass just once. You'll never regret it.

● ● ● ● ● ● ● ● ● ● ● ● ● ● ● ● ● ●

CHICKEN BREASTERS

"Yeah! Keith!" It was the late Dr. Ed Hahn, a Centreville, Maryland veterinarian, with his usual cheery greeting. "You won't believe this!"

"Try me."

"The hot trout bait in Delaware Bay is chicken breast."

Long pause...

"Yeah, right." (Normally, I believe what any angler tells me, because I want them to believe my stories).

"I'm not kidding. I caught 11 trout on chicken breast before Jimmy [Ed's son, Captain Jimmy Hahn] caught one on fresh soft crab." Ed even asked Jimmy if he wanted to reel in one of Ed's trout.

"No self-respecting fisherman would use chicken chunks," Jimmy sniffed. Dr. Ed went on to specify raw, unfrozen, uncooked chicken breast, cut into chunks. "Not slivers, chunks." He also said Perdue chicken breast was best. (One might suspect Perdue's ace ad agency conjured up this fad, but I don't think so).

"A beach tackle shop got 250 pounds of chicken breast on Tuesday morning, and they were sold out by Wednesday afternoon," Dr. Ed said. "And, the guys drifting slivers of chicken just off a local fishing pier caught limits of flounder on it." Normally, flounder pounders use a minnow and squid strip combo. That day, Dr. Ed and son, Jimmy caught about 50 trout, plus croaker and flounder on chicken breast. They kept 12 of the trout.

Next, Dale Timmons, publisher of the "Coastal Fisherman" out of Ocean City, wrote seriously: "According to a reliable source, the flounder and trout fishing has been very good in Delaware on the Cape Henlopen Pier, and the hottest bait going is... chicken breasts!" Dale also cited a tackle shop that planned to market a new bluefish lure called the "Fowlinator," a chicken leg complete with feathers and a treble hook.

That's not as far out as it might seem. I just finished rereading Hal Lyman's excellent book, "Bluefish." Hal mentions a late 1800s bluefish bone lure popular in Morehead City, North Carolina. When cats became scarce in the area, locals found that young boys had developed a lucrative market by securing a dead cat–or converting a live one–to get kitty shank bones for the angling market at 50 cents each. The bones were cut into three-inch sections and, being hollow, were through-wired and rigged with hooks. The wire leader was then wrapped around a broomstick to form coils. When pulled through the water, the lure made an irresistible bluefish bait. Hal reports that the future of Morehead City felines brightened considerably when it was found that turkey, goose, and chicken bones bleached in the sun worked equally well. Lately, plastic tubes and surgical rubber hose have been substituted, and "members of the S.P.C.A. can breathe more easily," Hal wrote.

Naturally, those of us who live on the Eastern Shore of Maryland, the World Epicenter of chicken-growing (as evidenced by the Delmarva Chicken Festival), are concerned that the overuse of chicken parts for fishing might cut substantially into our low-fat vittles. Think about it. Chicken necks for crabbing. Chicken livers are the hot new bait in a chum line. Gizzards are processed for fish food in aquaculture, so why couldn't you use it for chum? Naturally, breasts will be popular. Bones and feathers for lures. And, don't forget the report of a drumstick carelessly tossed into a chum line being greedily gobbled by a striper. All of the above, plus some uses not even dreamed of yet, could put a lot of pressure on Delmarva chicken growers to increase production. Otherwise, prices will surely rise as consumers, anglers, and the Colonel vie for chicken parts.

So, to concurrently advance the dual sciences of angling and chickenology, fishing buddy Jim Walker and I gathered up some baits for a trout/croaker trip. Minnows, squid strips, store shrimp, chicken breasts, peeler crab, and bloodworms were coolered for a research trip on the Choptank River. Jim Walker and I both tied on our world-famous "Do-Nothin' Rigs," or DNR for short.

We anchored my 22-foot outboard boat on the "Sands," a locally-named spot southeast of Blackwalnut Point where the bottom drops off sharply from 16 to 35 feet. We randomly switched baits from top to bottom hooks, and from rig to rig, a sloppy system sure to anger 'snickety scientists who like to keep detailed records.

Trout caught on chicken breast.

"Chicken breast gets mushy when it's on the hook for a while," Jim said as he changed baits and tossed the old chunk of chicken overboard. A gull swooped from out of nowhere and grabbed it before it sank. He called the gull back and tossed a piece of shrimp up high. The gull grabbed it in midair, and luckily flew away. Good. Gulls circling overhead make one think twice about looking up. It seems that you have to be anchored for a while before fish can find your bottom-fished baits. I think they follow a scent trail upcurrent to your bait like a Labrador retriever follows a scent trail upwind to find a duck.

During our long dry spell, I munched on a sandwich. I got to thinking about a recent TV news show that pointed out precautions to take when handling raw chicken that could harbor salmonella bacteria. After handling raw chicken (and other fish baits) you should wash your hands before holding your own food. Don't place food on an area where raw chicken was prepared. Clean and disinfect the area first. Since I saw that scary show, I make it a practice never to slice my sandwich on the baitboard.

When the ebb tide slacked, we started to catch fish. Trout were biting funny. You'd feel a good tug and pull it up to the surface to find an empty hook. It was as if they gave a tug on the line and then finned backwards and laughed as our DNR rigs shot skyward.

Atlantic croaker (called "hardhead") are, pound for pound, World Champion Tuggers. If a hardhead weighed 10 pounds, he'd pull you out of the boat. No doubt about it when a hardhead hits. The rod bends double, and he'll take out some drag, too, on a light outfit.

We were using the new superlines, FireLine and Fusion, on levelwind bass reels. Rods were graphite. That combination makes for such great sensitivity you can almost feel a fish change her mind. Graphite transmits the slightest twinge to the hand, and the new superlines have almost no stretch. If you don't believe it, you bottom-fish with a weepy old fiberglass rod and stretchy monofilament line while your partner uses a graphite rod/superline combo.

We did catch a fair number of trout, croaker, and a few white perch in our Bait Evaluation Test. Four of our seven trout bit on chicken breast, as did two of our seven hardhead. The rest of the trout, croaker, and perch hit bloodworms and crab baits, except one croaker bit on shrimp. The croaker were all between 16 and 17 inches. We kept two of our seven trout over the 14-inch minimum size.

Finally, a warning if you decide to try chicken breast for bait: Keep it below the gunwales until you're ready to use it! If the fish can see it, they'll jump right into the boat. Dangerous. Someone could get hurt.

• •

A SUPER SUNDAY

If you can't get up a fishing trip at the Bozman store on a beautiful Sunday morning you can't do it anywhere. It's a busy place on a day-off morning.

"I counted 27 pickup trucks outside the store one Sunday morning," Dr. Stan Minken, a world-renowned vascular surgeon told me recently when I had to park across the street on the Post Office lot.

A recent Sunday morning was cool for a change after a long, hot spell, and Carole told me she was getting worried about me since I hadn't been fishing for almost a month. (Actually, the hot spell was a great time to sit in the air conditioning and correct the proof pages of our new "Ingenious Angler" book, plus start work on another new one). I can take a hint. I headed for the store to see if anyone wanted to go fishing. Jim Walker allowed as it was a pretty day and he had been away selling skylights for a week. If he doesn't get out fishing once every three days, he gets grumpy. Ed Irre, a retired teacher, said he could possibly work a trip into his busy schedule. Doc Minken said "Aren't you going to invite me?"

"Well, you said you had some bushhogging to do, and Babs had a list," I replied. "Didn't think you could get away."

"Yeah, you're right," he said, "and I'm on call." Stan was recently the Chief of Surgery at Johns Hopkins. A psychiatrist friend, concerned about Stan's long hours at work, asked him if he'd "ever seen a Brinks truck following a hearse." That did it. He cut back a bit, and seems to be enjoying his 200-acre farm and its beautifully-remodeled 17th century farmhouse with two-foot thick walls. He called me later and said "Babs gave me the green light." I knew he was kidding about Babs letting him go

So, the gang gathered at my dock, armed with enough tackle and sandwiches to last a week. Walker asked if we needed any bait, and I said no, we would be able to catch fish on light tackle with lures, a prospect that became less likely as the day wore on.

My 175hp Johnson Ficht huffed and puffed a bit as the 22-foot walkaround cuddy cabin hull struggled to get on plane. We had three big 'uns on board, and one not so porky, plus a full load of gas, and the motor wasn't used to this torture. "Probably got some barnacles on the bottom," Walker suggested. "When was the last time you painted the bottom?" he asked.

"When was the last time you helped me?"

"Last August."

"Well, that's when it got painted."

A generous offer of assistance was forthcoming, and we will pull the boat, scrub, and paint in the near future, or sometime before fall rockfishing heats up. Or maybe next spring.

At the mouth of Broad Creek, eagle-eye Walker scanned the Choptank River up and down with my compact 7x20 Nikon binoculars for breaking fish, which had been reported recently. He grumbled about my binocs, "Wish I'd brought my 7x50s along." That's funny. They both have the same magnification, and the 20mm lenses gather plenty of light on a sunny day, though his 50mm's can be better at dusk. It was almost noon.

No breaking fish and their attendant gulls were visible, so I headed to the mouth of the Choptank. "We'll go see what that gaggle of boats is up to, then head for the middle of the Bay and run south looking for gulls. If we catch some small bluefish we can use them as cut bait for flounder. Our backup mode is shallow water perch fishing with the three ultralight spinning outfits in the cabin." We had four anglers. "I guess I won't be able to perch fish," Walker complained, "I didn't bring a perch rod." Tsk, tsk.

The gaggle of boats was anchored, tossing ground menhaden chum, attracting a few fish and a lot of gulls. We ran toward the shipping channel, stopping first to cast bucktails at the leaning Sharp's Island light. We once caught good numbers of spotted seatrout there.

"One of the locals used to bring his girlfriend out here for a little lighthouse lovin'," Stan said. This conjured up a mental image of love, not only on the sly, but on the slant, since the structure leans so much. "They had a fight one day, and he left her out here." Since the fish did not cooperate, we ran south about a mile here." Since the fish did not cooperate, we ran south about a mile to the Icebreaker.

The Icebreaker's rocks are huge, below the surface about three feet, and unmarked except for a buoy 100 feet away and a tiny mark on a chart. They are hard to find. Walker has caught black sea bass here, plus spotted seatrout. Fishing buddy Jack Wiley once looked down into the clear water at the Icebreaker and said, "That's a couple of funny-looking rockfish. Their stripes run up and down." When I looked at them, they turned out to be a pair of sheepsheads, often called "convict fish."

From the Icebreaker we headed south down the Bay looking for birds. There was a gathering of boats south of buoy #2 of the False Channel off James Island. They appeared to be trolling, so we checked them out. They were mostly charterboats circling around a channel edge between 45 and 60 feet of water. A few gulls circled above. Everyone started to leave. It - whatever "it" was - was over. We headed for James Island's stumps, where erosion had left tree parts offshore, submerged a bit, but still able to grab your outboard's prop. Inboards don't go there!

Up to this point, we hadn't caught anything. Stan allowed that since we had no fish for dinner, we should order a bushel of crabs and have some backup. So, he cell-phoned in an order for later pickup. Now we could relax and fish. If we got skunked (it happened to me once), we'd have crabs.

At James Island, we drifted around in the stump field and cast bucktails with white grubs. I caught the first fish, a small blue, which gave me short-lived bragging rights. Walker caught a 20-inch spotted seatrout, which I netted. He was fishing off the bow, and Ed soon joined him there. There was a lot of discussion about close quarters, but Ed soon caught two keeper rockfish in quick succession. He yelled at me to get the net out of the way, but I told him I was only trying to knock his fish off the line. "Yeah, I know," he replied. Stan was the only one who had not caught a fish, "Still a virgin," he moaned.

I knew another stump pile, and put Stan right over it where he caught an undersize rockfish. "No longer a virgin," he exclaimed happily as he released the fish.

I think one of the best things about fishing–or hunting–is the afterglow, getting together and telling lies about the trip. And so we did, at Stan's farm. He had the crabs cooked when we got there, and cold beer on ice. Stan's wife, Babs; my wife, Carole; and Ed's wife, Dot completed the group, plus the day's anglers. Walker, who Stan says is a "serial bachelor," came alone. Soon everyone was elbow deep in crabs, a fitting way to end a perfect day.

Left to right: Dot Irre, Jim Walker, Babs Minken, Stan Minken,
Ed Irre, and Carole Walters

DON'T ASK HOW MANY I CAUGHT!

"Meet us at the Bellevue launch ramp," Dr. John "Jack" Scanlon said on the phone, "Butch and I will pick you up at 0600. Bring some casting and spinning tackle, and maybe a perch outfit."

"My tackle box is growing by the minute," I replied, thinking of all the gear I'd have to bring along.

"That's nothing, Butch [Chambers] always says I bring too much gear."

A 4 a.m. get-up is not as bad as it sounds if you really want to do some serious hunting or fishing. It seems that the best fishing is always at first or last light. Butch wanted to be at his favorite spot by first light. And, we were.

"I don't remember this much grass the last time we were here," Butch said as Jack and I pulled in gobs of weed on our lures. The tide was very low, and more grass was exposed. It was going to get even lower as we fished that morning, which, in retrospect, "was a good thing"—as stock-market Martha might say.

Butch and Jack fish my kinda way – shallow, with light tackle. For shallow water plug casting, they used spinning gear, but I noticed that their levelwind rigs were rigged with spoon jigs for deep jigging under birds and breaking fish. This day, the wind was so ferocious we had to find a lee shore to fish.

Butch Chambers' boat is perfect for the fishing they do. His 20-foot Atlantic center console hull is powered by a 100 hp four-cycle Yamaha outboard with power tilt, which comes in handy for tilt-ups when fishing around the rocky shorelines they prefer. Butch stands on the bow and controls his Great White electric motor with a foot pedal while he casts lures at likely rocks or other structure. His center console sports a Lowrance 350 combination depthsounder with a GPS module. Each angler aboard stows his rods along the gunwale in a different spot for quick access, but after a few fish come aboard and a bit of pandemonium reigns, rods are mixed to the point it's hard to separate the gear. Vertically-stored rods would be in danger of getting broken when the anglers are casting.

"There are a lot of rocks in this area," Butch said, pointing to a string of underwater stones that was once protective rip-rap, but erosion had left them sitting on the bottom offshore.

Butch and Jack have settled on surface plugs for this area, since sub-surface lures are easily lost here. Cotton Cordell® jointed Redfins are refitted with single hooks with the barbs mashed down.

"We told a friend to mash down his barbs," Jack said, "He didn't. Fortunately, I'm a physician with a sharp jackknife, so I could dig out his barbed hooks." Jack said a lot of people don't realize that some nerves are next to the bone, and a hook buried there "can make you feel sick."

Another favorite is a four-inch popper: "Wal-Mart for four bucks apiece," Butch added. It has single barbless hooks, too. Many of the fish this pair catches are released, so single barbless hooks make it easier–and safer–to get fish off than it would be with two treble hooks on a plug: One hook is in the fish, the other is whipping around trying to catch your hand.

Dr. Jack Scanlon with his striper.

Surface lures are favored when fishing over the rocks, and they were deadly effective. Farther out from shore, where deeper water covers the structure, they used Cocahoe minnows, a Louisiana version of the sassy shad, but Jack says, "Cocahoes are tougher."

Jack caught the first striper, a 21-inch keeper. He has become a vegetarian, which has his weight, diabetes, and blood pressure under control, so he was going to put the fish back overboard. Butch vetoed that and held the cooler lid open.

The writer had several boils behind his single-hook Atom popper, but no takes. Naturally, he'd arrived at the ramp loaded down with the wrong plugs. His Red Fins were safe at home.

"Use this one," Butch said as he handed me a re-rigged Red Fin. Two long-shank single hooks with mashed barbs had replaced the factory twin trebles. Butch said he likes to see a V-shaped wake behind the lure as he reels it in. Then, I remembered what Joe Hughes told me years ago on Lake Cumberland in Kentucky. Hughes was then a PR guy for Pradco, the Red Fin's maker. He tied a Red Fin on my line and told me to cast it towards the shore and bring it back over an underwater point so slowly it made the V-wake. An eight-pound striper hit the lure; it was the biggest striper caught by an outdoor writer in that 1987 Striperama tournament. The largest fish in the tourney competition weighed 55 pounds, caught on a live gizzard shad bait.

Jack added an idea for keeping track of a surface lure in choppy water. He paints the back, or top of the lure with chrome yellow nail polish ("Go figure" he says), which makes it highly visible. I bet!

It's funny how an angler can abandon one type of fishing after a few bum trips, but that's what I did–got away from my shallow water roots and went flounder fishing.

Jack caught another keeper rockfish at 27 inches. I asked if he needed a net. Butch doesn't carry one, "Just gets everything all tangled up," he says. These anglers tie a shock leader (fly-fishing talk) to the end of their running line, which makes a nice handle to hoist the fish aboard.

Butch Chambers with a striper.

The whole time, I was getting bites and swirls behind the Red Fin, but couldn't connect. Then I noticed that the lure Butch handed me almost always had its two long-shank hooks hooked together! No wonder it wasn't hooking fish.

Meanwhile Butch hooked and released several rock, as did Jack. Butch put two keepers in the box. Both anglers had their limits, and decided to entertain the writer by catching and releasing many more fish while u-no-who couldn't hook up.

Jack regaled us with emergency room stories. When he worked at a hospital on Cape Cod, a diver came in with a spear problem: His spear gun had gone off and nailed his foot to the sand. "They brought him into the ER and I had to cut off his flipper," Jack said. "He was really upset, because he had rented the diving gear."

Jack said they keep reeling the Red Fins until they feel the weight of a fish. They keep following the lure busting at it "Like someone threw a cinderblock into the water." Guide Richie Gaines calls that a "Kelvinator Bite," as if a refrigerator was tossed in the water.

Butch said he was casting poppers at bluefish when he "Caught two singles, then a double—of sea gulls." Gulls often swoop down on surface lures and grab them since they look like lunch to a sea bird.

"You don't see any duck blinds along here," Jack said. "If you see kayaks in a yard, you won't see any duck blinds," he added.

"You're sort of a waterfront philosopher," I said, noting the same analogy could be made about Volvos.

The pair also regaled me with outdoors foul-ups that prompted the FUOTY Club, which stands for something like "Foul Up of the Year." They have an annual February dinner, where the appropriate awards are given. "Falling overboard almost guarantees you'll get one," Butch said. Hooks in the hand are a close runner-up. Jack sent me some of the top award winners, possibly enough for a future column—if they are suitable for a family newspaper.

The final bit of Jack/Butch philosophy is right on the money: "Surface lures sort out the fish," Butch says, "The larger fish will hit them. It culls out the smaller fish." He's right.

Just don't ask how many the writer caught.

White Perch: Schmoo of the Bay

Some of us who are longer of tooth will remember Al Capp and his 'Lil Abner cartoon strip. Capp made up a happy critter he called a schmoo that wanted to satisfy every whim of its owner. It would contentedly roll over and substitute for pork, beef, or chicken.

Well, our part of Chesapeake Bay has its own little schmoo; it's called a white perch. White perch are game fish closely related to striped bass, and will happily hit bait like peeler crab and chicken breast strips, or smack a small artificial lure with much gusto. To top it off their filets are great on the plate with corn on the cob and fresh garden tomatoes, all washed down with ice tea.

So, when flounder season was closed for a couple of weeks and rockfish seem to be taking mostly trolled lures in the main Bay, we scale down our tackle to four-pound-test line on tiny spinning reels mounted on ultralight five-foot rods and seek out nearshore white perch. Homemade tiny spinnerbaits weighing 1/8 oz. attract perch bites.

We have had days when every cast resulted in a lively, tugging white perch. Sometimes they are so thick and so close to shore we can cast our lures up on the beach and pull them off into the water for an immediate hit.

Jim Walker and I found good numbers of white perch recently by drifting along in the shallow water between the mouth of Island Creek and Chloras Point, casting our tiny lures. Rocky bottom near the shoreline in three to four feet of water at high tide seemed to reward us with the best perching.

The rocky bottom found in most of these areas can severely damage propellers and boat bottoms, so caution is called for, particularly at low water.

When he cast his spinner-and-grub into a foot or so of water, Walker was surprised at the ferocity of a strike. His 5-foot ultralight rod was bent double, his tiny spinning reel losing line rapidly.

"I think I've got a big rockfish on!" he hollered. I stood by to net his rock and get it back into the water quickly. A big silver fish finally showed color at boatside, but we saw no stripes on it. It looked like a world-record white perch at first glance. I netted Jim's fish, which turned out to be a 16-inch Atlantic croaker!

Croakers, called "hardheads" here on the Eastern Shore, have been caught in recent summers in good numbers in the Choptank. But, in deep water. On bait. Not in shallow water on lures.

"I'm glad you were with me when I caught a hardhead on a lure," Walker joked, "otherwise nobody would believe me." Really? Don't all fishermen believe all others? I do.

We had another surprise when a big striper exploded next to my struggling white perch and noisily chased it in circles as I tried to boat it. This was very unusual in shallow water near shore, and in bright sunlight when stripers normally seek deeper, darker water. That hefty rockfish churned up a big patch of water! It tossed spray 4 feet in the air, trying to pounce on my perch. Talk about exciting!

In past years, we've used live white perch as baits to catch big stripers. Also, while fishing deep with bait in November, I've had stripers chase my white perch to the surface in November and splash water on me. But, watching that big striper tear around in shallow water in search of my perch was the biggest thrill of all.

Walker and I found one spot where the biggest kind of perch were concentrated. It was where the deepest near-shore water met a rocky shoreline. The water was just deep enough to make our 1/8-oz. jigheads the most effective. In really shallow water, less than two feet, a 1/16-oz.-jighead is best since it is light enough to swim above bottom without snagging.

Slightly deeper water, about three to four feet or so, is better for casting tiny 1/8-oz. crankbaits, since their minute treble hooks are prone to snagging debris in shallower water. Berkley's new Power Rattle®, Storm's Pee Wee Wart®, Bill Lewis' Tiny Trap®, Heddon's Mini-Tad®, and in-line spinners like the Mepps are all perch getters. They also all have tiny treble hooks. My experiments with a single barbless hook on lipless crankbaits like the Tiny Trap have been slightly short of spectacular. But, more research is needed.

Our homemade spinner-and-grub lures are basically like the tried-and true Beetle Spins. We make our own because we lose so many baits in the rocks and bottom debris. They are essentially small spinnerbaits, with French or willowleaf blades about 3/4 inch to 1 inch long attached to #12 snap swivels. We use 1/16-oz. or 1/8-oz.-unpainted round jigheads. Paint makes the lure look nicer if you want to impress your friends, particularly if the jig head and grub are color-coordinated. But, hungry perch don't seem to care about paint.

Grubs to decorate our tiny jigs are 2 inches in length, and come in tube tails, beetle styles, swimmertail grubs, and paddle-tail grubs. Mr. Wiffle has a new 2-inch grub and a tiny octopus-looking tube grub. Both need more field-testing on perch. Stay tuned.

What color plastic tails do perch like? White, yellow, bubble gum, and clear sparkle plastic tails are all enthusiastically accepted by our Choptank River white perch. Scented tails include 2 inch-Power Grubs®, salty grubs, and those sprayed with fish oils by the angler. All will take perch, scented or not, since the fish are making split-second decisions about a moving lure, and probably don't have time to sniff it.

Our homemade lures on center fish net large white perch.

Between Oxford and Chloras Point on a later trip, Jack Stovall and I began a drift parallel to the shoreline, casting our lures to rockpiles and fallen trees. We caught some really nice white perch. Stovall wanted to keep the biggest ones, but I told him we'd catch some BIG ones later. He kept a few nine-inchers for dinner in case I was wrong. We drifted along, catching (and releasing) white perch of a size we would have been proud to keep just last summer. He kept a few more small ones, just in case.

Finally, I reached the place where Walker and I had caught the biggest perch. Stovall caught several. I slipped the small stern anchor over and we stayed a while.

"Why didn't we come here first?" Stovall asked as he unhooked another 11-inch perch.

"It would have been too easy," I answered, "I didn't want to spoil you!" That day, we only kept as many perch as we could clean and eat for dinner that night. We released the rest.

"Wow!" Stovall yelled. "Look at that!" There was a huge splash near the boat. Stovall's rod tip pointed at the center of a swirl that was 100 times bigger than one might expect from the tiny white perch on his line. A rockfish was after Stovall's perch. Since this was the same place where a striper attacked my perch a few days before, I wondered if it was the same fish.

This striper followed Stovall's nervous perch almost to the boat, tossing spray into the air like a feeding tuna. Stovall brought in the perch and released it. He later cast larger surface lures at the center of the striper's activity until his arms were tired with no success.

I've never seen anything like that!" Stovall said about the striper/ perch pursuit. "I'll probably dream about it tonight."

I knew how he felt. Who knew that white perch fishing could be that exciting?

• • • • • • • • • • • • • • • • • • • •

LAKE NAMAKAGON

(Hayward, Wisconsin)—I was completely surrounded by Nordic folks at Lakewoods Resort. All the waitpersons in the dining room overlooking Lake Namakagon could be on the Norwegian Bikini Team. (Photos of Nordic goddessii draped in tiny bits of string, however, would be out of place here).

So, back to the Norse angle, and the fishing stuff.

Resort owners Phil and Kathy Rasmussen are certified Norwegians; I think their PR lady, Naomi Shapiro, is one too. My late mother was a Knutson who foaled me in neighboring Minnesota. My fishing partner, outdoor scribe C. Boyd Pfeiffer, threatened to call himself Yearald Fjord so he could pass for a Norwegian.

The more astute readers will notice that Hayward, Wisconsin is not exactly near Chesapeake Bay, where my meandering in search of hard outdoorsy data usually take place. This odyssey, however, was in search of fishing facts we could bring home to the Bay, sort of a piscatorial technology transfer 'twixt fresh and saltwater.

Boyd came prepared to fish. He brought along 8 fly rods (I'm not making this up), 4 bait casters, and 6 spinning rods including 2 ultralights, matching reels for everything, plus 14 soft cases of fishing tackle, his wife Jackie, and a toothbrush.

I, on the other hand, came prepared to attend our annual Outdoor Writers Association of America meeting in Duluth, Minnesota, the following week. I brought only 1 spinning rod and reel, 1 baitcasting rod and reel, 1 (small) tackle box, my wife Carole, and 14 bags of clothing, toiletries, cameras and film, note paper and pens, shoe polish, snacks, a steam iron, hair curlers (hers), scotch (mine), and other absolute necessities. Fishing, of course, was secondary; this was a business trip. Ask my accountant.

The first business we conducted was a detailed study of the relationship between Boyd's Clouser flies, my Storm Thunderstick plug, and the polite refusal of several hundred northern pike to bite on either lure. Our test conductor was Lakewoods' chief chef and main fishing guide, one Dave Scanlon, possibly a Norwegian.

Lake Namakagon's 32,000 acres of blackish water is colored by the tamarack trees that line its shores, Dave told us. The water was really curious because you could see a chartreuse Thunderstick lure four feet deep in the inky water.

"We gotta find some cabbage [weeds]," Dave said, heading his 19-foot bass boat across the lake. "None here in this bay, but it'll be here later. All of a sudden in a week the cabbage will be here, and the fish'll be here too."

I caught a two-pound pike on a novelly-rigged jig/minnow combo that Dave had furnished me. The jig's 1/4-oz. round leadhead was in the minnow's mouth, and the hook protruded from its back. Dead minnows are not offended by this rigging.

Boyd, who throughout the next 3-1/2 days of concentrated fishing used only a fly rod, caught a pike on his "Invincible" fly design with 1/4-inch doll eyes. He thoughtfully liberated the fish 15 to 20 feet from the boat, what we conservationists call a "long-line release."

"Walleye hitting pretty good, eh?" Dave asked his friend, Don, in another boat. "Yep, you betcha," Don said with a Norwegian inflection, "but it's better near dusk. Had two muskies on - one hit a walleye at boatside. Wouldn't let it go. Had to lift the walleye out of the water before the dang musky'd let loose."

"We had a musky contest all set up," Dave told us, "with the [Wisconsin] Governor and everything. But we had to call it off— ice was still three feet thick on the lake the last week in May."

"I betcha y'all (Norwegian dialect mixed with deep south here) are bored stiff here in the winter with snow up to your nostrils."

"Oh, no," Dave said, "We're filled up year 'round. Lakewoods is the top-rated snowmobile resort in the country. We have miles of trails through the woods."

That evening, we took a dinner cruise on a big aluminum pontoon boat captained by 77-year-old Oscar Treeland, whose father started their Treeland Resort in 1928 after coming over from—you guessed it – Norway. Oscar remembered running cattle where the lake is now, before a dam was built to flood the beautiful, wild, 17,000-acre Lake Chippewa Flowage. Most of the property around the lake is undeveloped. "Great fishing," Oscar said, "One guide has fished the 'Big Chip' for many years and still hasn't explored it all."

Steak with all the trimmings, plus strawberry shortcake was barely tucked away when we saw a storm approaching from the west. Remember, we were on an aluminum boat with vertical aluminum poles holding up more aluminum poles that held up a canvas roof. Heavy rain and noisy lightening surrounded us. Captain Oscar pulled into the lee of an island and cheered us up with, "Don't touch the side rails!"

The next morning we launched guide Ron Weberg's 16-foot bass boat at Big Round Lake, an oblong watershed with lots of homes. Ron is a retired Chrysler auto worker who enjoys guiding anglers on several local lakes. Though of German extraction, I will hereby nominate Ron for honorary Norwegian citizenship.

"Within 16 square miles of my farm," Ron said, "there are 80 fishable lakes from 100 to 18,000 acres."

If Ron's chosen retirement area sounds like a rehab region for the piscatorially-challenged, it is, you betcha. We fished with Ron for 2-1/2 delightful days, caught fish and made lots of photos. Ron's eyes lit up when Boyd told him we needed fishing photos of bass, pike, or maybe a muskellunge (musky). Most folks Ron guides want to do walleye. Blech! All walleyes are is good to eat.

But, bass are an underfished species in Wisconsin. They need lots of

Fishing guide Ron Weberg with a nice smallmouth bass.

exercise. "Bedding bass is my favorite," Ron said, and we were off. Ron pointed out large homes and big boats at the docks, indicating this particular lake would be too busy with speedboat and jet ski traffic later on to be very good fishing. Lake water was so clear we could pick out the smallmouth bass on their beds and cast to them. Beds are rocky areas where male bass have swept aside the surrounding silt with their tails. The male then hustles one or more females to the bed, where they cast their eggs, and he fertilizes them. The females then swim away and go shopping.

It is up to the male to protect the eggs for a week or two until they become fry and swim away. Some anglers feel bedding bass fishing is a bit tacky, harassing fish while they are protecting their eggs. Ron refuses to bother bass that won't return to their beds after a strike.

The drill was to cast a Gitzit softhead and jig combo past the bed, then pull it slowly into the bed and let it sit there. Neatness counts with smallmouth bass, so the male fish picks up the jig in his mouth and carries it out of the bed. You can watch him do it in the clear water. Then, you set the hook and the smallie explodes, often jumping clear of the water.

Smallmouth bass will fight you right to the boat, around the boat, and right into the boat. Their popular cousins, largemouth bass, seem more lethargic; they thrash around a bit after being hooked, then swim over to the boat and hold their mouth open so you can remove the hook and release them. Yawn!

"I don't keep any bass anyway," Ron said, "they're my pets. My wife saw a picture of me kissing a fish before releasing it. She said 'You're kissing what?' I told her I only kiss the good lookin' ones."

"I heard it takes about 12,000 casts to catch a musky," I said. "Fooey," Ron said, "I catch seven or eight musky a day bass fishing with a white spinnerbait. Some guides will yell, 'There's a big musky right behind your bait!' and the dude goes back to the lodge happy. The dude never saw the musky, and neither did the guide."

Next day on Day Lake, a big musky followed my white spinnerbait to the boat. The fish was as big as my leg, and I have a long leg.

"Figure eight! Figure eight!" Ron yelled. Boyd and I looked at Ron. What? The mega-musky smiled at us and slowly sank out of sight.

Ron showed us how to "figure eight" by swishing his rod tip and lure in a rapid figure-eight pattern alongside the boat. Muskies will often grab the lure when it is manipulated like this. I wasn't sure I'd want a 40-pound fish that is one third teeth jumping into the boat with me after the old figure eight ploy. "I believe in small lures," Ron said. "Think about it. That 'ol musky can grab just about anything he wants to eat. Let's say he's just had a big walleye meal, and he's just sitting back, picking his teeth. He'll grab a small bait just like you'd grab a mint after dinner."

The running gag on these trips to different lakes was Boyd's tenacity and loyalty to the fly rod. Ron and I were bailing bass with spinning and bait casting outfits decorated with Gitzits and spinner baits. I'd hold up a nice bass to Boyd and ask if he didn't want to stick a fly in its mouth and we'd take all our pictures, and then the pressure would be off and we could have fun. I was kidding, but he ethically refused.

After 3-1/2 days of steady fly casting, he'd only caught that one pike. Finally, Boyd connected! A nice bass. We made dozens of photos, then released the bass. Next, we put Boyd ashore on a small island with some shrubs so he could frame his photos of Ron and I in the bass boat. We began casting for Boyd's cameras. "Wouldn't it be something if I caught a bass now?" I asked Boyd.

BAM! A smallie hit my white spinnerbait and went airborne for Boyd. Right on cue! A fitting end to our last day of angling research.

"Yeah," Ron kidded Boyd, "you could write that the other guys [Keith and Ron] were hammering bass, 50 or more a day, for three days on Gitzits, and you accidentally caught one on a fly!"

"Not in my damn article," Boyd said.

Spoken like a true Norwegian.

● ● ● ● ● ● ● ● ● ● ● ● ● ● ● ● ●

EASTERN SHORE POND BASSIN'

Norm Haddaway knows a special bass pond where he occasionally takes a friend, but only on Sunday mornings from dawn to 8:30 a.m.

"They quit biting then anyway," says Norm. The sun gets a little high over this shallow pond, maximum depth about 4-feet, and the fish turn off. But, in the dawn's early light one Sunday morning, our surface plugs and buzzbaits created fireworks equal to the Fourth of July display at Fort McHenry.

The first cool Sunday morning after our summer heat wave found Norm, Steve Henckel, and myself hustling a 14-foot aluminum jon boat across the well-manicured grass bank on a private estate, and down the bank to the water. More mud flat was showing than Norm liked, but the summer drought had ponds everywhere lower than usual.

"This pond is the best bass fishing I've ever had anywhere," Norm said as we put his electric trolling motor and our assorted bass tackle in his boat. Norm is a Bay fishing guide and has worked on the water all his life. He also takes sea duck hunting parties in the fall, and if the sea duck shooting is slow, there are usually breaking rockfish to keep his party busy. He has fished with all of the local bass guides. If Norm says this pond is the best, it's the best.

Norm rigged his 7-foot rod and levelwind reel, and tied a jointed Jitterbug to his line. Norm says a fairly stiff 7-foot rod gives him more leverage on the fish. Steve used a spinning outfit armed with a spinnerbait. I chose a clear plastic three-bladed buzzbait with a white skirt, and added a white 4-inch plastic swimmertail grub. My casting rod was a 6-foot graphite mounting a Ryobi V-Mag 3 levelwind reel loaded with 14-pound test Trimax line.

OK, bass, we're ready for you. Do your stuff. It was just beginning to get light.

"I love bass fishing," Norm said as we cast our lures, "When I first started bass fishing, I worked half-days for two years. The rest of the time, I was bass fishing."

Something followed my buzzbait, making a giant wave behind it, but didn't hit. Norm advised me to stop the lure and let it fall. Sometimes they'll grab it as it drops. On my next cast, something did grab the lure, and gave me a pretty good tussle. It was at least a five pounder. I was thrilled.

"Small one," Norm said, indicating it wasn't even a "picture fish." "There are bigger ones in here," he added.

How about that? I catch one of the biggest bass of my life, and Norm says it's a "small one."

Steve, who kneeled on the hard aluminum front seat of the boat all morning as he cast his spinnerbait, had a hit. Anyone who has the stamina to kneel on that hard metal surface and cast continually for three hours deserves a hit. Steve wrestled the bass to boatside and posed for a picture before releasing the fish. Another 5-pounder.

Norm Haddaway with his 7-lb. bass.

Norm plunked his Jitterbug down beyond a tiny twig sticking in the mud in mid-pond. He slowly reeled past the stick. Bam! A bass pounced on the lure. As Norm fought this bigger bass, he elatedly said, "See, I knew he'd be right by that stick." Bass guide Ken

Penrod says that if there is only one bass in a pond, and only one stump or stick, that's where the bass will be—alongside that stick. Ken was right, too. That's where Norm's 7-pound bass was.

"Told you there were bigger fish in here," Norm said, holding up his monster for pictures.

Two bass were noisily chasing a baitfish across the surface 20 yards from us. I cast a Hula Popper at the ruckus, and tied into a bass. Norm also cast at the melee, but his plug fell short. I had my hands full at the time, but I heard some spicy talk from the back seat. When I had time to look, I saw Norm picking at a world-class backlash. "A mega-backlash," he called it, but some guides he knows call it a "professional overrun." Norm did find time to lip grab and release my fish, another 5-pounder. Ho-hum.

We had worked our way around the 13-acre pond and we were back at ground zero, where another bass exploded like an atomic bomb under my buzzbait. I worked it toward the boat where Norm made a grab for the lip, the (5-pounder) spit the lure out, the lure zinged past my nose and hit Steve in the head. Luckily, no damage done.

Steve Henckel with a nice bass.

Steve pulled another bass out of some brush on shore, unusual because Norm hadn't been able to catch anything there in the past. Steve's success may have been due to the extremely low water.

Another bass had taken up residence next to Norm's stick when we came back to that part of the pond. It may have been the same fish, but it fell in love with Norm's Jitterbug again.

The bass were either so thick in this pond, or so hungry, that it didn't take much bass know-how to catch them. I mean, you have to understand, I call my own 22-foot

Angler boat, "Backlash." Does that tell you something? When I can catch bass after bass, almost all without changing from my old reliable buzzbait, then I know they are really thick in there.

With the sun getting higher, the bass suddenly got lockjaw. It happens every time, according to Norm. They hit really well until about 8:30 a.m., then just as if every bass was looking at the same watch, they all shut down. It was time to wrestle the jon boat across the mud flat and into the back of Norm's 4-wheel drive pickup

We stood on the grassy shoreline of the pond and sipped coffee from a thermos. I marveled at the number of bass we caught that morning. We didn't keep a running count. We had been too busy. But it had to be somewhere between two and three dozen bass!

"You don't get good fishing like THAT every day," I said.

Norm looked out across the pond. "You do here," he said.

● ● ● ● ● ● ● ● ● ● ● ● ● ● ● ● ●

GEEZER-FISHING

Outdoors writers should be more circumspect when they have strict grammarians looking over their shoulders. Recently, I wrote about a "geezer fishing" trip.

As soon as the story hit the printed page, I had an email query about how one could go fishing for geezers.

"What bait do you use?" the questioner asked. As geezers are mostly male (ladies long of tooth are called "matures"), my inquisitor assumed bait would consist of Poligrip sprinkled with Metamucil or Viagra. "Think of the size of net," he asked, "and whether lipping or gaffing (no release here) would be best. Do geezers hang around structure? (Sure, they lean on bars and set foot on brass rails). Dock benches are also good structure."

I shoulda wrote "geezers fishing." For the lack of the letter "S" the concept was lost. Sorry. I'll do better next time. Maybe.

THE CLAN FUOTY

Eighteen members of the Clan FUOTY met recently for their year 2002 Awards Banquet. One might suppose I got the year wrong, but such is not the case—the awards were for mostly negative events that occurred in the year 2002 that could be properly documented and approved by the board to be presented as soon as possible after the preceding year had shot itself in the foot. First, there were libations, tall tales, a sumptuous game dinner, and, lastly the awards.

FUOTY is an acronym for Foul-Up of the Year, or something close to that. FUOTYs gather data all year, with as much detail as possible about member's foul-ups so they may be properly—and negatively—brought before the membership. However, only board members can get the prestigious annual award—except for the chairman, who has declared himself permanently out of the running.

The earliest Fuoty, however, was documented in the seventh century in what is now Ireland's County Kerry, according to research by Dr. John "Jack" Scanlon. A huntsman and fisher, Priapus Fuoty, managed to drown himself because he wouldn't let go of his stout willow branch and horsehair line when attached to a monstrous salmon. He left seven children and his wife was heavy with an eighth. A picture of Priapus and his fish is limned in a seventh century Celtic tome.

Again, referring to Doc Scanlon's research, most of the male Fuotys had short—but adventurous lives. No fewer than four dozen male Fuoty headstones in the graveyard adjoining Innisglamorghan's Anglican Church bear eulogies such as:

"It weren't the whiskey but the water did him in." (Phadric Fuoty, 1793).

"Scion of the Fuoty Clan, victim of his own hand." (Malachi Fuoty, 1805).

"Hooked a great fish and, piously gurgling, lost the fight." (Sean Thomas Fuoty, 1839).

"Looked down the charged barrel and hastened to God." (Francis Xavier Fuoty, 1848).

Fuotys, Doc Scanlon found, kept popping up on the passenger lists of the Lusitania, the Titanic, the Hindenberg, and the Andrea Dory. Firearms skills got Fuotys positions with General Custer. Later, Fuotys bought property on a tiny Pacific atoll named Eniweetok. "There are few Fuotys left on the auld sod," Doc Scanlon says, "Need I say more?"

It is easy to see why the modern FUOTYs are loathe to have their names mentioned, though they do have a proud heritage. Several expressed trepidations about becoming famous, in a negative way, by having their names mentioned in a newspaper column. So, it might be better to include only the foul-ups without names in my report.

"Falling out of a boat," Doc Scanlon once told me, "Is a sure way to be nominated." Other sure-fire ways include catching a rockfish on one barbed treble hook of a plug, and impaling your hand on the other barbed hook, especially after being told to mash down your barbs. That's how the 2001 awardee gained recognition. One no-gas guy was so recognized, and another member ran aground in his home waters, actually near his house.

A board vote was taken to expand the board from six to seven, which, of course will allow another potential awardee. The new board member now has "all the rights and privileges thereto" pertaining to his elevated position.

Individual members proposed several candidates, including one hunter who shot his last three shells at a turkey, and missed every time. When more shells were offered to him, he admitted he had a 10-gauge. Everyone else had 12-gauge shells. Another was proposed for having a dead battery in his boat. Another member had forgotten his girlfriend's name at a public affair. A new award was suggested for an elderly gent with more interest in ladies than hunting - the Pfizer Award. Voted down or vetoed by the chairman, same result. It seems the FUOTYs were more worried about losing a good hunting farm than they were concerned about his new romance.

Ballots were passed around the room. To avoid mayhem, I abstained from voting. The chairman tallied the votes mentally, and tossed the ballots into the fireplace. Chairman's discretion, he called it. "There's a five-way tie," the chairman announced. "That means the present trophy holder gets to keep it for another year!" "Is that in the bylaws?" someone asked. The chairman picked up a three-ring binder, cracked open a page an inch or so, and quickly closed the book. "Yep, it's in here," he said.

"Ever seen the bylaws?" I asked the chap next to me. "No one has," he said.

Someone mentioned the chairman had enough "merits" to get the award himself, like burning a big hole in the back of an expensive hunting coat when he tossed it on a heater while disrobing to shoot (at) snow geese. He also wiped out an entire starling family with his smallbore rifle. The members voted unanimously that if eligible, The chairman would have won the 2002 FUOTY Award, hands down.

The meeting was adjourned in an uproar of parliamentarian babble, according to the secretary's notes.

But, a good time was had by all, and that's all that matters. And, a happy FUOTY new year to all.

CHICKEN-NECKERS

The extreme sport of chicken-necking has again reared its ugly head. For those not familiar with the sport, chicken-necking is the art of dangling the neck of a dead chicken in the water at the end of a string, with a spark plug or some other plebeian weight to hold the bait on bottom. The other end of the string is attached to an anchored boat. From six to twelve such rigs, plus a dip net and a bushel basket with a cover are all that's needed for a chicken-necker's holiday.

When the boat is properly anchored in six to eight feet of water and the crab lines are spread out around the boat so they'd look like a spider's legs from above, the wait begins.

When a crab picks up the bait the chicken-necker string puller slowly picks up the line and drags the crab back toward the boat where an assistant, called a "chicken-necker netter" waits with a

long handled net. If the net is suspended over the water, the crab will see it and drop off the bait. This is the part where experience is necessary. Seasoned chicken-necker netters wait until the moment before the crab lets go, then they come from behind and dip the critter. A ruler is handy to make sure the crab meets the minimum size and the crustacean is dropped into the basket. Unfortunately, chicken-necking seems to have been imported from the western shore (not capitalized) to the Eastern Shore (always capitalized),

Carole Walters

which then led to the present term of derision where professional trotline crabbers call non-professional chicken-necking crabbers "chicken-neckers." The same term is used, along with some cuss words, when a non-professional trotliner lays his line over a pro's trotline.

This battleground between crabbing philosophies began years ago in the crab-infested waters around Kent Island (KI), and has since spread eastward, causing hard feelings all the way to the ocean, or as chicken-neckers from the western shore (ws) say "downee ocean." Kent Island, slowly agglomerating population from the western shore, has become an extension of that great wasteland west of the Bay. What seems to have happened is that so many ws people have moved to KI, it has become more or less attached to the ws, moving the dividing line between the ws and the Eastern Shore (ES) eastward to Kent Narrows. Some might say that means that Kent Island should no longer be capitalized, since it is now just a suburb of Anne Arundel County on the western shore.

Two events got me to pondering about this weighty subject. First, Queen Anne Countian Bill Evans, wrote an entertaining column for the Bay Times. Evans, in an entertaining fashion, seems to be developing a whole new chicken-necker ethos, ethic, and philosophy. He was selling a T-shirt emblazoned with a crab picking away at a chicken-neck, a fancy garment that could be worn to the toniest of Queen Anne County cocktail parties.

And, secondly, since a local waterman with an unmufflered diesel engine and a loud radio has awakened us at 5 a.m. every morning, seven days a week, for over two months, I had a lot more time to think about esoteric subjects like chicken-necking. By the way, it may surprise you to know that two types of vessel are exempted from Maryland's disturbing the peace and noise ordinances: airboats and watermen's boats, according to Natural Resources Policeman, Sgt. George Ball. "I can do something about the loud radio," Sgt. Ball said, "but I don't have any teeth on the unmufflered diesel." I told him that if I were to ride up and down the waterman's street with an unmufflered diesel engine and a loud radio for six hours when people were trying to sleep, I'd wind up in jail. Soon after, the waterman made an attempt to hold down the noise by running slower and turning his radio down. But, still, old people get grumpy when awakened by noisy diesel engines every morning at 5 a.m. Then, they write cantankerous columns.

Before moving to the Shore, we lived on the Little Magothy River, a shallow creek bordering Cape St. Claire on the ws. A few of my neighbors would get together on weekends and lay a short trot line baited with chunks of salt eel out in the shallow creek. They would run the line in a small skiff, whooping and hollering each time a crab was netted, then retire to a shady lawn and drink beer until it was time to run the line again. This procedure was repeated all day until evening when the crabs were steamed. One might imagine by mid-afternoon they were fairly well oiled, and that's when we non-participants began watching the shenanigans. They'd start out with three or four people in the boat, one of them netting crabs off the trot line and tossing them toward the basket, often missing the toss so their barefoot companions could dodge snapping claws.

If the netter missed a crab, he was shoved overboard. Luckily the water was only about four feet deep. By late afternoon, there was usually only one person in the boat by the time it reached the end of the trot line, and he ran a wobbly course back to the dock. That was 40 years ago, and all of the participants, strangely enough, have since died of natural causes. I do not condone this type of irresponsible behavior, nor do the water cops, and it's a wonder no one drowned. I only relate it here to serve as a bad example. Don't do this!

When my wife and I first moved to the ES, we'd leave our dock at daybreak, motor to the end of a sandbar across Broad Creek, and set out our chicken-neck baits. We did rather well, too, often catching enough crusty crustaceans to invite friends for a feast. Later, we switched to the standard two crab pots off the dock baited with perch carcasses left over after fileting off the meat. We don't catch as many crabs as we did when we chicken-necked, and the action is not as fast and ferocious, but we get along better not yelling at each other about our misses with the net.

The ultimate irony for us chicken-neckers occurred recently at the local post office. Parked outside was a pickup truck belonging to a retired college professor who now is a professional waterman/ trotliner. I couldn't help but notice a square box in the bed of the truck. It was marked "chicken-necks!"

From that point on, the watermen's derisive description "chicken-necker" has no teeth. Excluding profanity, what will they now call "come-heres" like us?

• • • • • • • • • • • • • • • • • •

OLD DOCKS AND OLD DOCS

"What we usually look for is an old dock," I said with great authority. "Hey, that's me you're talking about!" Doc Scanlon said, with even greater authority.

"I'm talking about piers that gather up white perch. Not doctors. Unless, of course you have barnacles growing on your pilings."

We were white perch fishing in Broad Creek and thereabouts, and old docks with marine growth attract critters that attract white perch, and sometimes small white perch attract rockfish, and so on up the food chain—to us.

Dr. John "Jack" Scanlon and Butch Chambers had arrived at 0630 hours at my dock (which holds no white perch), loaded down with fishing rods. Butch only had six, but Jack had at least eight. Each of their rods was rigged with a lure, so they didn't have to re-tie when a new lure became necessary. Both also had huge soft pack tackle boxes that contained just about any lure you'd need to fish anywhere in North America, well, maybe you could add South America and Australia.

My favorite perch outfit is a 5-1/2 foot ultralight spinning rod mounting a small spinning reel loaded with 4-pound test monofilament line. I use small spinner and grub lures about 1/8-

ounce in weight, copies of the Beetle Spin I make myself. They are decorated with small spinner blades and 2-inch white Power Grubs.

Butch and Jack have a different spec for "ultralight." They use 6-foot spinning rods with medium spinning reels loaded with 6-pound test line. Jack uses superline, and Butch uses Stren® purple mono so he can see where his line is. Both cast 1/8-ounce Tiny Traps in silver finish. They buy their Tiny Traps by the dozen. I soon found out why.

At 0645 on a sunny morning the perch were hiding in the shade of a dock that ends in 6 feet of water. We caught several on our various lures. Most were near the dock pilings but a few struck our lures in open water. If I had kept score, I'd guess their Tiny Traps caught larger perch. Both commented that Broad Creek held the biggest white perch they'd seen this year. Jack lives on the Little Choptank, and both usually fish from Butch's 20-foot Atlantic center console hull in the big Choptank and out across the Bay to the Power Plant and Gas Dock, plus anywhere in between. That's why they brought so many rods, we didn't know where we'd wind up fishing.

But first, we ran to several points on the high tide to cast lures like the Cocahoe Minnow® for rockfish. A few undersize "dinks" came in, but no keepers. I put the anglers on top of a stump pile in open water. They both rigged up with deep-jigging spoons at the end of a leader and a hook decorated with chartreuse bucktail hair two feet ahead of the jig. They fish their jigs with levelwind reels. Very effective. Jack caught a few small rock and Butch caught a doubleheader of 12-inch rock. All were released.

Butch thought it would be productive if we ran out to 17 feet of water and bottom-fished for croakers. He caught some big croakers out there several days before. We tried three different spots, but no luck.

We watched the western sky all morning, and it looked more threatening every minute. Butch said the radar showed a big, bad storm coming our way, but "it was in West Virginia at 0530 hours." It was now about 11 a.m. Hmmm... Five and a half hours at 30 miles per hour. How far away is West Virginia? The vote was to head back into the Choptank and fish "France" for hardheads. When we arrived at France, so did a 30-knot wind and rain. Luckily, I had left the Bimini and side curtains up, because it poured buckets. "A car wash rain," Butch called it.

So, now we needed to get in the lee of Nelson Point at the mouth of Broad Creek, about 3-plus miles at compass heading 030 degrees. There was no way to bang into those waves and it wasn't very comfortable to run at 3,000 rpm in the wave troughs, either, but I had no choice. It was an uncomfortable 20 minute ride, and I couldn't see much through a windshield solidly washed with rainwater.

"I thought you said there was only a 30-percent chance of rain," I scolded Butch, our weatherman. "That's right," Butch replied, "all 30 percent is coming down right now!"

When I finally got a glimpse of the shoreline, I was way off to starboard; the wind on our port side had pushed me off on quite a tangent, so my 030 course was pretty much useless. I corrected course but could barely see Nelson Point. Butch said "It's over there," pointing off the port bow.

Dr. Jack Scanlon – soaked.

We passed a workboat on the way in. He was headed into the waves, just riding it out. His boat was long enough to span two or more waves, so he looked pretty comfortable. Butch sat in the passenger seat, I steered from the captain's seat, and Jack was wedged in between us, trying to keep dry, since we didn't have time to drop the rear curtains when the storm hit us. With his left shoulder forward, Jack's right side was exposed to the tempest.

Finally, behind Nelson Point, it was calm. There was a dock handy.

The guys wanted to try casting around the dock for white perch. In the rain.

Butch was moderately unhappy because he hadn't hooked a cownose ray, or "doublehead" yet; Jack calls him the "Doublehead King."

Jack looked grumpy up on the bow as he re-tied a messy line and lure wrap-up. Jack said his Tiny Trap had "come loose and crocheted itself around the guides and the rod itself." A carwash

Butch Chambers in the rain.

rain added to his mood. He was now soaked to the skin. So was Butch, who smiled happily when I took his photograph. Fishing in a downpour requires a considerable amount of chutzpah. I stayed in the (dry) cabin and positioned the boat so they could cast.

For some reason, these guys hunt ducks on sunny days and fish on rainy, windy ones. Jack says they don't plan it that way – it just happens.

When the sun finally came out, we tried some more docks and caught more big perch. We were in by noon, all dried out and happy again. Even the Old Doc.

Some guys are nuts about fishing; some are just nuts.

SIDEWAYS THINKING ABOUT REEL HISTORY

Fishing line storage devices are thought to go as far back as Cleopatra. She reportedly had a slave dive underwater and hook a fish on Mark Antony's line. As Mark reeled in the fish, she reeled in Mark Antony. Here, fishing history takes an ominous twist: Julius Caesar had a hissy-fit about the fishing deal, and William Shakespeare, the first outdoor writer, did a story about it.

I think reel history goes back a lot further to Og, the caveman, who stored his monkeyvine fishing line on a dumbbell-shaped rock. Between carrying a big club for hunting and his weighty fishing reel, Og gained a pretty big set of biceps, a fact not lost on today's bodybuilders. They groan and strain lifting modern-day dumbbells, whereas if they put some fishing line on them, they could abandon pain and gain some fun in the outdoors—breathe fresh air instead of inhaling sweaty gym air.

Og thought if he could refine his "reel" enough he could get a patent on it, and live on royalties instead of bashing dinosaurs for dinner and having to carry that $%#@ big reel from stream to river, then back to the cave dragging a huge stringer of fish. But, hunting and fishing took up most of his time and his dream of a patent never happened.

Actually, there are only two commonly accepted ways to store fishing line on a spool; rotate the spool to cast and retrieve line as is done on conventional reels, or wind the line around a stationary spool with a rotating flyer and bail mechanism, and cast it off the end of the spool, like modern-day spinning reels.

In the mid-1800s, Malloch invented a swiveling spool that would swivel to cast line off the spool's end, and swivel back to allow rotating the spool for line retrieval, much like a modern fly reel. The only problems a modern angler would find with Malloch's invention were: 1) It was machined of solid brass and weighed four or five pounds, and 2) The fishing lines of that era were made of horsehair and cast much like bailing wire.

Actually, there is a modern version of the Malloch reel, made by Alvey in Australia. It swivs in exactly the same way as Malloch's reel, but it has the advantage of modern lines and a drag system.

Later, more sophisticated spinning reels were invented. Illingworth's first spinning reel in the late 1800s was a wobbly contraption, but it worked. In a parallel universe, William Shakespeare, Jr. (not the earlier outdoor writer) made one of the first (never, ever, say "the first." Someone else was always there first) levelwind reels in 1897. He called it the "Handmade Model C" and ran his model numbers backwards to the turn of the century; i.e., 1898 was "B" and 1899 was "A." After that he went to a straight numbering system. What's novel about Willy's first brass (yes, brass) reel was a dual-machined cam that carried the line-levelling loop back and forth to evenly spread the line on the spool to keep it from lumping up on one side and jamming the works.

Spinning reel technology didn't really blossom until better fishing lines came out after WWII, but levelwinder technology raced ahead in order to extract a lot of loot from rich early 1900s bass anglers.

Then, some watchmakers in Kentucky came up with beautifully-made bass reels that modern-day tackle collectors call, surprisingly, "Kentucky Reels." Meek and Milam and Snyder engraved their names on these shiny winders, and those names today bring incredible prices.

Meanwhile, down on the ocean, (Baltimore pronunciation: "Downee Oshun"), big game anglers wanted larger versions of conventional reels, but without the extra weight of the cumbersome (in that reel size) levelwind mechanism. Their non-levelwind reels required one to have an "educated thumb" to spread the line evenly upon retrieval. The problem with catching a 1,000-pound swordfish with your thumb on the reel spool is that you lose a considerable amount of thumb-print and its underlying flesh. So, a man named William Boschen, working in the dungeon under the Vom Hofe reel company's factory, came up with a "star drag," to put on his benefactor's reels.

On the left coast, J. C. Coxe adapted the star drag to his big game reels, and so did everyone else of that era. You see, Boschen

The star drag on the Vom Hofe reel on the right revolutionized sea fishing.

never patented his wonderful invention, which was simplicity personified: stack some washers on a bolt, thread on a nut and tighten it until the washers won't turn on the bolt. Every modern reel drag is based on that simple principle, using alternating washers of metal and compressible stuff like leather.

Levelwind technology hasn't changed much over the years. Modern bass reels do gain some casting distance by disengaging the levelwind mechanism when the free-spool thumb bar is pressed. Their makers are now engaged in a competition to see who can stuff the most ball bearings into a reel case, but one of the best features of modern levelwinders is backlash suppression. They came up with several ways to keep the novice from scrambling his (and today, her) superlines into such a mess you need to take the reel onto the workbench to cut everything apart.

One of the first anti-backlash reels featured a floppy wire that bore down on the escaping line evermore exuberantly and slowed reel speed at the end of a cast; this was on early South Bend baitcasters. Then, there is the adjustment, a bearing cover on one side of the reel; it can be adjusted to keep the reel from overrunning at the end of a cast. Here's how: With a favorite lure on the end of the line, press on the thumb bar to put the reel in free spool. Watch the lure. Does it drop slowly? If so, the adjustment is about perfect for casting minus a backlash. If it drops not at all, the adjustment is too tight and your lure will not go as far. If it drops really fast, a backlash is certain. In the two last cases, readjust.

New reels like the EON have a planetary gear system that allows the spool to spin more easily. But, the end cap can be adjusted, as above, to avoid (most) backlashes. Fishing buddy, Chuck Prahl, has been an avid baitcaster for several decades. He has an educated thumb and can manually stop his lure at the end of a cast and avoid backlash. Most of the time. This free-spool system allows lures as light as 1/4 ounce to be cast accurately with levelwind reels.

The levelwind mechanism is popular on some trolling reels, too. The Penn 309 and GTI 320 have levelwind capability that allows the angler to know how far his line is out. When a fish is caught, the number of traverses of the levelwind traveler can be remembered and you have repeatability. When trolling a certain lure and weight combination, say you let line out for 14 traverses (one way across is one traverse). At about 10 feet of line to a traverse on a 309 reel, you know you have about 140 feet of line out behind the boat. Catch a fish, reel in, then let your lure out 14 traverses again. Bingo! Another fish.

If Mark Antony had a new levelwind reel, he might have ignored Cleopatra, and William Shakespeare would not have written "Julius Caesar," and been acclaimed as the first outdoors writer.

Fishing reel history would never have been the same.

● ● ● ● ● ● ● ● ● ● ● ● ● ● ● ● ●

Snow Hill, Maryland scenes in 1955.

UNCLE ERF AND THE SNALLYGASTER

The Pocomoke is a river of my youth. It has changed little since I fished there in the mid-1950's, perhaps not at all since Indians plied its waters in log canoes. The tide floods and ebbs along a shoreline uncluttered with houses or industry. The main channel is deep, the deepest river for its width in the country, some say. Three-masted sailing rams once plied the deep Pocomoke as far as Snow Hill, Maryland, loaded with lumber or fertilizer.

Lily pads near shore provide a home for bass, pickerel, and crappie. Ardent bass anglers imagine lunkers alongside cypress knees in the coffee-colored water. Afloat on the river, casting lures to each stump and lily pad and drifting along with the tide, one can imagine things have been pretty much the same here for a thousand years or more.

Snow Hill's old brick Snow Hill Inn is gone now, the name now used by a bed and breakfast. In the 1880s, the original Inn was often filled with drummers (salesmen) traveling the Eastern Shore. Carole and I honeymooned at the old Inn 48 years ago, when it was owned by my bride's aunt and uncle, Edee and Erford "Erf" Barnes.

If anyone ever bought the Titanic of hotels at the wrong time, it was Edee and Erf. In the 1950s, improvements in vehicles and roads made it possible for drummers to visit Snow Hill and return home the same day. After that the Pocomoke River and the Snow Hill Inn were left pretty much alone. Erf promoted the Pocomoke's excellent bass fishing to attract hotel guests, but most who came to fish went back home the same night.

Erf loved to bass fish on the Pocomoke. His rental skiffs were tied to a small dock on the river shore about a block from the Snow Hill Inn.

One summer day, I loaded our fishing tackle and two-horse outboard engine into the least leaky rental skiff and Erf got aboard. A 16-foot wooden skiff had marginal freeboard left when you added Erf's considerable bulk. He was a big man, so large we nicknamed him "Erford the Hereford." He steered us up the Pocomoke. We usually drifted back downriver with the outgoing tide, casting our lures around cypress stumps and lily pads.

I was anxious (impatient, actually) to try my new spinning reel on freshwater fish. Striped bass had tested it on the Bay, and now I wanted to catch largemouth black bass with it.

Erf was a traditional bass fisherman. He preferred surface plugs like the classic Devil's Horse and Lucky 13. Erf would cast his lure right next to a cypress knee and let it sit for what seemed like hours to this restless youth. (I had just returned from the Korean War with a good case of the twitchies).

"Gotta have a lot of patience for this kind of fishing," my elder counseled me as his lure lay still on the surface. He took at least six leisurely puffs on his cigarette before twitching the lure. Then six more puffs. Twitch again. Tiny concentric rings spread across the calm surface of the Pocomoke, with his plug in the center of the circle. He wanted to make the bass lurking below his lure mad enough (or wait until it was hungry enough) to engulf the offering. After the rings spread at least to China, he twitched the lure again. I thought I heard a bored bass below, yawning.

"Hell with this stuff," I thought. "Takes too much bleeping time. If he wants to watch a wood chip float all day, let him. I'm gonna catch some bass."

I quickly tied on my favorite lure of that day, a number 14 Tony Acetta chromium-plated spoon with a yellow feather. If there was a fish that wouldn't hit a Tony I didn't care to know about it. Faith in any lure, I know now, comes with the constant use of it. Sooner or later, something stupid will grab it.

I lobbed the heavy spoon through space and clunked a cypress knee with it. The hollow stump echoed like a bass drum. My lure ricocheted from the stump and splashed noisily across the water's surface. As I began a rapid retrieve something made a giant swirl and grabbed my spoon. Play the fish on a light drag? Phooey! The drag on my spinning reel was almost tight enough to pop the 20 pound test line. I could learn finesse later. As a novice angler in 1955, I wanted meat in the boat. Now!

My strike had come as quite a shock to Uncle Erf. His mouth hung open and the cigarette he used as a lure-twitch timer dangled in mid-air, stuck to his lower lip. His Devil's Horse lay floating next to a cypress knee. Untouched. In Erf's mind, the same fish that moments earlier eyed the underside of his Horse was now busy fighting my Tony.

When Erf netted my three-pound bass, his air of disdain plainly said that he considered himself beneath this low-life style of fishing. He was a purist. I chuckled and offered him my extra Tony. He mumbled something under his breath. Dang kids. No #@%$& respect.

More swirls behind my unorthodox bass lure did not go unnoticed by the Good Uncle. My thunky presentation to stumps likely gave Erf the willies, too. He had learned classic bass fishing tactics from the literature of the day. As a novice angler, I was unburdened by all that knowledge and tempted bass after bass with the Tony. Erf's plugs floated pristine and new on the chocolate waters of the Pocomoke. Unscathed.

Out of the corner of my eye, I saw Erf rooting around in his tackle box. "What do you think of this lure?" he asked, holding up an old 1940s Pflueger Limper spoon.

"Why not?," I asked. Hot Dang! If Erf would convert to klutz-casting, we could get on with it, maybe cover more than 10 feet of shoreline an hour.

Erf tied into a monster on his first klutz-cast. Round and round the leaky old rowboat boat he went, fighting his fish. The boat tilted this way and that, shipping water when Erf stood too close to a gunwale.

Erf surely contemplated a new record black bass and a dandy mount for his wall. Perhaps a congratulatory handshake from Maryland's governor, even a letter from President Eisenhower. It was like watching a prize fight: The pugilist in this corner weighing who-knows-what gained some line, then the whatever-it-is under the boat took some back. Finally, the bell.

A prehistoric monster raised its ugly head from the Pocomoke's chocolate waters. Erf's Limper spoon dangled from its toothy mouth.

Erf's smile turned to puzzlement as we viewed a Stone Age snallygaster of a fish glaring up at us beside the boat. The armor-plated alligator gar was three feet long, and one-third teeth—it was not smiling.

Its slender, spotted, olive-colored body had big fins at the rear like the fletching on an arrow. Strange fish. "Snallygaster" really described this critter.

"I'll take him home to show Edee," Erf said. Getting 10 pounds of angry garfish into the boat presented some problems—and a heated discussion. I voted to cut Erf's line and let Snally have the Limper spoon to show his/her friends. Filet of alligator gar was not high on my dinner menu. Losing a finger was out of the question.

But Erf persisted. It was his call.

We were totally unprepared, net-wise. Snally slipped through Erf's tiny (and rotten) trout net like a knife through hot butter. Now we had another problem. Erf had to continue the fight with his fishing line through the aluminum bow of the net. We were beginning to make the Keystone Cops look like amateurs. Then the scientist in Erf came out.

"They are probably like alligators in that they can bite down hard but they don't have much power to open their mouths," Erf surmised. "I'll hold his mouth shut with these pliers while you tie this piece of string around his snout and that will keep him from biting us," Erf continued, handing me a dubious piece of twine.

The garfish was not tired enough to go along with this plan. Any 10-pound animal that doesn't want to cooperate can stir up a terrible fuss at boatside. The gar wound up its propeller and sprayed water, as Eastern Shoremen say, "Ev'r which-a-way."

Two wetter - but no wiser - anglers finally got the string around the toothy snout of the disgusted garfish. Now, to get that snallygaster in the boat. Four hundred pounds of anglers finally rolled 10 pounds of gar over the gunwale, as we shipped 100 more gallons of Pocomoke River aboard.

Finally, success. Snally was aboard, tired and weakly flopping in the skiffy swimming pool we had created.

"Aw, hell," Erf said. He snipped Snally's snout twine and slipped him/her overboard. Snally swam downward into the Pocomoke's murky depths. Erf surveyed the messy interior of the skiff like Genghis Kahn surveying remains on a watery battlefield.

"Helluva battle, huh?" Erf asked.

"Ya sure, you damn betcha," smiled the Korean War vet in his native Minnesotan dialect.

Erf smiled and tied his old favorite Devil's Horse back on the line. He made a perfect cast alongside a cypress knee where the tide swirled around it. He heaved a sigh of relief and lit a cigarette. Not catching bass was more relaxing, he decided, than fighting prehistoric monsters.

I went back to klutz-casting my Tony spoon. Could be another snallygaster out there.

● ● ● ● ● ● ● ● ● ● ● ● ● ●

BASSER CATCHES MONSTER DOWDY

I have it firsthand that famous bass angler, Jimmy Huston (or a possible look-alike), has been fishing the Honga River with assorted reprobates, and that "Jimmy" caught a possible world-record oyster toadfish (Opsanus tau) while bottom-dunking $1.75 peeler crabs for hardheads. He was using a $200 Shimano Calcutta reel mounted on a $200 rod. Now, that's class.

Poor 'ol Walter Britt. Everywhere he goes, people stop him and ask for his autograph. Down Norfolk, Virginia way, where Walter lives (he actually fishes and hunts in Dorchester County, Maryland), a kid stopped him and asked "Hey, mister ainchu that guy on TV?" Can't blame the kid; Walter could be Jimmy Huston's stunt double.

Normally, 'ol Opsanus is a bottom-feeder, not a character you'd expect to see on a listing of IGFA

Walter Britt–Jimmy Huston look-alike.
Photo by Butch Chambers

(International Game Fish Association) game fish. They don't seem to take artificial lures, particularly surface poppers. They feed on oysters, so oyster shell bottom is preferred.

Opsanus has a wide-gap mouth, and crusher teeth, so don't reach in there to get your hook back. Big, buggy eyes, plus warts and slime, just make him more lovable.

However, "Jimmy" loves to catch fish, no matter what kind. "A tug on the line is all I want," he's been heard to say.

Some years ago the good 'ol boys at Tilghman Inn hosted a toadfish contest, but the contest winner's fish was nowhere the size of "Jimmy's" fish.

The trick to catching prize-winning oyster toadfish, also called "dowdies" locally, is to act like you're fishing for something else, like trout or hardheads. This is the strategy Jimmy uses, look innocent and grin like you're catching really good stuff, and you might luck out with 'ol Opsanus.

IGFA rules state that only the angler can touch the rod. No one can set the hook, not even a mate. Stand-up tackle is recommended. Check the IGFA rule book for leader length, etc.

Keep trying for that monster dowdy. You, too, could catch a World Record.

● ● ● ● ● ● ● ● ● ● ● ● ● ● ● ● ●

COOKING DOWDIES

Lucretia Krantz, wife of Dr. George Krantz who studied toadfish at the Oxford Lab, has eaten toadfish since she fished with her grandfather, Luther Garvin of Tilghman. "He made me bring my own tub because he didn't want slimy dowdies in with the 'good' fish," she said. "I grew up eating dowdies. We all did. We never knew anything else. When I go fishing now, I toss the blues back and keep the dowdies."

Mrs. Krantz cleans toadfish the same way you skin an eel - she pulls the skin off the dowdy's tail with a pair of pliers. Then she filets two pieces of meat from the tail.

"It's excellent eating," said Mrs. Krantz, "The meat is gray and glossy, much like eel in texture. It has a light, delicate flavor, very moist." Mrs. Krantz pan fries the filets, either plain or after dipping in batter. Larger dowdies provide the best filets.

ANGLERS' LUNCHES

Canned Vienna sausage, jalapeno crackers, and gas-producing beverages, all mutually combative in the stomach, have long been staples on sport fishing boats.

Jack Stovall and I were catching lots of white perch at mid-day on Chuck Prahl's boat when our stomachs started to growl. We hated to give up the fishing, but since we had only planned on a short morning trip, there were no vittles aboard.

"I know I'm gonna die," said the 80-year old Stovall, whose wife keeps him on a fat-free (read taste-free) diet, "But, I'm damn-sure not gonna die hungry." He reached into his tackle box for his emergency can of Vienna sausages.

Prahl allowed as how there were some jalapeno-flavored crackers he'd stored under the gunwale for just such a predicament. "Not sure how long they've been there," he said, pulling out a moldy package of doubtful ancestry, "but these are really tasty."

I contributed various canned beverages and my hunting jacket coughed up a pack of semi-powdered peanut butter crackers, the latter of which I am never without in case of a world cataclysm.

Actually, it wasn't a bad lunch. It's truly amazing how one's stomach can be pacified, temporarily, by groceries that would turn a dietician's hair gray overnight.

Lesser concoctions, when combined with rough seas, have had many a stalwart mariner hanging over the side talking to "Raallph."

Queasy stomachs can be controlled, as I found out on my way to visit the Korean War on a rolling, pitching troop ship. Grease seemed to be the mainstay of our cuisine, so I found that lying very still in my bunk after a meal would keep my bubbling belly from erupting. Until the guy in the bunk next to me, well, you know. Let go.

On the ship, several of us provided afternoon entertainment by swaying to and fro in unison while we told barf stories to our latest victim, who was soon heading for the rail. Just ahead of us.

Once in Korea, we found the grease in C-Rations could be somewhat liquefied by heating the cans on a deuce-and-a-half truck's exhaust manifold. Fifty years later, just mentioning C-Rations makes my stomach do flippy-flops.

In Korea, kim-chi is a delicacy of fermented cabbage and fish, buried until it reeks so rancidly even starving dogs won't dig it up. I saw a can of it in the deli section of a local supermarket. While tempted to buy it for the boat's emergency rations, I gave some thought to its history. Nah.

Vic Dunaway wrote in Florida Sportsman Magazine that Europe has its share of stomach-bubblers, too. Icelanders have hakarl, Dunaway said, which, boiled down to its essence, is Rotten Shark. He also reminded the reader about haggis, sheep stomach stuffed with various body parts, which is what made Scotch whisky so popular over there.

My own Norwegian ancestors brought lutefisk (fish soaked in lye) with them to this country, but the literature is rife with hundreds of reasons not to try it, like the poem that includes: "Oh lutefisk! Oh lutefisk! You smell so strong, you look like glue, you taste just like an overshoe."

Consider Thor the Viking on the open ocean holding a sword to Eric's throat at Middag (noon, or dinner time) making him eat lefse (potato bread) and lutefisk. "Now, Eric, you hold the sword on me," says Thor, "make me eat the damn lutefisk." Lutefisk has been promoted as an aphrodisiac, and one Norse wag says that's why the Vikings wore those horny helmets.

Present day fishing boats on the Chesapeake bay chum rockfish to the boat with ground-up menhaden, a modern-day lutefisk smell-alike. On a rocking boat in a rolling seaway, one needs to stay upwind of the chum bucket. 'Nuf said. The above hints are just a few of the food items one must avoid on a rolling, pitching fishing vessel.

All ignored by one of my fishing buddies, Sid Dickson, who tips, and I do mean tips, the scales at somewhere near 280 pounds. I wondered what was in the giant cooler on his fishing boat. "Lunch," he said. "Never can tell when you'll break down out here. Don't wanna starve."

I must have a dozen photographs of anglers, who, when suddenly called upon to reel in a fish, stuffed a sandwich, apple, or other foodstuff into their mouths as a convenient place to park the goodie until the fish was coolered. I'd also like to repeat a warning about not cutting up your sandwich on the bait board, and keeping slimy fish and canned beverages apart in the cooler.

Two other fishing companions have the ideal solution to settle their stomachs after a fishing trip. A large thermos of martinis awaits them on the dock. Whether they caught any fish or not, a toast to a successful return from a perilous voyage is in order. By the time they've cleaned their fish and the boat, they're a coupla happy puppies, indeed.

•••••••••••••••••

LAKE OUACHITA STRIPERS

On our way through Hot Springs, Arkansas to striped bass fish with guide John T. Hall, I saw a bumper sticker on the rusty pickup truck driven by a pony-tailed blonde girl ahead of me at a traffic light: "Fight Crime," it said, "Shoot back!" My kinda people.

Hot Springs proclaims itself the "Boyhood Home of Bill Clinton." When I asked a number of natives what they thought of their boy going to Washington, several said, "I hope they keep him there." I wasn't sure whether they thought he was doing a great job, or they didn't want him back – and I was afraid to ask.

Lake Ouachita (pronounced "wash-i-tah") means "good hunting, good fishing." An Indian meaning, but a French spelling, John T. says. The lake's striper population is stable due to stocking programs, but the size of the fish is ever-expanding. The 45,000-acre lake has 1,000 miles of shoreline, counting all the indents and squiggles, with only a few access points, actually resorts, that were "grandfathered" when the Corps of Engineers filled the lake. The shoreline is forested. Behind the shoreline, mountains rise.

John T. Hall's slogan is "Catch a memory," and he made one for me. More on that later. We launched his 21-foot Kenner bass boat powered by a 200 hp Yammy at the Brady Mountain Resort. John T. (There are so many John Halls in town, he has to add the "T") pointed to a spot about 300 yards off the ramp. "That's where we fish," he said. Usually anglers run past people who are bailing in fish so they can try a rumored hot spot at the other end of nowhere where there are no fish.

"My boat had the state record for rockfish for four days," John T. said, "It was 57 pounds, nine ounces."The reason he didn't claim it was his own catch is that he hands a hooked fish off to a client. The client reeled in the striper, and he netted it.

"The record was broken by another guide a few days later in the same spot with a 57-pound, 13-ounce rockfish," Hall said. He had told the other guide where he caught the previous winner.

"My biggest striper was 32-1/2 pounds," I told John T. "It was the Maryland state record from 1964 until a 50-plus pounder bested it." He said most of the stripers they catch are big when they fish with live 5- to 15-inch gizzard shad baits. Smaller fish are usually caught on artificials near the surface.

John T. rigs up several rods and places each one in a holder around the boat's gunwale. His hooks are 7/0, because "when you bait with a 15-inch shad, your hook needs a lot of throat." He fishes one cut bait on the bottom, two baits down with sliding sinkers, one near the surface under a balloon float, and two baitfish swim around with no weight or floats, free-lined.

The first place we stopped was a clearing in the trees that might have been a field when the lake was filled. The surrounding timber in 55 feet of water came up about 25 feet off the bottom. You could see big stripers on the depthfinder; they looked like an inverted "U"on the screen. John T. angles his transom-mounted depthfinder transducer forward so he can see his baits when bottom fishing at anchor.

These stripers came up, nosed around the nervous baitfish, then they slowly sank back down to the bottom. "They're doing a lot of window shopping today," John T. quipped. He constantly tended the rods as the boat swung around, taking in line here, checking a bait there, and letting out line as needed.

John T. used Shimano Calcutta 400 levelwind reels loaded with 17-pound test Super Silver Thread monofilament line. Rods are stiff seven foot "trigger sticks," made for casting live baits. I told him about the Calcutta 400 I won at an outdoor writer's meeting, and how I use it to cast 1-1/2 ounce bucktail jigs for stripers in Chesapeake Bay. But, his Calcutta reel made a clicking sound when a fish took line.

"What's that noise?" I asked. He looked at me strangely and said "That's the clicker. Right here on the bottom of the reel." Though I had used the Calcutta 400 for several years, I'd never baitfished with it, never needed a clicker. But, there on the bottom of one side plate was a small sliding button to engage the clicker. Live and learn. And, perhaps occasionally, read the reel's instruction sheet.

As a well-known guide in the Hot Springs area, John T. has been in a number of magazine articles and on several TV fishing shows. He wears designer sunglasses. "The other guides call me Hollywood," he said.

After some time with no action, I admitted I'd jinxed the area. "I've been known to jinx a whole river at home."

"I don't believe in jinxes," John T. said. "I'd stay here until midnight to break a jinx." He fishes 260 trips a year, sometimes two a day. He can't afford a jinx. To break the possibility of my jinxing this hole, we moved to another part of the lake.

We were drifting along over some tree tops about 20 feet below. John T. catches fish here on plugs. I tried a popper from Chesapeake Bay, and several other surface baits. A 3-pound largemouth bass hit my Super Spook lure. After releasing the bass, I saw a big striper come up to the surface chasing a baitfish. The striper's upper body was half above the water! I'd never seen that before. I tossed the Super Spook at him several times as he swirled around after the baitfish, to no avail.

"Time is right to fish that first place," John T. said. "The evening bite is always best." He mentioned that cows were now standing up in the field and feeding, a sure sign the bite was imminent.

The sunset silhouetted a mountain top when John T. had a bite. His free-swimming shad baitfish nervously made tracks for tall timber as the rockfish finally grabbed the bait and dove into the trees.

John T. slowly and carefully worked the fish out of the tree tops. The "U" bend in his rod indicated a big striper. Back and forth the battle see-sawed, each opponent gaining and losing line. He thought this might be the largest striper he'd ever caught. As a guide, he always hands a bucking rod to the client, so he rarely catches a big fish to call his own.

Three times the monster fish went into the trees, and three times he finessed it back out. When we saw color at boatside, we couldn't believe the fish's size. I netted it head first, and John T. helped drag it in over the gunwale. I took photographs with a beautiful sunset outlining the mountains.

John T. Hall with his
Lake Ouachita striper.

The fish measured 43 inches long and had a 24-1/2 inch girth. We estimated it would weigh 30 pounds.

Back at the building where John T. keeps his boat and huge bait tanks, the big striper tipped the scales at 32-1/2 pounds. Exactly the same weight as my 1964 record rockfish! What goes around, comes around.

And, that's a wrap.

ROADKILL FLY-TIERS

Fly anglers march to a different drummer. Many of them look down their noses at us mere mortal spinning and casting anglers. Theirs is a higher calling.

Their sport, its history dating back through the dim mists of time, richly deserves to be set up on a pedestal so as not to be tainted by earthy tackle like spinning rods or levelwind reels. Say the word "trolling" and be forever banished from their lofty circles.

This myth has been perpetuated by fly fishing manufacturers who think nothing of charging $1000 for a rod or $800 for a reel.

I'd like to debunk the fly-fishing myth, at least in part. I know a few fly fishermen who are pretty normal folks.

On a somewhat lower social scale, I know some who haunt roadside ditches for road-killed critters in search of fly tying materials. My kinda people.

A retired dentist of my acquaintance carries a filet knife in his van in hopes of finding a road-killed deer. Picture my well-dressed friend in a muddy ditch, filet knife in hand, separating an unfortunate deer from its tail. Deer hair is one of the most desirable materials, and the after end of a deer is the only place to find it. Live deer are understandably reluctant to part with their tail hair for artificial flies, so road kill is the next best place to look for it.

"Oh, yes," says Dr. Karl Malik, a microbiologist who decided running an Internet outdoors site was more fun than medical research. "I'm always on the lookout for road kill deer, foxes, and other critters. I carry tin snips in my car. Black underhair makes excellent dubbing." Malik soaks critter tails in salt, air dries the hide, then washes the hair. "Nutragena soap doesn't leave any residue," he says, "it leaves the fur in finesse condition."

Other friends take a different tack, figuring to collect a freezer of venison in addition to fly-tying materials. This involves the purchase of a deer gun and suitable hunting clothing, hunting license, and hunting property rental. Some even buy hunting property, which runs the cost of a single fly up considerably.

Fly-tiers are continually looking for materials. Some haunt craft stores for items like doll eyes or yarn. Others, like me, adapt everyday items. For instance, wine corks make excellent bluefish fly rod poppers. My wife, Carole, mentioned my need for wine corks at a ladies' meeting. One of the ladies, who always seemed cheerful and happy, brought Carole a bag of wine corks from time to time. Presently, I'm overcorked, but I don't want to shut off the supply.

Some outdoor writers, like C. Boyd Pfeiffer, see fly materials everywhere they go. "Ed Russell has the beautiful long-haired cat named 'Tyler," Boyd says, "a Persian or something, and its hair color was perfect. Every time I went to Ed's house, I looked at that cat as a possible supplier of fur for a popular fly called a 'Zonker' that includes a strip of rabbit fur. I started to call that cat Zonker."

"Every time I went to visit," Boyd said, "Ed's wife, Doris, would holler 'Hide the cat!' I suggested cutting off its tail. A cat doesn't need a tail anyway–look at bobcats." No dice. Doris wasn't

receptive. This is a lady who talks to worms when she baits up: "I'm sorry little worm, really sorry. Please forgive me."

Then, Boyd, who once taught anatomy at Johns Hopkins, offered another suggestion: "How about taking out a strip long enough for a Zonker? We could stitch him up and you'd never notice. I used to sew up cadavers after various procedures. A cat would be easy." Ed balked at that suggestion, so Boyd offered" I'll do the suture if you'll hold the cat."

Getting no sympathy for the Zonker project, Boyd offered a final solution. "I told Ed that if Tyler

C. Boyd Pfeiffer dips a bass he caught on one of his special flies.

ever died, Ed had to skin him quick before the hair starts to fall out, which would ruin the cat for fly-tying."

Boyd is also the originator of several very imaginative flies, including the Chita Pet Fly, "As soon as it hits the water, it grows hair," and the lamprey fly, which has a "hook-and-loop sucker and attaches itself to the fish."

Boyd wound multicolored pipe cleaners around a hook, an idea I used in my "Ingenious Angler" book.

It has been said that if you steal an idea from one person it's called "plagiarism," but if you steal from many it's called "research." I do a lot of research for my books.

Ever the self-depreciating inventor, Boyd is the first one to admit he didn't develop the "Egg-sucking Leach Fly." In Alaska they call it the "Lawyer Fly."

Professional fly-tier, DL Goddard of Easton, gets his deer tails honestly. An avid deer hunter, he takes several deer a year for the freezer. He warns that road kill fly materials have a rabies potential, but adds that all sorts of weird stuff finds its way into flies. Pipe cleaners are a given, and anything in a craft store is fair game. Velcro buttons make great crab flies. Braided nylon upholstery piping in many sizes and colors becomes bodies for fur flies. Doll and taxidermy eyes decorate flies, and toilet bead chain makes good flies, too. Punch yarn that is normally used with a needle to pull to fill in pre-painted portions of a canvas is used for fly bodies. Doll hair, originally "craft hair" finds its way into flies, too.

DL's wife, Stephanie, notes that Scientific Anglers' 20-pound test monofilament line is used to sew doll bodies, a fitting feminine payback for using doll materials in flies.

"Ha, that's nothing," DL says, "I use women's fake fingernails in spoon flies."

DL also used women's nylon stockings to make bait-holding bags to catch crawfish when he lived in Florida. Crawfish came to nuzzle the dead bait, and their multiple belly-mounted legs became entangled in the nylon mesh.

"You used the craws for fish bait?" I asked.

"Heck, no, we ate 'em," he said. (Imagine 'ol DL saying "heck?"). Geez!

When I told DL about Boyd's efforts to nip a little fur from Zonker, he said "I guess that's not as bad as the fly-tier who snipped hair from his wife's mink coat."

Stephanie! Quick! Lock up your mink coat!

● ●

GATOR-MAN AND "E"

"Oh, yes," Walt Rhodes told me, "E loves to fish."

"E?," I said, Who's E?"

"My wife, Elizabeth," he explained. "She doesn't like Liz or Beth, so I call her E for short."

"O. K.," I said, "We'll go out and catch something. How about perch on ultralight tackle? Four pound test line, small lures?" He allowed as that would be a lot of fun, since we only had two hours to fish between his afternoon visit to an aunt, and my wife, Carole's, rockfish dinner.

Walt and E were visiting their home turf in Maryland for a week, and he had promised to get in touch with Carole and I ever since we met at an outdoor writers' meeting in Cherokee, NC. Walt was from Kent Island and E was from Salisbury originally, both Eastern Shore folks who had gone off to college, he for a master's degree in wildlife management, and she for a masters in coastal geology.

They didn't know each other before meeting in South Carolina, but theirs was a marriage made in the swamp. While Walt was examining alligator stomachs in the lab where he later met her, E was leading tours in the Okefenokee Swamp. Both loved to slosh around in muddy water, a common bond they soon found out about when they finally met over a pile of gator guts in Walt's lab.

"I'm everything to do with alligators in South Carolina," said Walt, who is the Alligator Project Manager for the SC-DNR. E teaches geology at the University of Charleston in the same state. Walt also writes an outdoors column for the Charleston Post & Courier and writes stories for numerous magazines. E is a partner in everything including helping build their log home—and gathering gator eggs.

"You have to rassle gators?" I asked, wide-eyed.

"Oh, I catch dozens a year," he said sort of offhand, like gator-grabbing was something every wildlife biologist would aspire to. "Some are up to 12 feet," he added. He said some gators are fed by people and get used to them, so they wind up in garages or under the family car in a driveway. They move at night from one body of water to another, and if they don't find water by dawn, they seek shade for the hot daylight hours.

"They rarely attack someone unless they are harassed," Walt said, "most of the time they're not aggressive." That's reassuring, isn't it? I mean, Floridians are always missing small dogs and cats, burp!–you know what I mean? Walt cautions to stay away from gator nests in the marsh, big piles of dirt that resemble beaver huts. "Momma gator is often nearby just lying there keeping an eye on the nest."

Some gators charge with their mouth open, so Walt carries a canoe paddle to tap them on the nose (don't try this yourself, O.K.?). Sometimes they are so protective, Walt has to hold them off with the paddle "while E digs out their eggs." The average nest holds 44 eggs. This takes a while. Eggs are placed in crates that are kept separate with the nest location recorded, and the couple takes them home to hatch them out in mid-August. The incubation period is 63 to 65 days.

"The data we're looking for is the sex ratio," Walt explained. Weather has an effect on the sex of the critters. "Dr. Jeff Lang of North Dakota developed a way of sexing them without killing them." If they waited until the gators hatched out, it would be too labor-intensive to gather them up. After hatching and sexing, the tiny critters are returned to their original nest site.

The purpose of the study is to look at sex ratio in relation to temperature and weather changes, since they don't want to overharvest the females. South Carolina has a hunting season on American alligators. The only significant population of crocodiles in America, he says, is the American crocodile in south Florida, a usually shy croc that has no documented human fatalities associated with it.

"Crocodilians have an incubation range of 14 degrees F" Walt said," and many think that's why they outlasted the dinosaurs." They were here before and after the dinosaurs? Yep. Dinos are thought to have had a limited incubation temperature range, so the Ice Age could have wiped them out.

The hunting season on gators has been beneficial for them and for other species on private lands in South Carolina, Walt said. When landowners found they could market the meat and skins, they began to configure their property for gators, which benefits not only the alligators, but bird, and other critter's habitat.

The alligator is also a keystone animal indicator species for the health of the environment. They are long-lived, and they are the [absolute] top of the food chain.

"E" Rhodes photographs Walt's white perch.

Well, one might suppose fishing for white perch would be pretty tame stuff for gatorologists, eh? Not so. A trip out on Broad Creek for two hours kept the Rhodes family busy yanking in white perch on almost every cast. We probably caught about 50 perch on ultralight spinning gear and 4-pound test line with my homemade Beetle Spin type lures. We kept only a dozen or so perch, including a few "picture fish."

Outdoor writers need pictures to go with their copy so people will be more likely to believe the story. Walt and I took a lot of pictures, and E did too, but with a digital camera.

"Move in closer, Fred," Walt admonished E.

"Who's Fred?" I asked.

"Fred is the fictional character who goes around our house leaving the lights on," he said. E wrinkled her nose.

Back at the Walters home, Futility Base (apologies to NASA), we sat down to a great dinner of Carole's baked fish on Vidalia onions, a hash brown potato casserole, and fresh green beans. Dessert was apple crumb pie.

"We had crates and critters when Hurricane Floyd came in with 80-knot winds," Walt said after dinner. They protected 50 crates of eggs and gators by moving them under their crawl space, boarded up the windows, and sat in the dark during the hurricane.

It's funny," Walt said: We met over alligator stomachs, and slept over alligators during Hurricane Floyd."

Can you imagine a more perfect romance? Gator guts in the lab and little toothy critters all over your house?

"It's a good thing you both grew up on the Eastern Shore," I opined. "The webbed feet you grew in 'Shore marshes certainly came in handy in Carolina gator swamps!"

I bet they never even thought about it that way. Swamp romance is like that.

• • • • • • • • • • • • • • • • • •

"I CAN JINX A WHOLE RIVER"

Sometimes it pays to notice the little things. One morning, on my way home from the post office, I noticed Gordon Ries' truck was not in its usual spot, but someone else's van was parked nearby. I deduced that Gordon was out fishing, also not unusual except the wind was huffing along over 15 knots and the temperature was hugging 40 degrees, making the wind chill on the water something ghastly.

When I got home I called Gordon on the marine VHF radio. "It's great here," he said, meaning the fishing.

"Where are you?"

"Off Buddy World," which is Eastern Shore (ES) code for the Choptank River near Buddy Harrison's Chesapeake House, so only 5,000 ES citizens, if they were listening, would be privy to that information. "Birds everywhere," Gordon added, "and these fish are big ones."

"See you in about 20 minutes," I replied. "Even if it's all over when I get there – as usual."

Well, it took me about three seconds to line up a fishing partner after I told him Gordon's story. Dick Clayton said he'd be right over.

"The action's died down," Gordon called as Dick and I ran out of Broad Creek, "Birds are scattered," he added. Anything to cheer me up. Dick shrugged his shoulders, been there before. We kept on course.

"I knew I'd jinx it," I told Dick. He smiled, unbelieving, since we've caught a lot of fish together.

"I can jinx a whole river," I added. He grimaced. This was going to be a long day.

I found Gordon's boat. He was drifting along with two other anglers aboard. They had their limits and were, thankfully, marking the hot area for me. He said yellow bucktails were hot, so naturally, I cast out my white one-ounce homemade bucktail jig decorated with white deer tail hair and a six-inch swimmertail grub. My rig was a levelwind Shimano Calcutta 250 loaded with 50/12 white Whiplash braided superline, ended with doubled line secured to a black snap swivel. The bucktail was tied to a three-foot shot of 20-pound test Vanish® fluorocarbon line, and this leader is ended with a Perfection Knot that clips into the snap swivel. This rig lets me change lures quickly.

Dick prefers spinning tackle and he had two outfits ready, both rigged with small bucktails decorated with small plastic eels. Stripers love eels most of the time, but were not overwhelmed with plastic ones this day.

The wind was blowing us along at about one and a half knots, a good trolling speed for rockfish. We were in 16 feet of water most of the time, and these elements combined to keep our lures above bottom when the rods were in their holders. Dick likes to hold his rod and give the lure some action. My 22-foot Angler hull is now more comfortable with its "winter cabin" of canvas side and rear curtains in place. Clear plastic "windows" in the panels give us good visibility, and the temporary cabin keeps us a bit warmer in chill autumn winds, but, only when we're running. We fish from the open rear deck where the wind can chill hands to the point they are stiff and almost useless.

My rod in its holder caught the first striper, one about 23 inches long. It was taking out a lot of line against a medium drag, so I knew it was a keeper. Dick netted the fish head first for me as I drug the fighting critter toward the boat. If you make a mistake and touch the fish's tail with the net, it will take off and may get away, since we use barbless hooks. "Don't you ever touch me there again!" the fish seems to say as it waves goodbye.

These are the fish we've waited for since early fall. The rock we caught were sassy, fat, and shiny. Some have sea lice in their gills, suggesting they came up from the Atlantic Ocean to see what's going on in our neighborhood. The fat fish's stomachs were packed with menhaden about four or five inches long; some of the baitfish were partially digested.

We caught a few undersize rock, but they were only an inch shy of the 18-inch minimum. Then, I caught another tackle-buster. It measured 24 inches, a fact I proudly radioed to George Fromm fishing nearby. "I beat you by an inch," he replied, deflating my ego balloon. Moral of that story: Always tell your story last so you can add a pound or an inch to your fish!

Dick caught one that beat the minimum size by only an inch. We were shy of a limit by one fish.

I can mark the spot on my Lowrance GlobalMap 1600 GPS where we catch a fish, and when the wind takes us away from it, I can run back to exactly the same spot and give us another shot at the pod of fish. Strangely, I never did see "marks" on my depthsounder that indicated a school of rock. The water was very clear and perhaps that made the fish shy off away from the drifting boat. While some drift with the motor running, I feel that puts the fish off their feed, or chases them away.

We made about six or seven long drifts before Dick yelled, "Holy Cow," and grabbed his spinning rod from its holder. He'd decided my luck in catching the first fish was somehow tied to having my rod in a holder (so I wouldn't mess up a bite, "Let the holder catch the fish," I say). His spinning rod was severely bent, and the fish took out a lot of line before it was within range of the net, which favor I performed for him.

We decided we had punished our bodies in the cold long enough, and ran back to my dock, restoring body heat by hiding out in the cabin.

I had un-jinxed the waters off Buddy World. Temporarily.

Dick Clayton with two nice stripers.

KING MACKEREL AT YOUR FEET

"The kings are boiling right next to the point," Al Smith radioed us from his boat anchored near buoy R"4" off Power Squadron Spit near Cape Lookout, North Carolina, as we returned from gathering pinfish baits, "If you can anchor near Stan (Seufert) or Dale (Arbogast) you should get some action." Marylanders Stan and Dale had been floating their live pinfish baits along in the current right next to the point where the bottom drops off sharply from six- to 30-feet. Hookups had been fast and furious for them but there was no room for other boats to get in on the action until the lucky anglers anchored their boats uptide from their most productive spot.

Omar Stoltzfus and Mert Cowger readied the anchor in my 20-foot Mako as we slowly motored toward the edge of the beach. We positioned the boat uptide from the spot Smitty recommended. Omar was the first to get a bait in the water. His live pinfish floated slowly along in the current suspended by a balloon float, not 20 feet from the edge of the shoreline.

The expression of surprise on the face of a lone surf fisherman standing at the tip of the point must have been classic—if only I'd had time to look that way. A big king mackerel exploded on the surface right next to the beach as it grabbed Omar's live pinfish bait, less than 100-feet from the surf jockey. Just imagine the surfcaster's amazement when Omar's balloon burst in a shower of spray, his rod bent double in its holder, and the reel's clicker screamed in protest! The king was headed across the inlet toward Smitty's boat. If the surfcaster had balloon-floated a live pinfish along the edge of the steep dropoff at the point the way Omar had from our boat, he might have been fighting Omar's monster king.

"Told you they were busting bait right next to shore," Smitty called on the VHF radio. "I believe, Smitty, I believe," I called back as I photographed the battle. Mert stood by holding the gaff.

Omar is a firm believer in heavy tackle. No less than 60-pound test line graces his conventional star drag boat reel, and his short boat rod has all the resilience of a tire iron, but this king mackerel wasn't taking any guff from him, horse tackle or not. There was much splashing on the surface of the water near the boat as the king gave us all a bath. From his boat anchored nearby, Frank Shaffer joined Smitty on the radio to offer Omar moral support. "Quit playing with him, Omar," Frank said, "you're messing up all the water in the inlet." "Yeah," Smitty agreed, "we'd like to catch some fish, too."

Finally, the double line touched Omar's rod tip. The fish's silver coloring showed six feet down in the clear water. When the king

Omar Stoltzfus with his King Mackerel.

was near the surface, Mert gaffed it in a shower of spray and swung it aboard. At 34-pounds, it was a nice king in anybody's boat, and our largest of the trip.

We learn something new every year we fish for kings at Cape Lookout, but finding the fish this close to the shoreline, and within easy reach of surf casters was quite a departure from our usual procedure. For several Octobers, our 12-boat contingent of 30 Maryland anglers converged on the Harker's Island Fishing Center near Morehead City, North Carolina to float-fish live baits for the kings. Our group are old friends from the NASA days, some still working at the Goddard Space Flight Center in Greenbelt, Maryland, and some are retired, but we keep in touch. The annual king mackerel trip is much like a reunion, and there is a good bit of kidding (plus shared fishing information) back and forth on the radio.

The successful king mackerel system we have evolved over the years usually begins at first light as we troll along the edge of the breakers at Cape Lookout to catch our favorite small bluefish baits for the livewell. Bucktail lures in sizes 4/0 to 7/0 produce all the bluefish we need, and the heavier king mackerel-sized spinning gear lets us get them into the livewell quicker to avoid stressing them. Then, a run back toward Barden Inlet to anchor outside the stone jetty off buoy R"2" for the rest of the day. Four bluefish baits are floated under balloons behind the boat, with their rods placed in gunwhale holders. During lulls in the king mackerel action, we gather more baitfish for the livewell by bottom fishing with #4 gold hooks on a standard bottom rig. Squid or cut fish baits produce spot, croaker, blues, and pinfish baits. There is always something to do, either catching baitfish, or keeping the balloon rigs apart as active baitfish swim back and forth.

Never boring, this fishing can explode into action when you least expect it. With two fishermen aboard and a fish on, the fishless angler has to quickly reel in the other lines to avoid tangles. If two kings hit at the same time, pandemonium reigns. Once, with two 25-pounders on in rough seas, I loosened the drag to let my king swim wherever he wanted, storing the rod in a holder until Omar's fish was gaffed, then I fought my king to the boat. A calculated risk paid off.

While some of our Marylanders alternately tried slow-trolling with cast-netted live mullet, made forays to an offshore wreck, or tried spots off Beaufort Inlet—all with some degree of success—sooner or later everyone returned to the same method and place that had produced year after year: float-fishing live bluefish baits outside buoy R"2" near Cape Lookout.

Light drag settings can cause some problems if no one grabs the rod on a strike. "The next fish is yours, Mert," I kidded, continuing the running joke that had plagued Mert for most of the trip. Every time a king hit, Mert was almost trampled in the rush for the bent rod in the gunwhale holder. Overpolite on his first king mackerel trip, Mert finally gave up and jumped out of the way when a balloon burst signalling a king's strike.

"Your fish, Mert," I hollered as a king grabbed the bait on the spinning rod in a holder next to me, "grab that rod!" Mert ducked and looked back over his shoulder expecting to get clobbered in the rush for the surging rod. Omar and I outwaited him. Mert finally took the rampaging rod from it's holder. With a light drag, there was a lot of line out, almost halfway across the inlet, and the king was dangerously close to other boats. As Mert began to crank the two-drag spinning reel, the dual-drag lever snapped forward and the heavier fighting drag came into play. He pumped and reeled the king, gaining line like a pro until the silver-colored fish showed just under the surface. Omar gaffed a 15-pound king for Mert, the last fish of a successful trip.

King mackerel can be found by boat fishermen in many areas near Morehead City and Cape Lookout in October. The wreck at buoy N"16" due west of the Beaufort Inlet held kings last October, but sizeable tackle-testing amberjack were mixed with the kings. We release amberjack, but the similar-fighting (and delicious) cobia are definitely not released, and it is sometimes hard to tell which is which until you get them to the boat. Kings were caught right in Beaufort Inlet, too, and that got us to thinking that king mackerel can be caught by shore-bound surfcasters at sharp drop-offs like Power Squadron Spit just as easily as we caught them from a boat only 20-feet off the beach.

Word gets around. Perhaps surf casting would offer some comfort advantages over boat fishing when the ocean kicks up and the rains come down. Solid sand would feel better under your feet than a pitching boat, and the heated cab of a beach buggy might seem pretty comfortable at times. I expect, though, that we'll be bouncing around in a sportfishing boat in the inlet surf come October, wearing slickers to ward off the rain and gulping hot thermos coffee to keep warm while we wait for that heart-stopping king mackerel strike.

Old habits are hard to break.

SNUKE LIGHTS

Snook, called "snuke" by real Florida natives (if you can find one), are much like our Chesapeake Bay striped bass. They are both great gamefish, taking bait and lures with equal abandon, then suddenly shutting down entirely due to some whim of tide or weather. Snuke, and stripers, hang around structure like dock pilings, rocks, exposed tree roots, jetties, and sandbars, any structure with a strong current running past it. And, both species seem to feed better at night.

Like stripers, snuke gather up around schools of baitfish where the dining is easier. Baitfish gather under lights at night. Gamefish lie in wait in the dark water and dart into the lighted area when a tempting meal swims past, then go back into their dark ambush place to await further developments.

Knowing the snuke's habits, Floridians attach floodlights to the end of their docks that illuminate a circle of water about 30 feet across. The lights are on a timer so they come on at dark and go off at the owner's bedtime. Floridians often sit at the end of their docks in the evening and sip various liquids as they watch snuke smash into the schools of baitfish attracted by the lights.

In "Snook Alley" near Venice, Florida, fishing guides have learned how to fish snuke lights from a boat. They silently sneak up on the lights using electric trolling motors and quietly slip an anchor over to position their clients within fly casting distance. This writer took one such a trip, and even caught 1.5 snuke. The experienced guide caught 8.5 fish. The half-point represents "long line releases," or those fish that were conscientiously let go a long way from the boat.

So, it made perfect sense when a fishing buddy called me (I'll call him "Buddy") one evening and told me he had a "snuke light" at the end of his dock here in Maryland. He said there were scads of rockfish hanging around the edge of the light in the dark. There were also some monster stripers under his dock watching the smaller ones feed on tiny baitfish attracted by the light. Buddy had caught some of the smaller rock on a fly rod from his dock, but casting a fly up under the dock where the big bass were based presented a problem.

"Come on over, and bring a pair of waders," Buddy said, "we'll get in my canoe and paddle out in the creek so we can cast up under the dock where the big ones are. Oh, and bring a fly rod and some streamer flies."

"Six weight O.K.?"

"Fine, and hurry up!"

Isn't it amazing how much clearer and more logical everything seems after the cocktail hour?

I gathered up my chest waders and a fly rod. My hip waders leaked, so I had cut them down to boot size. I later found that my chest waders leaked, too, when water poured in over the top.

All was in readiness when I arrived at Buddy's. He had the canoe at the water's edge, just outside some rocks on the beach.

"You get in the front," he said. "You can cast better from up there. I'll paddle."

Did you ever try to get into a tippy canoe while standing in several inches of mud wearing chest waders? Particularly when your aging joints don't bend as far as they used to?

I placed my cloth camera bag in the bottom of the canoe and my fly rod longways in the vessel along the far side. Then I put my left booted foot into the canoe, keeping my body low as Buddy recommended. I hadn't been in a canoe for about 50 years, so getting my right foot and 200-pound rear end in the canoe was a bit tricky. With one hand on either gunwale, I tried to lift my right foot out of the mud. Bad move. Instead of hauling my foot over the gunwale, the mud held onto the boot, and I pulled the canoe over. I found myself in a foot of cold, muddy water and the top of my waders was under the water. I thumped a rock pretty hard with my back. My left foot was still anchored in the canoe, my right boot stuck in the mud, and the icy water pouring into my waders was quickly dampening my ardor for this mission.

"You O.K.?" Buddy asked.

"I guess."

"O.K., I'll hold the canoe and you try again." I could imagine all those rockfish under the dock laughing their gills off.

My next try was a bit more successful, if you don't count my weight coming down on my right leg that was bent up under my rear end. I screamed in pain. That hurt!

"You O.K.?"

"I guess, as soon as I can stop screaming."

Now, my back and my knee both hurt, and there was a gallon or two of cold, muddy water sloshing around inside my waders. This trip was getting off to a bad start.

Buddy paddled us out into deeper water off the end of the dock far enough to cast a fly to the outer edge of the light. We could see fish silhouetted against the illuminated water at the edge of the light circle. I made several casts and caught a few small stripers.

"Look at the big ones under the dock," Buddy said. There were six or eight big stripers suspended near the surface. They were as long as your arm. I tried several times to rifle a cast under the dock, but my fly-casting ability is to laugh at.

"Hand me the rod," Buddy said. He is an expert fly caster, and placed the fly gently on the water under the dock near a big striper. He gave the line a few short strips. A slightly smaller rock raced in and grabbed his lure.

I groped around for my camera bag, since this was probably the only "picture fish" we'd get that night. The bag was soaked. That's why I carry waterproof cameras on missions like this. Buddy held up the fish, and I popped a picture, not a great one, but considering the circumstances—the black of night, a dim snuke light in the background, and a camera that doesn't want to focus in the dark.

I tried a few more times to get a fly up under the dock, with sometimes hilarious consequences, like hooking the dock, the canoe, and almost –Buddy's ear. I gave up on underdock casting and tried for smaller fish outside the light with better success. My fish were not big enough to photograph, saving me some embarrassment.

"Come on up to the house and get a nice gin and tonic in you," Buddy said, "warm you up."

"O.K., but please – no ice!" The drink chilled me even more. Buddy's wife came to the door: "Come on in," she said.

"I'm all muddy, and you don't want me tramping on your oriental rugs, but thanks for the thought."

"That's nothing," she said, "last night Buddy took our Lab out with him, and she laid a big pile right in his path just before he returned from the dock. He came in the house and tracked it all over. Mud is nothing compared to that!"

I bid them a fond farewell, and slowly peeled off my waders for the ride home. They still had a quart of water in them. The car heater felt good.

Fishing a snuke light from a canoe is a lot of fun. Try it sometime.

• • • • • • • • • • • • • • • • • •

FRANK SMOOT: WORLD'S OLDEST OUTDOORS ARTIST

Frank Smoot loves to draw animals for the kiddies at outdoor shows. I called him recently to see how he was. Frank, now 98, is still sharp as a tack. I reminded him of a discussion we had at a show in Salisbury, Maryland: "Frank, I don't want to know how old you are, but someone told me you had to fight dinosaurs all the way to school as a kid." "No, but, we hunted pterodactyls and it was always in doubt whether we could catch them or they'd catch us. Actually, not many people know I invented the Jurassic Fly. It's three feet long–so big IT does the fishing! It has corkscrews that impale the fish. You don't even need a barbless hook." Then Frank drew me a picture of his invention, The Jurassic Fly. Scary, isn't it? I asked Frank if I could use his drawing in this book and I would see that he got a copy. Frank said "sure, but you'd better hurry."

The Jurassic Fly
by Frank Smoot

EVERGLADES

"DUCK!" our guide, Larry Demere, shouted. Clay Gooch, John Shields, and this writer ducked as low in the 16-foot aluminum skiff as we could get. We had been warned about this.

Larry made a 90-degree turn to the right and crashed into a wall of mangroves. Suddenly, we were inside a tunnel of horrors, a creek about two feet deep and about a foot wider than the boat, with sunken logs to jump over, and low-hanging limbs decorated with spider webs to duck under. This was our introduction to the Florida Everglades near Chocoloskee, a small fishing village just off the Tamiami Trail.

Larry sat cross-legged on the rear seat and guided the boat around stumps and across logs with the calm demeanor of a preacher out for a Sunday drive. His 40 hp Nissan outboard motor was taking a terrible beating.

"Ever shear a pin?" John Shields joked. John does some Everglades guiding a bit west of here.

"No," Larry answered, "we don't have shear pins any more, but I spin about two hubs a year." Modern propellers are made in two parts separated by a rubber hub that, in theory, absorbs the shock of hitting stuff like rocks and logs. When the hub has had enough abuse, it lets go of the bladed part of the prop and lets it spin. That's when you don't go any further into, or out of, the swamp.

"I'm gathering up a lot of spider webs up here," I told Larry from my spot at the bow, not complaining you understand, but somewhat uncomfortable about things crawling down my back that I can't identify.

Larry picked off a piece of tree limb. "Here," he said, "swish the webs with this."

Spider webs were not the only entertainment on our voyage down this gully. Larry swung the boat around hairpin turns, dodging stuff the pointed bow didn't deflect. We marveled at the lack of light in our tunnel; the mangrove canopy overhead shuts out most of it, to the point where these narrow channels are not even visible in aerial photographs. Larry stopped once to show us a wild orchid plant. Mangrove roots that hung down into the slimy water were not always shunted to one side by the bow, sometimes they slopped mud in our faces.

Larry seemed to have an encyclopedic knowledge about the Everglades and its flora and fauna - and he remembered every twist, turn, and submerged log in what he called a "creek." How did he do that? "I've been in here all my life," he answered. He and his father commercial-fished out of Chocoloskee, and he is a fourth generation fisherman. When he and his dad were hunting and fishing in here, his father would let him make a few casts for what Larry calls "snuke," the Florida native's name for snook. "He'd only let me catch enough for dinner," Larry said.

"Ever eat manatee?" I asked. Manatees are protected now, and a protective cult has formed around the gentle mammals. Many Florida waterways now have slow zones to lessen propeller wounds to the animals. But, remember, Chocoloskee is near the end of the world. Things go on here you'd rather not know about.

"Yes, I tried it when I was about 10 (he was 62 then)," Larry said. "I didn't like it. But, I'll eat these ibis."

"You mean Chocoloskee Chicken?" John asked.

Ibis were hunted almost to extinction in the early 1900s for their beautiful white plumes, which were used in women's hats and boas. They shot them on their nest, and the young would die. They have been protected ever since.

"You mean ibis tastes sorta like bald eagle?" I kidded. Larry smiled. Eagles are fish hawks, and would most likely taste fishy, like the bottom of their zoo cages smell.

We were about 15 minutes into the swamp. I asked Larry how much farther. "We're about halfway," he answered. Groan. I continued swishing spider webs. Clay and John kept their heads low. My fishing cap was knocked off several times.

Larry told us not to grab any snake curled up on a limb. "Wait until they fall in the boat," he advised. "Do many snakes fall in your boat?" I asked.

"Not in a long time," Larry said. "Because I haven't been up here in a long time."

"WHOA!" Clay hollered. I looked back to see his left leg hoisted up in the air, trapped by the single oar Larry carries. A limb had grabbed the oar and lifted it. Clay's leg was over the oar. His boat shoe was knocked off. Larry stopped the boat right away and we straightened everything out.

Two eternities later, we emerged from the tunnel into a wider, but still shallow, channel. It was about 20 feet wide. Mangroves formed a slight arch over the channel.

"Is there a shorter way back?" I asked.

"That WAS the shortcut," Larry said. Groan.

Larry stopped the boat and anchored 50 feet from a curve we had just passed. "Cast your lures back there," he said. We had just run over the fish we would be casting to. I thought every fish in the area would have left. Not so. These fish rarely see a boat.

Clay and John tied green fleck Fin-S soft baits on their wide gap hooks with no weight. The water was only about two feet deep. Clay and I use 20 pound test Whiplash® superline, and John uses 17-pound test mono. We all used spinning gear on this trip.

John caught a small snook and Clay caught one. We caught (and released) several more snook from this hole. And, right after we had run right over them! Go figure.

Next, we ran to a lake that Larry called "Hell's Half Acre." After casting around the shoreline for some time without a bite, we decided to try another small lake.

"You're here at the wrong time," Larry said. "The best snuke fishing is in March, April, and May." That's also the time local mosquitoes are feeling their oats, too. So, here we were in January - the wrong month.

"And, the moon is full, too," Clay added. Experts say the full moon is the worst time to go fishing. Clay travels quite a bit for his fishing, which is mostly with a fly rod. He checks moon phases and tides before he schedules a trip. My window of opportunity, however, was at that particular time, and we had other activities scheduled.

The other lake was smaller, but we had to go through another tunnel to get there. If it was possible to find more spider webs, I knew we would. We did. The webs were not only larger, but the spiders had built them three or four deep, so a bug would have to fly through four layers of web to survive. My old tree limb swisher was barely adequate. On the other side of the tunnel we had two inches of debris (leaves and limbs) in the boat, plus so many bewildered spiders crawling around, they were hard to count. This was another lake where the snook swam past the boat, but were not interested in our lures.

"Ever try live bait in here?" John asked.

"No, I only use lures," Larry said. "If they won't bite lures, I leave them here. Hey, look guys, there's an alligator swimming this way!" The alligator was about half the length of our 16-foot skiff. Our guide was not impressed. The gator turned and disappeared into the mangroves.

"Whew," I sighed, "I thought that critter might be hungry." Clay Gooch and John Shields never saw it.

"DUCK," Larry said. We hunkered down in the boat again as he plowed into another waterway so narrow the boat scraped the bank on both sides. The mangrove limbs were not quite as low as in the long winding channel that got us in here.

"This a freeway through here," Larry said. Well, not quite. His idea of a "freeway" and mine are a lot different. A "freeway" in here would allow two boats to pass. This was, by comparison, a country lane with cobwebs. It was too narrow for a gator to pass us, which, fortunately, didn't happen. We came out of the channel into a wider one.

"Finally, some fish in here," Larry said. The channel, locally called a "river," was about 25 feet wide. Air bubbles on the surface told us tarpon were present in the three-foot deep water. We could see them rolling on the surface.

Larry kneeled on the bow and moved us up the creek with his single oar, sculling us toward the tarpon by rotating his oar so the blade was aligned with the hull as it drifted through the water, then he turned the flat side of the oar around 90 degrees so he could pull us forward. His sculling was silent, and we made no sound in the boat, but the fish moved away from us about a long cast.

Picture this: a narrow channel with mangroves on both sides, the guide kneeling on the bow, and the three anglers behind him casting lures past his head toward the tarpon. The fish appeared to be about 20 pounds or less, not the huge 200-pounders seen at Boca Grande Pass in midsummer. But, if one of these big herrings grabbed a lure and went airborne as they usually do, they'd likely come down in a tree.

Trees. That's where most of our lures landed. Sometimes you can shake a weedless rig out of the branches, but a lure with two treble hooks is another matter. Larry called us "Tree fishermen." Each hung lure made it necessary to row to the mangrove and untangle the mess.

Larry remarked he didn't like it in here. "Water too dirty?" Clay asked. "Yep." We tried every lure we could think of for these tarpon. No strikes.

"It's the dirty water," John (also a guide) said about the tarpon's lack of interest in our lures. "And the full moon."

"I saw one snuke coming in here," Larry said, "But none since."

Clay had a hit on a Bass Assassin rigged with no weight and a bassin' wide-gap hook.

"I guided a fly fisherman from Montana in here," Larry said. "He caught snuke, a 34-incher, a 31, and two 29s. He never broke any of them off. Most of them break off anything over 30 inches."

The live bait suggestion came up again. "If they won't hit artificials I leave them here," Larry repeated. He's never used live bait in these lakes, though he conceded others may have.

Demere told us one of his clients had two follows right to the boat by a river otter. "If he'd caught that one, I'd have to get the hook out some way," Larry said, "I didn't want it in the boat—it's all claws and teeth."

As we headed back out the first channel that brought us into these lakes, I noticed that some of the spiders were really enterprising. They had rebuilt enough webs to renew my interest in swishing them out of the way again with a tree limb. Again, it was like a scary Disney World jungle tour, minus the elephants, but with snakes and spiders added.

"A lot of women like to come in here," Larry said as we plowed through mud, bounced over submerged logs, spider-swished, and ducked overhead limbs.

"More then once?" I asked.

"They like to see the critters and the environment," Larry answered. "Then, the Park Service thought I was taking out 'eco' tours and they told me I had to get another license. It costs $250." He already has a $250 park fishing license, plus a guide's license, and insurance. The extra 250 bucks was a bit much for a poor guide to absorb.

"I told this lady she had to fish if I took her in here," Larry said. "She said she didn't fish. I told her if she didn't fish, I couldn't take her."

"How far back in the Glades have we been today?" I asked. "About 100 miles?" "No," Larry said, "maybe 15 or 20."

I noticed that Larry seemed to be on a first-name basis with every log and limb as he twisted and turned his aluminum hull through hairpin turns and around stumps. "Waal, I was raised in here," he said.

"Hold on tight in here, I may hit bottom" Larry advised, and later, "Hold on a LOT tighter in HERE!" We made it without hitting anything. "Did that surprise you?" I asked.

"Waal," he drawled, "I wasn't real sure."

When we again saw daylight at the end of the tunnel, Larry dropped anchor near a deep hole next to a sandbar. We cast 1/4-ounce jigheads decorated with a brown soft plastic shrimp imitation. John caught a nice spotted seatrout. Clay hung into a big fish that threatened to spool him, but it broke off before we saw what it was.

Clay caught a gafftopsail catfish. Larry very carefully took the four-pound fish off the hook. They have spines that can give you quite a nasty wound. Larry mentioned that "Sail cat slime is now a damned drug." Clay expressed surprise.

"Yeah," Larry said with disgust, "They lick it off [the fish]."

As we returned to the dock, Clay reminded us it was the wrong time of year to fish for snook. And, avoid the full moon, Clay said. And dirty water is bad.

"Yep," John Shields, also a Florida guide, said, "We guides are required to buy a thick book of excuses." Real thick.

● ● ● ● ● ● ● ● ● ● ● ● ● ● ● ● ● ●

KAYAK FISHING

Clay Gooch and I were fishing with Captain John Shields out of Port of the Islands on the edge of the Everglades when I noticed a fly angler casting his line from a small kayak. He was drifting along the edge of a shallow sandbar where the back-country mangroves meet the gulf of Mexico. While Captain Shields' flats boat can travel in some pretty skinny water, the kayak was drifting in just a few inches. The angler was catching a fish now and then on his flies, and we were doing pretty good with shrimp baits. He was catching and releasing – we were catching and keeping some for dinner. If someone had a happy meter to measure our different pleasure auras, I expect we were about even-Steven with the kayaker.

Kayaking the 'Glades wouldn't suit me, since these crafts are so low to the water they put you eye-to-eye with alligators or other crocodilians, none of which I ever met seemed very friendly.

Fishing, though, from these low-lying craft has some advantages. First, your profile is lower to the water, so you are less likely to scare fish as you would by standing up in a flats boat while wearing a "Florida Camo" shirt that looks like an explosion in a shabby paint factory.

Even the dumbest snook or tarpon would exit the area at warp speed after seeing that much tacky in one place.

VENICE FISHING

"Why don't we share a guide?" Pete Taylor, a retired metallurgist from Maryland's Talbot County who winters in Venice, Florida suggested. We wanted to catch and release a few Florida fish, and learn some new techniques in the same sport. A local guide is the best way to learn.

Pete and I made this decision on my annual winter fact-finding trip to warmer climes with my wife, Carole. Snow and ice appeals to us a lot less every year. And February is the month when Chesapeake Bay winters float over us like a lead balloon.

I met Pete at his condo in downtown Venice, a town that exudes a St. Michaels-like charm with its upscale shoppes and wide tree-lined streets. Pete had agreed to meet our guide, Captain Steve Warren, at Longboat Key just off Sarasota.

Steve's boat was already overboard, and we ran out a narrow channel to Sarasota Bay. He headed south for Bird Key as we talked. Steve hails from Sugar Loaf, Maine, where he had a restaurant at a ski resort. Long hours? Yes, "but there is a window," he said, "when the snow melts in the spring." Then he fly-fished local streams for trout. When he moved to Florida, he bought an 18-foot Shoal Cat boat and a 50 hp Honda 4-stroke outboard, and passed the requirements for a Coast Guard captain's license. Florida does not require a guide's license as does Maryland.

"Bird Key is 100 percent man-made," Steve said, pointing to several decidedly upscale waterfront homes built on reclaimed land. "Maria Schriver and Jerry Springer have homes there," he added.

Many Florida guides supply the tackle. Steve's gear was Loomis rods mounting Penn Spinning reels. He makes his own lures, as do most guides. He believes in casting small bucktails dressed with feathers and hair in the colors du jour. Small lures duplicate the baitfish found in these waters, he says.

We stopped on a channel edge in six to seven feet of water. Steve knows these shallow waters so well, he doesn't need a depthsounder. "The sand holes here are good trout habitat," he said. He likes the incoming tide.

For pompano, you bottom-hop the jig. Let it hit bottom, then twitch the rod tip to bounce the lure along the bottom. On past trips in waters south of here, Carole and I saw pompano skipping along on the surface on their sides, but Pete and I saw none this day. Nor did we catch any of these tasty fish.

Spotted seatrout are a Florida favorite, great gamefish that will take a variety of baits, and lures too. And, they are great eating, with a firmer flesh than our Chesapeake Bay weakfish (yellowfin trout). Speckled trout like the lure moving slowly. And usually near the bottom.

Our next spot was a rocky shoreline in Big Pass between Lido and Siesta Keys. Live shrimp on number one Teflon-coated hooks are Steve's favorite here. Pete immediately caught several large sheepshead. It is often said about wily sheepshead, "You have to set the hook before they bite." Pete really had the knack. Steve

Pete Taylor with a sheepshead

held his own with the striped sheepshead, also called "convict fish." These were the largest of that variety I've ever seen, running up to five or six pounds. "No!" Pete kidded me, "not that big!?" I replied "They grow in the telling. By next year they'll be double that size!"

Convict fish are great bait stealers. After we had fed a good number of shrimp to the fish, Steve said, "We've got them right where we want them now!"

Pete pointed out an inkfish floating around on the surface sunning itself. Inkfish must be a local name, because I couldn't find it in my research materials. It looks like a small bat or ray. It is double-ugly, and the ink from its name must be disgusting, too, because it didn't seem to be worried about predators.

On our left, a large island covered with mangroves was densely populated with hundreds of water birds, including great blue herons, wood storks, snowy egrets, and pelicans, to name but a few.

"We'll drift across this channel, and if we don't get a redfish (channel bass), we'll go inshore and look for specs," Steve said. Several drifts across the channel produced some close-running yachts (some actually slowed for us), and a skate. We went inshore to a dock where Steve caught redfish up to 12 pounds the day before.

Steve anchored just off a deep-water dock so we could cast our shrimp under it into the shade where we hoped big reds were snoozing. Pete had this lobbing side-cast down pat. He could place his shrimp between the dock pilings into shaded areas with great precision. But, after all, he spends his winters doing just that. I caught the dock several times before getting the hang of it. You keep low in the boat for a low profile, let the fish take the bait for just the right amount of time (certain amount of witchcraft involved here), and "Horse 'em out," says Steve.

"You have to get his head up first," Steve coached us. I played a big fish between the pilings and lost it to a barnacle. Steve re-rigged for me.

Pete hooked a nice red and handed me the rod. I said "You fight it. You hooked it!" I guess Pete thought this would be my only chance to fight a red to the boat, so I politely fought the fish to the boat, where Steve lipped it. It was 23-inches long and weighed

5-1/2 pounds. Like most fish landed on this trip, it was released.

Pete caught a 14-inch trout, but the boat was surrounded by cormorants all too eager to grab any fish we tossed overboard. Steve said, "Look, there are two cormorants hiding under the boat to snatch this trout when I release it." He faked out the two birds with a "Statue of Liberty Play" and slowly released the fish over the opposite side, but a third cormorant zipped out from under the boat, grabbed the fish, and swallowed it whole. The birds had faked US out with their old "One guy hide under the boat" trick. We were snookered, but the fish paid the price for our gullibility.

Back at the ramp, I had a discussion with a young student who was gathering fishing statistics for a study. "Is this for the MRFSS?" I asked. He seemed surprised. "Yes, it is," he answered. The Marine Recreational Fishing Statistical Study (MRFSS) is distrusted by knowledgeable fishermen. It's known to be full of inaccuracies. One data point showed anglers catching limits of Chesapeake stripers in the middle of a Bay sailboat marina!

Later, Pete and his wife Molly, Carole and I, all had a great dinner at a restaurant with a pond where a big sign stated "Please don't feed the alligator!"

It was a great trip!

• • • • • • • • • • • • • • • • •

GATOR HOLE BASS

"Carole doesn't want me to go on an airboat," I told Clay Gooch. "Says she'll divorce me."

"Okay," he replied, "then I'll write you a check for court costs."

What a pal! That's what friends are for.

Clay continued to give me the airboat bass-fishing pitch. He'd done the thing, and had a great time. Besides, he said, it's a great story. A bass on every cast, some up to 7-1/2 pounds. Airboats are not dangerous, he continued. He said he feels safer in an airboat than in a flats boat. After he conned me into taking a trip into the innards of the Everglades where I was the spider swisher and snake catcher, I had some reservations. Naturally, I kept these trepidations from Carole.

"Besides," I told her, "Clay says he'll pay my court costs." She got out the insurance policies to see if they covered airboats. So, I met Clay and our guide, Lee Boyd, at the Florida intersection of Route 75 near the turnoff to Marco Island, just outside Naples, Florida.

Lee's airboat is a 17-foot Hollman fiberglass hull, built along the lines of a rugged barge. Mounted to the aft section of the craft is a huge stainless steel wire cage to keep people and other undesirables from getting in the way of the propeller. The prop is attached to a 260 hp Continental aircraft engine. Lee said these engines are used in several airplanes. The rig was perched on a trailer fitted to the craft. Pulling the rig was a four-door pickup truck.

Clay and I climbed into Lee's truck, and we motored eastward on Route 75 toward Miami as the Florida sun rose in a clear sky.

"How far do we go toward Miami," I asked Lee.

"About 60 miles," he said. An hour or so.

We got acquainted as we rode. Lee was a Florida Game Commission officer for 22 years, and has been guiding for 12 years. This area was his territory, and he knows it well. That was reassuring; the title of his business is "Gator Hole Fishing Charters."

I told Lee I had been this way before. In fact, for a previous fishing trip when I met Clay in Chocoloskee to fish in the spider-infested jungles of the 'Glades. I was interested at that time to see so many signs warning motorists to be on the lookout for panthers—not the gray panthers some call "snowbirds," but real ones with claws and teeth. Lee said he rarely sees them. They really don't bother anyone unless they're hungry, or if you have a bite-size dog along.

We launched the airboat at a turnoff somewhere between Naples and Miami. We got aboard and Lee handed us sound-protective earmuffs before he started the engine. Then we began a run southward along trails marked by bent-over grass. The grass was about a foot or two tall, and a great prairie stretched before us, with occasional clumps of trees. What has been called "a river of grass"

Lee Boyd revs up his airboat.

is fed by a few inches of slowly-flowing water, but I think the airboat would have coasted over dew-covered grass.

The airboat ride was surprisingly smooth, as if we were zooming along on a level sea. Engine noise was barely discernible through the earmuffs. I occupied the front seat and "broke wind" for the captain sitting two feet higher and slightly behind me. Clay's seat was above and slightly behind Lee. We wore heavy coats, since the temperature was about 60 degrees F, and the open boat was moving at about 30 knots. It was coolish, but not uncomfortable.

I noticed a tall microwave tower, where Lee turned west along another trail across the grass. In a few minutes, we entered a canal about 50 feet wide. It had been cut through coquina rock in the 1930s during the WPA days to "drain the swamp."

Lee said, "They tried to drain Florida back then. Now they're spending jillions to get the water back."

I looked down into the clear water, only slightly stained by tannin from the bald cypress tree roots. Garfish were stacked up like cordwood in the 15-foot deep canal. What looked like many logs floating in the canal were actually the backs and snouts of alligators. It was not unusual to see up to a dozen at a time. Every so often a gator would throw up a mighty geyser of water as it grabbed a bite of lunch.

Clay Gooch with a nice largemouth bass.

Lee opened a compartment and sorted through several rigged spinning outfits. He handed Clay and I rigs with plastic worms, and took one himself. Lee also brought out a white electric trolling motor, clamped it to the starboard gunwale, and attached the wires to a battery down below. With this motor so positioned, he could move us slowly down the canal at a slight cattywampus angle. This allowed each of us to cast without snagging someone else.

Several largemouth bass were caught by Lee and Clay, but my worming technique didn't suit the fish. Lee handed me another spinning outfit rigged with a mid-sized Zara Super Spook®, Junior. I "walked the dog" across the surface of the canal, getting strikesbehind the lure. Lee said I should slow my retrieve, and I did for a while, but I'm used to retrieving at striper speed. I did catch several nice bass, but most of what we caught was small. Lee said the largest he ever caught here was 7-1/2 pounds. Clay and Lee were soon rigged with topwater lures, Clay with a Pop-R, and Lee with another Spook. We caught a bass on almost every cast.

"Look at that," Lee said, pointing to a previously-ignored 12-foot gator lying on the bank about five feet from the boat, sunning himself. It was smiling, but luckily not hungry. I guess it sees a lot of anglers, and maybe doesn't like the way they taste.

One of my casts went over a floating gator. The only way to get it back was to drag it across his back. This was one critter I really didn't want to catch, but I drug it quickly across the animal's armor-plated hide. He erupted in a spray of water and dove out of sight. "Guess he didn't want it," Lee said. Lucky me. "But, when it gets warmer, he'll go right after it," Lee continued.

A green heron kept diving at my surface plug. He'd make a pass at it, then, missing it, would sit on a nearby tree branch and scowl at it. But, on the next cast, he was back. "In all my years out here," Lee said, "I've never seen a green heron go after top water lures."

Lee advised me to throw my lure, "Right off those lily pads. I bet you can catch 20/30 fish off that ledge." I did catch a few bass there, as did Lee.

"See the roseate spoonbills," Clay said. Several of them were dipping and slurping in a small pool off to one side. We saw so many different species of critters, I can't recall all of them, but they included all kinds of herons, plus wood storks, curlews, cormorants, anhingas, and of course alligators. Orchids grew profusely on trees, and lily pads were in bloom. Strangely, there were no bugs.

We didn't see any wild pigs, but I told my companions about the "pig slapper." One very brave chap from the Orlando area would sneak up on a wild pig and slap it on the back. Pigs are notoriously myopic, so all the slapper did was freeze and keep still while the pig ran around in circles looking for the source of his provocation. A word to the wise: Don't try this at home.

On the way back, Lee stopped to point out an Everglade kite. We stared and he stared, maybe figuring an airboat didn't look like his regular diet of snails. It finally flew away.

Lee powered the airboat back onto the trailer, and we headed back toward Naples and our cars.

● ● ● ● ● ● ● ● ● ● ● ● ● ● ● ● ●

Know how to tell a happy airboater?

By the bugs on his teeth.

ROD MAN REDUX

Our annual book sales excursion to a mid-January Fishing Show was a hoot, mostly because my wife Carole and I were assigned the booth next to the Kellner brothers, Steve and Eric, who meld themselves into one persona to trade as "The Rod Man."

This is the only show where we peddled our books, since we respect our retailers' right to make money on us the rest of the year.

The ebullient Eric Kellner again placed tape on the floor in front of our booth, labelled "Buy Zone. Step in this box for two minutes, and you must buy something. Enforced by the Booth Police."

To retaliate, I placed paper footprints through their booth from left to right labeled, "In," "Spiral guides, 25 cents extra, new technology," and "Exit Here." One guy asked about getting a rod with spiral guides; he was not kidding!

Some of the folks that stopped by our booth to get shook and howdied were interesting. One asked if I was the book author, and noddingly assured me he read a book once.

Another guy had visited a fly fishing exhibit, and was not impressed with fly folks: "They don't wanna tell you nothing. They act like it's a damn secret religion or something." He then proceeded to tell us about his favorite bluefishing technique (We do striped bass books). "First you put some 60-pound test line on a Hatteras Heaver outfit [14-foot rod]," he said, "then wind the drag down tight. When you catch a blue he skips all over the ocean. You really FEEL the fish." Light tackle be damned, he said.

I think people respond to you in the same way you approach them. I have wonderful friends in the fly-fishing community. All have shared information with me. Several even attempted to improve my fly casting, something most other fly folks frankly consider a lost cause.

Captain Eric Burnley said he loves fly fishing parties on his boat. "They catch one fish, and they're ecstatic," he said, "then they release it so it doesn't dirty my cooler. They don't toss beer cans all over the place, they just sit around and drink wine and eat that funny cheese. I love 'em!"

Touring the show, I was challenged by outdoor writer Gary Diamond to a fishing match, fighting a computer with an offshore rod and reel while a computer displayed a jumping marlin on a screen. I thought 900 was a good score against Gary's 600, until an attendant told me low scores are the most desirable.

I shopped for some fishing gear I had to have for our annual Florida fact-gathering trip.

Back at our booth, Carole called my attention to the Kellner's rod-selling techniques. By using sexual undertones, they described fishing rods with all the fervor of White House dandies checking out the latest interns: "This one has a nice butt," Eric intoned in a low, earthy voice.

"Gimbal butts are better offshore than this regular butt," Steve told a customer, who asked, "What's the difference?" "About five bucks," Steve answered.

Those who don't think there is something sexual about buying a fishing rod should have seen the young chap I watched handling a spinning rod. He reverently picked up the rod, caressed its silken finish, then eyed it from its tip top to – if you'll pardon the redundant expression – butt. Each guide was slowly examined. His hot breath condensed on rod wrappings. He seemed to be panting a bit, and drooling. It took me back to my youth.

Eric spied the chap, and advanced toward what looked like a sure sale. He pulled a bagel of questionable ancestry out of his pocket and said, "We're giving away a bagel with every rod."

Hesitant to butt in, we heard a lot of butts discussed in the booth next to us, including: "This rod has a: nice butt, stiff butt, fancy butt, aluminum butt, extension butt, foam-handled butt, slick butt," and, I'd like to see this one – a "featherweight butt."

Carole says that's enough of this callipygian discussion from a guy who's basically mammalian. Let's talk about the bomb.

When we arrived at our booth on the Sunday morning of the show, there were two suspicious grocery bags upended on our table. I joked, "Is anything ticking?" Eric in the next booth chuckled.

Since there were no ticking sounds, I made Carole back off a bit and I lifted one bag. Under it sat a small stuffed toy in the shape of a Valentine heart with legs. Carole pronounced it "cute."

The other bag hid something more ominous. On first glance it looked like a bomb with batteries and a coiled wire hooked to both ends of a small salami. A poem with the "baloney bomb" stated: "Roses are red, violets are blue. This time bomb was made especially for you. If you don't turn over all your cash by one o'clock – your booth will blow up and your books will rock! P.S. No rolled coin, please."

Eric and Steve Kellner pose with the "evidence."

The Kellners were in stitches, and so were we. It certainly was hard trying to figure out who did this dastardly act. Steve and Eric were rolling on the floor.

The brothers finally fessed up. They had shopped a local market the night before; fortunately they didn't mention they were building a bomb. Eric volunteered: "Baloney time bombs built to order," he said, "any size from one pound to Ryder truck."

I returned the favor later. When Eric ran out of reels to sell with his rods, he'd buy more from another vendor at the show. He came past our booth with an armload of reels, bumping his way though hundreds of people in the crowded aisle.

"Hey, Eric!" I hollered, "are those the reels you're selling for five bucks?" A dozen people followed him into his booth.

A card mysteriously appeared on our table: "Tick-Tick-Tick-Tick" it said.

• •

FLORIDA SHALLOWS ARE SHALLOWER

When Pete Taylor said we'd be fishing shallow water with Captain Brandon Naeve, I thought "shallow" like here in Chesapeake Bay waters, maybe three or four feet. No way. No sooner than we left the dock at Placida, Florida in Brandon's 17-foot Maverick tunnel hull, I looked down alongside into four and a half inches of water. Now, that's shallow, even for the small bays off Charlotte Harbor.

Brandon's 70 hp Yamaha outboard prop spins in a tunnel, leaving only the motor's skag to slow the boat in skinny water. The advantage of this shallow-running boat is that only a handful of guides in the Boca Grande area can fish Bull and Turtle Bays. You have to run in extreme shallow water for miles before you can fish depths of three or four feet!

"We'll jig for trout and reds in Gasparilla Bay until the sun warms the dark-bottomed holes," Brandon said. "Then we'll have a bit higher tide to get back into Bull Bay. We're fishing 54 degree water - that's like ice fishing to us. Snook like warmer water before they get active." But first, we fished the "Redfish Rectangle," named for the schools of reds that frequent the area certain times of the year.

While we rigged up with spinning tackle Brandon told us about his dart-playing days. He played for 10 years, all over the country. He was in the top 20 players worldwide. I had no idea that darts were so popular. He said it was possible for a top dart-tosser to make 100 grand a year, playing mostly on weekends.

"This is the slowest time of the year for fishing," Brandon said, "because of the cold." It was 65 degrees F! I wore a light sweater over my shirt. At home it was in the 20s and 30s. Floridians complain about cold weather that we Marylanders would love to see.

Tom Goodspeed, an Annapolis outdoors writer who moved to Florida, once said he could tell the snowbirds by their shorts and sandals—the natives were wearing heavy coats when the temp dropped below 60.

On the Gulf side of Gasparilla Island, we cast small jigheads decorated with 3-inch CAL green fleck paddle-tail minnows by DOA. We caught some spotted seatrout, small redfish, and a loot of ladyfish. Ladyfish are smaller cousins of tarpon, and usually go airborne upon feeling the hook. Pete, standing on the bow, caught several ladyfish on jigs, then switched to a fly rod. Any small fly seems to interest ladyfish.

Brandon had a novel use for his Boga Grip. He'd surround the angler's line with the circular jaws of the grip and slide the grip down the line and over the small lure's hook. It was then simple to flip the fish overboard without harming it, or getting ladyfish slime on his hands.

While we caught several more ladyfish, three dolphin swam nearby, perhaps cleaning out the fish we'd found, or waiting for a handout. Before long, the bite was off, and it was time to move.

After lunch Brandon figured the inside waters had warmed enough, and we entered Bull Bay. There was an interesting structure on stilts that looked abandoned. It was an icehouse, built with thick walls for insulation. "After the net ban," Brandon said, "several were sold to sportfishermen. The commercials, who blamed sportfishermen for the ban, burned a couple of them to get even. They really burned their own heritage."

Brandon was free with his fishing information and tips. Information makes a person want to come back, he said. The more you know about this fishing, the more you want to return. He's right. Would you go again with a taciturn captain who won't tell you what's going on?

Brandon has tarpon anglers who come for three days after a two-day front moves through, and that still gives you at least one great day. "Looking for tarpon is like hunting elephant," he says, "it's not like shooting rabbits."

"We have 110 islands here," Brandon continued, "and 30 square miles of the Ding Darling National Wildlife Refuge below Pine Island. There are 200 square miles of flats." It took him five years to learn the islands, since one mangrove island looks pretty much like another, but he's waded around every island in here, and he can now identify each island the way we'd tell where we are by the Mickey Ds and road signs at home.

I noticed he didn't have a depthfinder on his boat. "Don't need one here," he laughed, looking down at three inches of clear water spotted here and there with sponge and turtle grass. "I'm about the only one that can get in here."

The shallow back waters are always clear, even in 30 knot winds, so sight-casting is always possible.

We stopped and drifted the deeper water, about two feet or so, casting lures at sandy patches on the edges of drop-offs. Brandon poles his craft, but he has installed an hydraulically-operated device on the transom that operated much like your arm if it was attached outside the boat at your shoulder, with your hand pointed downward, elbow bent in an "L." This hydraulic ram drives a pin (where your fingers would be) into the bottom to hold the boat in position like an anchor - without the bother of resetting an anchor at every stop.

Brandon had fished 40 days straight and wanted to do something with his wife. When he asked her what she wanted to do on his "day off," she said, "I'd like to go fishing." Groan.

A couple of miles back in the islands, Brandon cut the motor, and began to pole toward a small bay he called a basin. He called for quiet. He didn't use the hydraulic device because of possible noise. A small anchor was quietly lowered.

This fishing was a bit different. Live shrimp were tail-hooked on 1/0 short-shanked stainless steel hooks and cast without additional weight into four feet or so of water toward the shore. When the shrimp started twitching, it meant somebody out there was sniffing the bait. We could feel the shrimp through the graphite rods and the taut FireLine on small spinning reels. Using the feel technique (you feel and the fish feels, and whoever feels the best, wins), we caught (and released) several nice snook. You have to give the snook a bit of time to get the shrimp: "Just wait until the rod bends," Brandon says, "then wind it in." It's like fishing with circle hooks.

Pete Taylor with a snook.

Pete, on the bow, hooked a steamroller of a fish. After a line-peeling fight, Pete had the fish near the boat, and it was a big one! Brandon lip-gripped the fish with his Boga and brought it aboard for pictures. The 25-inch snook broke Pete's previous record, and it was released after photos.

When the bite turned off, Brandon took us on a sight-seeing tour of Boca Grande on Gasparilla Island. As we passed the golf course, Brandon told us he recently caught a nice snook on the other side of the course when a nice lady asked him if he would sell her that fish. He doesn't have a fish-sellers license and told her so. She finally talked him out of the fish, and cradled it in her arms as she started to leave the course. Brandon asked her if she wasn't going to finish the rest of the course.

"Heck, no," she said. "I'm a lousy golfer!"

FISHING CAP MEMORIES

A recent column on ball-team shirts got me to thinking about the angler's equivalent—the baseball-type caps we use to keep the sun out of our eyes when we are searching for fish.

These caps seem to multiply every time you close a closet door and they have all that darkness to play in. Outdoor writers accumulate ball caps at an alarming rate, and most advertise something. When the closet is full, I put the surplus caps on a table at a yard sale at $1 each, and people grab them like they were the last fishing caps in the world. Heh, heh, now their closets will be full of caps. Neat.

Fishing caps come in many different styles and colors. Some have an open-weave top that is cooler in the summer. It lets air circulate. However, if you are bald, or slightly so, you will get a bad sunburn on your pate.

Other caps are more suited to fall and winter, since they are constructed of solid material, no mesh. They all have some advertising on their front panels. Two of my favorites (because they are comfortable) are Humminbird's "Piranha" and Shakespeare's "Ugly Stik." The first one gets some puzzled looks and calls for a bit of explanation: Piranha is a new Humminbird depthsounder. The other cap got a funny response from a lady at the post office, who pointed at my cap and giggled about the Ugly Stik (fishing rod) logo emblazoned in large letters on the peak of my cap, but I was too embarrassed to ask the source of her humor. I may not have wanted to hear it.

A cap I picked up in Florida has the most incredible mix of colors imaginable. I call it "Florida Camo." Brilliant yellows, greens, purples, and reds are splashed around on the material like an explosion at the Ticky-Tacky Paint Factory. The ad on the front panel is barely legible. It advertises Port of the Islands, a Florida fish camp. I assume the wild colors were concocted to scare off alligators.

One of my treasured caps is a blue one with a logo that says, "Participant Striped Bass Restoration." These caps were given by the U. S. Fish and Wildlife Service (Service) to anglers who caught a tagged striper that was part of the hatchery recovery effort partnered by the Service and the MD-DNR. The funny part is I never caught a tagged striper, although Carole has a cap (I told her where to cast). At the time, I was a contract writer for the Service, scribbling about the striper recovery effort – and the Service's Charlie Wooley handed me the prized cap. Later, Charlie was casting a lure from MY boat when He caught a tagged striper. Humph.

Charlie Wooley's replacement at the Service's Annapolis office, Jorgen Skjeveland, gave me a green "Sturgeon Conservation Participant" cap, although I've never seen a sturgeon.

I left a price tag on another treasured cap. It was given to me by a tackle shop owner when we were going fishing and I didn't bring a cap. This chap is known far and wide as a great businessman (read tight-fisted), and the gift of a cap bearing his shop's logo is a remembrance of that trip.

An American white shad is embroidered on a tan cap that also says "DNR Fisheries Division." DNR biologist Dale Weinrich gave me that one when I fished with him below the Susquehanna River Dam for shad during the restoration effort for that species.

A Cape Lookout cap with a silk-screened lighthouse takes me back to the days when we fished near there for king mackerel and cobia.

Other caps from Pasadena Sportfishing, Salt Water Sportsman, The Mariner, Coastal Fisherman, Memorial Hospital's Rockfish Tournament, Miles River Angler's Club, all bring back some great memories. I expect that's why I keep them, although there's never enough time to wear them all.

Last on my extensive list of caps is a barf green cap embroidered with "Keith's Ale" I picked up in Nova Scotia. Carole carefully picked out the "Ale" threads and matched them, to replace "Ale" with "Hat." I get some really funny looks when people read "Keith's Hat" on my headgear of the moment.

Sorta takes your breath away, don't it?

OPENING DAY MEMORIES

I never sleep well the night before Opening Day. Any Opening Day, hunting or fishing. Makes no difference. I lie awake, staring at the ceiling, worrying that the alarm won't go off and I'll miss my buddies at the dock. Or I'll get there with all the right rods and no tackle box. Hunting, I worry I'll have the right gun, wrong shells. Or, in both cases, vice versa.

In that magic twilight of half-sleep I imagine myself in a deer stand about 9 a.m. when my stomach begins to grumble about missing breakfast. Then I realize my lunch is in the refrigerator, at home. At my age, I've suffered through a half-century of Nights Before Opening Days. Luckily, most Opening Days made up for everything, even though they were not all star-spangled successes.

Opening Day experiences I remember—some bitter, some sweet—include the morning Baseball Hall-of-Famer Brooks Robinson shot a buck that ran at me so fast I couldn't get out of the way. Kneeling in a ditch, all I could do was turn my back and hunker down. The buck ran right over me, and fell dead 50 feet away. My back was numb, my blaze orange hunting coat covered with blood. Luckily for me it was deer blood, not mine. Sports Afield's Gerry Almy took photos.

Deer hunting on that same farm a year later, I talked to octogenarian Froggy Wheedleton in the frosty pre-dawn darkness until it was time for us to go into the woods. Froggy wished me luck as I walked toward my stand and I wished him the same. We both knew that his son, Burton, would drive a buck past him as he sat on his favorite stump. Twenty minutes later Froggy died sitting there on his stump. Looking back, I believe he died exactly where he wanted to, deer hunting with friends.

On a farm near Chestertown, some dirt-ball road hunters shooting from a moving truck drove a herd of deer in our direction. Five of us were walking across the field to drive the adjoining woods. I swung on a running deer 135 yards away and fired one slug. The deer fell. Our guys looked at me in awe. The dirt-balls in the van cheered. I smiled. Do it all the time.

One icy morning, a big buck fed slowly across a corn field between me in a tree stand and the late Bill Perry across the way in a goose blind. The buck's rack was so big he could have passed for an elk on one of those phony TV nature shows. He was at least 200 yards away from both Bill and I, too far for either of us to make a clean shot with slugs. The buck fed across the field for what seemed like an eternity, and slowly walked back the way he came, never coming close enough for a clean shot. I'm glad neither of us shot. So I was a little short on venison. I still have that Opening Day memory.

Waterfowling Opening Days began for me 45 years ago when my late cousin Cres and I sat on a wooded bank in back of the Ice House in Glen Burnie and shot mallards swinging toward the marsh below. We waded waist-deep in the icy waters of Sawmill Branch to get our ducks. Who could afford a dog? Much later, I had a chocolate Labrador retriever big enough to eat hay, one who loved water retrieves, but she made me get my own geese in the field. She loved to swim, but why should she get her mouth full of feathers when I could walk out in the field and pick up a smelly bird?

Opening Days afield (some aswamp) include heavy rain and high winds on the Choptank River when Canada geese wouldn't stay out of our decoys, and sunny Southern Maryland classic hunts where I proved over and over again that doves could fly fast enough to dodge shot.

Recently, I hunted mourning doves on Dr. Stan and Babs Minken's Lostock Farm. No early get-up here. Hunting doesn't start until noon. Banker's hours, much more civilized. We got out to the field at 1 p.m., but the birds didn't fly until 3 p.m. Then there was a lot of shooting. Did I mention not hitting? I shot a box of 25 shells, plus a few, for three doves. You see, doves can dodge shot, or have this stealth-bomber type of configuration that includes armor plate. Dove hunting, luckily, is mostly about socializing, and we had plenty of that with our hosts. A very memorable opening day.

Did you ever try to hit a feathered buzz-bomb of a sea duck while standing on a slippery boat deck bouncing in a heavy sea off Tilghman Island? Now that's an Opening Day to remember! I swung on a string of ducks and the fourth one dropped. "Nice shot, Keith!" guide Norm Haddaway yelled over the storm. I didn't have the heart to tell him I was leading the FIRST duck an Eastern Shore mile!

Recently, after a six-year closure, we were anxious to get out and hunt for migratory Canada geese again, even though the bag limit is now one a day per person. But my hedgerow blind had to be rebuilt and brushed. Decoys needed spiffing up a bit. Hunting licenses needed updating.

So, old-time hunting buddy, Warren Clarken, helped me rebuild my blind. The whole time, we had geese watching us from the field, my lawn, or from Broad Creek out in front of the house. They were not at all nervous. They hadn't been hunted for the previous six seasons in Maryland.

Warren Clarken, Lois Clarken, & Carole Walters painting decoys.

The decoys stored in the shed were muddy from the rainy day we'd put them away several years ago, and mud dauber wasps had built many tunnels on them to lay their eggs. A brushing made them look almost presentable. Warren and his wife, Lois, and my wife, Carole, and I decided we needed to repaint the decoys so we set up an assembly line. See photo on previous page.

Opening Day finally arrived, along with Warren, at about 7 a.m. on the November 19, 2001. We started to put the decoys out in the field, but it was tough getting their metal stakes into the dry turf and it took a while.

Meanwhile, we heard geese flying and calling to our incomplete decoy set, wanting to get in the field. We stood in awe in the dekes, looking up at a sight we hadn't seen for six years, determined geese with their wings set, heading toward us.

As the birds settled down toward a pocket in the decoys, we each took a shot. Two geese down. Our limit. Warren and I looked at each other. "OK, what do we do now?" he asked. It was about 7:30 a.m. and hunting was over for the day. Guns were unloaded, gear was stacked outside the blind. It was much like a honeymoon— months of planning, then 10 minutes later it's all over.

But, what an Opening Day we had! Sort of repayment for all those days in past years when we sat all day in a cold rain or snow without even seeing a goose. That Opening Day couldn't have been better. We might be spoiled now, and expect that same fantastic reaction to our calls and decoys in the future! It may not happen. But, this Opening Day just couldn't have been any better.

Of such memories, great Opening Days are made.

● ● ● ● ● ● ● ● ● ● ● ● ● ● ● ● ●

THE WONDERFUL ONE-BOX SEASON

He was still elated when he told me about his morning in the goose pit. A morning of easy and tough shots, of some geese downed, but mostly missed. Geese coming in with wings set, the cacophony of the guide's goose call mixed with that of the honkers. Suddenly, the guide's shouted direction: "Take 'em."

His eyes were a-sparkle and the smile never left his lips as we talked about shot patterns, how far to lead a goose, shot sizes and the like. It was his first hunt for the majestic Canada goose. His partners in the blind were just as impressed. They were teenagers and he was an adult, but it was a first waterfowling trip for all.

Now, this was not a first-time hunter, this man. He had hunted deer and small game in his home state, Wisconsin. Big game had fallen before him. He worked for a national association active in gun affairs. He traveled and wrote about hunting. It was plain to see that he was enthused—and he would be back to Maryland's Talbot County to hunt the goose. A brand-new waterfowler had been created.

Then came the jolt: "I shot a whole box of shells this morning," he said, beaming. One Canada goose lay on the pavement with his kit. One goose! One box of shells!

What happened? Did the guide let his hunters sky-bust at geese out of range? Not likely, because guides must go back to the same places to hunt, day after day. They don't like to educate any more geese than necessary. Were the hunters poor shots? Hard to tell, but they were not novice gunners, all having passed rigid testing on hunter safety and marksmanship.

Our happy hunter's entire goose season was wrapped up in one morning, one box of shells, one Canada goose. And was he happy!! It made me think about other outdoorsmen, other styles, other goals.

In fishing, it is said the angler progresses in three stages: First he must catch as many fish as possible; next, he wants the biggest fish that will take a hook—a record; and lastly, in his dotage, he most enjoys "quality" fishing—contemplative angling. He stops to experience the "ambience." He no longer has to prove his prowess with rod and lure.

One wonders if there is a similar analogy in hunting. Perhaps there is. First comes the gung-ho, get-up-before dawn and set out the decoys, shoot at anything in (or out of) range skybuster, who hails from the "if they fly, they die" school of thought. A few never grow out of this stage. That is sad, because they are the ones that anti-hunters point to as "average."

The second stage in a hunter's life might be chasing record big game, standing in front of a charging Cape buffalo and wondering if a single .600 Nitro Express round will keep him from being trampled into a grease spot. Somehow, luckily, most of us miss this stage, and go right to "The Quality Hunt" stage.

You must know of a Quality Hunter. One old-timer calls him the "Abercrombie & Fitch Hunter," but that derisive description is not really fair just because our gentleman wants the best—classic clothes, guns, decoys, dogs, field experience, fellowship.

He feels there is much more to it—not having to kill game to enjoy the hunt—the thrill of seeing birds working downwind of the decoys, wings set, even if they don't come in; the heft of a fine double barrel shotgun; watching the dog find game that otherwise might have been lost; a classic hunt over a stool of wood blocks; the clean, crisp air of autumn; and after the hunt, fellowship and conversation with his peers. Those who have never experienced these things are poorer for having missed them.

In our own blind there are seven marks on the wall, indicating that *only* seven Canadas were taken here last season by owner and friends. *Only* is a relative term. Ours is a small field, not one that a seasoned goose guide would consider. A brushed hedgerow blind at one end of the 6-acre field, just 150 feet from the house, and 1,200 feet from the county road. Six dozen beat-up hardboard silhouettes are placed in front of the blind at the beginning of the goose season, and stay there. Most sit cattywampus until the season closes in January. Sometimes, we experiment with exotic decoys like "wind socks" or "stuffers," but we have reached a truce with the geese.

If the geese begin to fly, it is only a short walk to the blind with gun and dog. If they toll to the silhouettes, fine. We will not sky-bust. If they hang suspended with feet lowered at the outer edge of the decoys only 35 yards away, their mark *might* go on the wall—if we are lucky. We watch the dog retrieve with awe and pride. Our zone of fire is narrow. No shots toward the house. If the birds ignore the seductive blandishments of the goose call and fly away to some other field, that's O.K., too. We like to watch them. They are as valuable to us in the air as in the freezer. Non-hunters, please don't try to understand us. You never will.

"Know how many shells I fired last season?" one sport hunter asked me. With the quality of his hunting and the number of birds present, we silently guessed that a case or two would be about right.

"Less than a box," he said, "As I get older, I enjoy fellowship as much as the hunt."

Come to think of it, boxes of unshot shotshells are accumulating around home, too. A friend reloads, and every time he comes to hunt, mountains of shells tumble from his car trunk. With the change from lead to steel shot, we returned tons of lead-loads to him.

An inventory of the amount of shells we expended last season was in order. Unbelievable! Less than a box. And now, it is time to get some steel shotshells for the goose season that is upon us.

One box should do it.

● ● ● ● ● ● ● ● ● ● ● ● ● ● ● ● ● ●

SPORTING CLAYS

This writer and old-time hunting and fishing buddy, Warren Clarken, had an interesting day of clay target shooting (not necessarily hitting) at a sporting clays range in Sudlersville. Talk about a way to sharpen up your aim and increase your humility index!

The range must have at least 100 different trap setups, each one giving the shooter a new challenge and each one representing a different hunting situation—incoming or outgoing "birds" and crossing targets both high and low. The toughest is a "rabbit" target rolled on its edge between two stacks of firewood about 25 feet apart. By the time your shotgun meets your shoulder after you call "pull" to your trapper, the tiny edge-rolling rabbit target runs behind the stack of logs. Tough one.

Our trapper, Tommy Simpler, let us newbies look at a target or two before we fired for record. I found that I could hit more targets if I saw where they were going to fly while I made one or two practice swings with my 12 gauge. Then, shooting for the record, I'd miss one and hit one. We shot 50 rounds, two rounds at each of 25 different stations. Warren, who is an experienced trap league shooter, hit a few more than I, but not enough to embarrass me. He's very polite.

It's a great way to sharpen up for field hunting situations, although many non-hunters get hooked on the challenge of sporting clays. Some shoot in league competition almost every weekend. If you go, take along a good set of ear protectors, or buy them at the lodge. You won't regret it.

EASTERN SHORE DOVE HUNT

"One coming straight at you," Sam Willman hollered at me from the corn stalks. I never did see that dang dove. And so it went for most of opening day of the mourning dove season, Sam calling to me about doves coming my way, and me missing most of them.

I have a number of excuses ready: I have numerous vitreous floaters sloshing around in my eyeballs that all look like birds; my Remington 11-87, 12-guage shotgun has a crooked barrel; the dirty rats that loaded my shotshells at the factory left out the lead shot; and the earth's magnetic field changes every time I shoot—all of which combined, earn me the title of "Conservationist" every time I hunt.

We were dove hunting on Dr. Stanley and Babs Minken's 200-acre place, called "Lostock Farm" near Bozman. Also hunting the same field were Tom Bozzuto and his wife, Barbara; Tom Schaffran; Jim Smith and his son, Nick; Alan Faulkner; the Minken's son-in-law, Larry Schwartz; and the owners, Stan and Babs Minken.

"Here comes another one in back of you," Sam called. Tom Schaffran fired twice, I missed with two shots, the dove circled around over Sam, then Larry, with a barrage of shot filling the cool fall air. Then the lone bird flew past the two Bozzutos' hail of shot, and left the field of action.

"Wasn't THAT an embarrassing display!?" Sam called out. Heck, I thought it only proved the old theory that doves can dodge shot.

There was a lot of shooting down where the Minkens were hiding. Sounded like a war. I thought after that, everyone had their 12-bird limit. Later, that assumption proved incorrect.

Alan Faulkner, huntmaster, told me this would be like last fall's western shore vs Eastern Shore Canada Goose Tournament, but with this dove hunt, it would be the "city boys against the country boys." I said you'd better count me in with the city boys so it wouldn't make Eastern Shoremen look so bad. He laughed, but it was a hollow one.

Alan placed the hunters far enough apart so falling shot wouldn't reach the other hunters, and made it clear, "No LOW shots!" that might hit someone. While number 7-1/2 shot may not be fatal at long range, it can sting. Shots aimed at high-flying doves will fall harmlessly.

Faulkner told about one hunter who shot him not once, but twice. "Right here," he said, pointing to his posterior. The careless one didn't get another invite.

Larry saw a dove coming and made a perfect shot, and Sam called "Nice shot!" Larry, a chef by trade, later said he'd come up with some good recipes.

We had started at 1 p.m. We could have hunted until sunset. As the day wore on, with mostly embarrassing consequences, the hunters changed locations. Larry was about to move near Stan, when I said, "You could do worse than join me on this berm." Larry brought his new dove bucket with the fancy rotating seat (like mine) and enough shells to start an insurrection. His new pump shotgun was loaded and ready.

I had been concerned that I was sticking up in the air like a sore thumb sitting on top of a dirt berm four feet higher than the surrounding field level, but Alan said it wouldn't make any difference. The birds just came a little closer and flew directly over my head, probably to get a closer look so they could laugh louder and longer.

Keith Walters on dove bucket.

I rose from my swivel-top bucket and followed a dove around in a circle—until my footing on the bank was, well, a bit unsteady. When I had a good lead on the dove, I fired and the gun's kick almost sent me over backwards into the pool of water behind me.

Stan later said, "That was quite a little dance you did there." Terpsichore ain't exactly my thing, but I admit it was a pretty graceful recovery.

A small plane flew over us. I asked Sam if he'd seen the game warden in it. He said the ground was too soft for them to land. I said they don't have to land, they have cars in the area, and the overflight was to record our GPS coordinates for the land-based officers. There was a long, contemplative silence.

Alan parked his truck under a nearby tree and brought an insulated bag filled with cold sodas to the hunters. He took care of all the hunters, then set up near Stan and Babs, who had moved closer to me–about where the Bozzuto's had been hunting.

I was getting plenty of action sitting on the berm, though I was missing a lot. I did knock down a couple of doves. One dropped into the water and Sam retrieved it. Another fell into the roadway behind me, and Larry picked it up as I gave him directions. If I'd walked around the corn rows between me and the road, I would have lost my "mark" on the bird.

"Nice shot," Stan hollered when I hit that bird. He was probably so surprised to see me hit anything, he reacted automatically.

Stan moved behind Larry and I to sit with Tom Schaffran. Stan asked me a question about when we should quit and quaff a libation. At least, I thought that was what he asked. I replied, "About 5:30." It was about 5 p.m. We prepared to leave for the house and replenish the liquids we lost out there sweating over hot gun barrels.

Alan was sitting near Babs, and hit a dove. "Did Babs shoot that one?" Stan called. Embarrassed silence. "Yeah, I think so," Alan said gallantly. He soon found the bird in high grass.

Back at the gazebo, we splashed some liquids in cups and cheerily downloaded our field experiences. Jim Smith and son Nick had eight doves; Nick shot five of them with his 20-guage pump gun.

"Did you write down my eight birds?" Tom Schaffran asked. I was hunting near him, and hadn't seen eight birds even come near him. He said that was his total score for the last three years.

Stan asked how late we could have hunted. "Until sunset," I

Left to right: Babs Minken, son-in-law Larry Schwartz, his wife Cindy, and their daughter Maddie, and Dr. Stanley Minken.

replied. "I thought you said until 5:30," he said. "No, I said that was when the sun is over the yardarm—somewhere."

Babs volunteered her recipe for dove breasts: Marinate for a half-hour in Italian dressing, then grill for 10 minutes until pink inside (not rare), with one quarter strip of bacon on top. Sam said he dredges the breasts in flour, and sauteès them in peanut oil.

The group broke up after that, all were about half marinated by then and happy with their classic Eastern Shore dove hunt.

When I got home, I had nine doves in my bucket to clean. Maybe I got the wrong bucket.

● ● ● ● ● ● ● ● ● ● ● ● ● ● ● ● ●

LOOSIANA GATORS

"I had no idea Walt Rhodes handled alligators," outdoor writer Etta Pettijohn wrote. (See Gator Man and "E" on page 133). "I'll have to tell him about the time I went alligator hunting in Louisiana. It is one of those things you like to say, 'I've been there and done that,' but would NEVER, EVER do again."

"When I was riding around in a 14-foot jon boat with a seven-foot alligator I made a lot of promises to God that if he ever got me out of this one I'd attend church regularly, and be a much better person."

"At one point early into the trip as we were cruising down the bayou I told my hosts, 'Huh, I haven't seen one alligator yet.'"

"The guy stops the boat and says, 'You want to see an alligator?' He makes this weird sounding call and alligators pop out of the water all around the boat. Needless to say I didn't make any more suggestions the rest of the trip!"

"When they (there were two guys and me and a seven-foot alligator in this little jon boat) pulled the gator up out of the water and casually tossed him back at my feet I came very close to jumping out of that boat, despite the fact they had shot him between the eyes."

"I had heard seasoned old cajuns talking about shooting an alligator and throwing it in the boat thinking it was dead, only to find out it was just stunned and then they were facing one very upset alligator."

"So, when the nerves in the alligator's tail started causing the tail to slam back and forth banging the sides of the boat, I thought about jumping out of the boat again, but then I remembered all those unseen alligators that guy had called up earlier."

"I was a lot braver in my youth than I am now."

• • • • • • • • • • • • • • • • • •

A BIRTHDAY GREETING FROM OLD FRIENDS

I heard the strangest goose call yesterday, my birthday. It sounded like a greeting, perhaps from some old friends, though that may be a bit of unnecessary anthropomorphism. Anyway, I looked out in the yard where 15 Canada geese were gathered at the riprap. They didn't seem alarmed when I opened the window and clucked at them, though my mouth goose calling leaves much to be desired.

My guess is that these birds are our regular winter sojourners. Since we built our home here on Broad Creek in 1981, a small group of Canadas have enjoyed our 40-foot x 100-foot pond, and a small field when it had crops in it. Now they feed on lawn grass, and drop the processed remains all over the place. Early on we had five birds, then seven, and now 12.

When more birds arrive, we'll have as many as 200 or so munching grass and swimming in the creek out front. I think the small cadre of birds has been imprinted on our place, but have no way to prove it unless the birds wore neck collars.

It was a fitting birthday greeting.

WHAT DO WE DO NOW?

POW! POW!

Two shots, two geese down. Our morning hunt was over. We each had a limit of one bird for the day. It was pretty much over before it started.

"What do we do now?" Warren Clarken said, looking at his watch. It was only 7:20 a. m., about three minutes after our decoys were in place. Here's what happened: I was right, our migratory Canada geese were incredibly naive on opening day. No sooner

had Warren and I placed our shabby goose silhouette decoys, than a flock of geese came over and set their wings, drifting toward the decoys on silent wings.

Oops! We were still standing in front of the blind! The geese were a bit high, so they sailed on by. We dove into the blind and grabbed our shotguns. The geese came back around over the trees silently, dropping lower. They sailed over the decoys, going away. We hunkered down behind the blind's brushed front.

Warren Clarken checking his watch.

Then, the birds turned around 180 degrees–into the wind again –and came to the dekes like they were on wires leading to an open spot in our placement. "Always leave a hole," say old timers about their decoy sets, "gives them a nice homey place to go."

Warren made a call or two when the geese were further out, but sometimes it is better to say nothing. We kept quiet, except for poking shotgun barrels out through the blind's brush and softly snapping our safeties off.

The farthest decoy was a measured 40 paces (about 40 yards) out from the blind, about the maximum reliable range for our 3-inch magnum steel BB loads, considering we've missed closer shots. "Experts" will chide us for shooting at that close range; some say they can drop a goose at 75 yards with a 20-gauge. Maybe, but we hate to see birds crippled because some egotist thinks a long shot with a small bore gun is something to brag about. Canada geese are big, tough birds, and can survive beyond imagining.

As the birds ghosted in, we took aim and fired one shot each, and it was over. Weeks of planning, rebuilding the blind and brushing it, cleaning our shabby decoys, getting our geezer lifetime hunting licenses, buying shells, checking out shotguns—and learning how to miss clay birds at a sporting clays range. Well, it paid off. A Canada goose was invited to dinner.

As Warren and I took our gear out of the blind (my thermos of tea was still hot), more birds set their wings for the blind. Again, we were standing out in front of it, talking. I jokingly voiced some goose-like noises, sounding sort of like a herniated crow with a bad case of asthma. They liked it! They dropped in, then stood at the outer edge of the decoys and smiled at us. Never have waterfowlers been more severely tempted. But, our guns had been unloaded right after we shot, and our gear (including shells) was in neat piles outside the blind.

Warren and I walked back to the house carrying our birds. It seemed they were larger than we remembered from the "old days" before the six-year moratorium. OK, we are older now, or perhaps the geese were heavier, but mine seemed to weigh more than the 13-pound Thanksgiving turkey I got out of the freezer to thaw. That's a big goose.

Back at the house sipping my hot tea, Carole called out, "Look at that," she said with great enthusiasm, "All those geese dropping into your decoys!" Her gleeful comment was a throw-back to the pre-moratorium days when Warren and I sat out some pretty cold mornings. Nothing flew, and as soon as we were getting our body heat back in the warm house at lunchtime, the %$#@% geese would pile into the decoys, just mocking us. Carole likes to point out stuff like that. Even her poodle smiled.

For the rest of the day, the geese taunted us by swimming up and down past our dock as more and more of their friends set their wings and came to them. There must have been a hundred or more by midafternoon.

Carole made fresh goose stew from cubed meat and a variety of veggies. The toothsome aroma of that sure-to-be-delicious stew wafts down the stairwell to the Dungeon as I type this. Pure ambrosia! Her delicious recipe is on page 190.

If the rest of this week is as great as the first day, it might make up for the long, dry spell when we couldn't hunt migratory Canadas. At this writing it is one goose per hunter in possession on the first day, no more than two geese in possession from the second day on. However, we must remember to always check the regulations as to the allowed number of geese. I know game wardens who'd be happy to count them for us!

● ● ● ● ● ● ● ● ● ● ● ● ● ● ● ● ●

SMELLY GEESE

Outdoors artist, Peter Ring and I often team up at meetings of the Southeastern Outdoor Press Association and go antiquing. We talk a lot about his favorite outdoors sport, hunting. Naturally he drags his game home to be cooked for dinner by his wife, Fleda.

When asked by Peter how a snow goose tastes, their daughter answered, "It tastes like my dog smells when he's wet!"

GOOSE BRUNSWICK STEW

FIRST, COOK YOUR GOOSE

Place cleaned goose in a pot of salted ice water and soak for at least an hour. Pour off water. Then place goose in a large, deep soup pot. Cover with cold water. Add one stalk of celery with leaves, 4 whole black peppers, one bay leaf. Bring to a boil, then cover and simmer 1 hour or longer until goose is fork tender. Discard water and seasonings. Cool meat and carefully remove from bones (watch out for shot), chop and prepare for recipe below or your favorite recipe.

4 medium potatoes, peeled and diced
1 small onion, chopped
2 carrots, sliced
2 stalks of celery, chopped
4 cups of water
Simmer above 5 ingredients in large pot about 30 minutes until potatoes and carrots are fork tender.
Add to above:
Two cups of water
1 teaspoon dried sweet basil leaves
One 16 oz. can of diced tomatoes, undrained
One 16 oz. can of yellow or white corn, drained
One 16 oz. can of cut blue lake green beans, drained
One 6 oz. can of tomato paste
Goose meat, small cubes
Salt & pepper to taste

Simmer all about an hour then add:
One or two 1.1 oz. packets of instant beef broth
1 to 2 tablespoons of corn starch to thicken
(blend corn starch in a little cold water first then add to stew)
Simmer 20 minutes more or until thickened.

Tastes like beef stew. Freezes well.

HAPPINESS IS A WARM (CHOCOLATE LAB) PUPPY

Start with a six-week old chocolate Lab puppy. Call her "Solitude's Cinnamon of Aerie" to give her a little class if you like, but we use "Cindy" for short. Listen to tortured howls from a big cardboard box in the kitchen for two long, long nights until she wins—her bed next to yours seems more suitable anyway. Watch her fall, actually fall, on her dish at meal times. Realize that something that small and uneducated is bound to fall in the pond on her first day home and off the pier into the creek on her second. She shows no fear of water. She lies down to drink from her dish. After all, she's a water dog, right?

It was only when she grew to the size of Carole's 15-year old miniature poodle we realized that within Cindy's rotund chocolate-furred body beat the soul of a terrorist. Anything within reach became her own personal chewie toy. Hands, feet, shoes, plastic bottles, poodles—whatever. Puppy teeth are like sharp needles.

Noel, the poodle, was getting a little grumpy in her old age. "Touch my body to pet me if you like," she said, "but leave my feet and tail alone." Guess which part of poodle anatomy was the first target for The Terrorist? And the second target?

People are fair game for terrorists, too. Imagine a 12-pound furry chocolate rocket launching herself from the far corner of the room through your newspaper and into your rib cage. Now, she weighs 90 plus pounds, and it pays to keep one eye on her over the top of your magazine. Each additional pound on her frame has the potential of cracking two more ribs. It's a war of nerves. That's what terrorists do for a living.

Carole's needlework proved a little harder to get at. Unzipping a needlework bag is not puppy's work, you know. It takes attention to duty and a fiendish doggy delight to unzip a bag like that with your teeth and chew the corners off a needlework piece that has been 11 months in the stitching.

Cindy's first foray into Carole's sewing room was like the proverbial kid in a candy store. "Let's see what you have in your mouth," Carole asked a guilty-looking puppy. Cindy went "ploop" and out popped a soggy spool of thread. The sewing room door is closed now. Tightly.

Later, Cindy came to Carole and whined that the sewing room door was closed. She kept it up. Carole investigated to find that Noel was trapped inside. Did the Terrorist warn Carole about Noel's predicament out of the goodness of her heart? Fooey! I think she wanted to get at her favorite chewie toy—the poodle. Why hadn't Noel barked about her predicament? Fear. Inside the sewing room, peace and quiet. Outside, stark terror in a chocolate overcoat.

Kitchen noises seem to appeal to growing dogs. Pantries contain the staff of canine life. Dog food. Doggie snacks. Bones. It is truly amazing that a dog that can't hear a shouted **"SIT"** command can manage to show up from the other end of the house at the slightest creak of a pantry, or refrigerator, door.

Ice cubes are Cindy's downfall. She's a cubaholic. Crunching ice cubes is great fun, and she magically appears whenever the freezer door opens. Cubes are fair game even if they happen to be in a glass. Cocktail parties are a real blast in this household. Cindy found early in her career that a wet, cold dog muzzle, properly placed, will launch ice cubes toward the ceiling. Cover your drink and hold it close to your body. Don't worry if you spill it, though. Once it hits the floor, it belongs to the Terrorist. She doesn't mind cleaning up the booze. Runs in her family, I'm told.

Cindy climbed into my lap as a puppy, whining. A small tooth fell onto my trousers. "Put it under your bedding," I told her. "The canine tooth fairy will leave you a dog biscuit for it." She gave me an unbelieving look but hid the tiny fang anyway. Discretion is the better part of sound snack management.

Investigating mechanical things is a part of growing up. You haven't really tested your powers of concentration unless you have been under a tractor's mower with an air-driven impact wrench in one hand while juggling a bolt, three washers, and a blade in the other—while a puppy is licking your ears.

Lately, when I check under the hood of a car, she has taken to putting both front paws on the grill and peering into the engine compartment with a knowing smile. Just waiting for me to screw something up.

We all have blue days. It might surprise you to know dogs do, too. Only problem is, when you have chocolate fur, blue stuff shows up pretty good on it. If it's blue epoxy paint, it will stay a lot longer. Did you know that one little ball point pen holds over a gallon of the bluest ink you ever saw? Shows up exceedingly well on brown fur—and on brown carpet. It is a lot more permanent than you might think.

One might suppose that a dog who laid on the floor to get a drink of water and slid slowly backwards off the pier or into the pond had no potential as a Trained Retriever. Not so. When she was a seven month old dog and living with one of the worst trainers in the entire hemisphere, she showed a lot of hustle. She flashed out into the field or water to get the rubber training dummy and returned it on the run. Whistle commands were not really taken seriously, but I can't say that her trainer knew how to tweet one of the dang things right anyway.

Cindy showed us she also had goose hunting potential when she was a few months old. A show about the Chesapeake Bay was on her favorite educational TV channel and when they showed the World Championship Goose Calling Contest at The Waterfowl Festival® in Easton, Maryland, that puppy snapped right to attention. Yessir. She liked the voice callers best and growled at the tube calls. So do I. Now, that's class. She paid rapt attention to the scenes of Canada geese landing and guys banging away with shotguns, but lost interest when they cut to scenes of sailing skipjacks dredging oysters.

I was in the process of teaching her to read, using a waterfowler's magazine as a primer, but she got way ahead of me. I thought when she was sufficiently literate I could just hand her a copy of Dick Wolter's *WATER DOG* and let her take it from there. Save me all that time tossing rubber dummies around the yard. Now she's writing her *own* book.

Cindy grew from a lallygagging, bamboozling, butterfly-watching puppy to a (mostly) Trained Retriever.

Now, that's progress.

THE CRAIGHEADS

Picture this: You are in the middle of a herd of 13,000 elk. Half of them, the bulls, have huge antlers that seem to reach the clouds. It's a dream that big game hunters often have between seasons. But, it's not a dream. It happens every winter at the Elk Refuge in Jackson, Wyoming, often called "Jackson Hole" because it sits in a valley.

As elk migrate southward in late fall, they are stopped from proceeding farther by ranch fences south of the Jackson Hole area. So, the federal government, always the benefactor, created the Elk Refuge so they could feed the animals all winter, and let them migrate northward in the spring. Before their spring migration begins, the bulls, perhaps to thank their hosts, shed their antlers, which are then graded as to quality and stacked in piles. Then an auction is held. Oriental buyers bid high prices for the antlers which are then ground up and sold to clients in their home countries. Profits are donated to the Boy Scouts.

"Why do the orientals buy the powder?" I asked Dr. John Craighead one evening in a Jackson Hole restaurant.

"They use it as an aphrodisiac," he replied.

"Does it work?"

"If you THINK it does," he answered.

I had a chance to see the elk herd as a part of my job with the National Aeronautics and Space Administration (NASA). Jim Lynch, who was then the Assistant Public Affairs Director at the Goddard Space Flight Center (GSFC), called me about a photo assignment. I was then the Photographic Section Head.

"NASA is supporting an experiment in elk migration," Jim explained. "Drs. John and Frank Craighead (twin brothers with great credibility in grizzly bear research in Yellowstone Park), proposed an experiment that allow them to track an elk's migration north in the spring using data relayed to a space satellite from a transmitter on an elk."

Chuck Cote of GSFC was the NASA Principle Investigator (PI). A collar was soon fabricated that included solar cells to recharge the batteries, instrumentation, and a short antenna. A cow elk was the best candidate for the collar, since a bull elk's neck can swell in rut. The collar would use position location data from OPLE (Omega Position Location Experiment) which had a resolution of about one mile.

After installing the collar on a captive cow elk at the National Bison Refuge near Missoula, Montana, researchers found the elk's position sent to the satellite was within one-half mile of her actual location. Next, there would be a full-scale test, with national press invited, at the National Elk Refuge in Jackson Hole, Wyoming.

It was bitter cold that February in Jackson Hole. I had to take my mittens off to operate the three cameras I had along, a Nikon 35mm, a Hassleblad, and a 16mm Bolex movie camera. "We have a dry cold here," locals said, "It doesn't bother you like your damp cold back east." Fooey! Take your mittens off at minus 15 degrees anywhere and see if your fingers don't tempt frostbite! Cold is cold wherever you find it.

To get a biologist close enough to a cow elk to shoot a tranquilizer dart, we hunkered down amid bales of hay on a large sled pulled over the snow by a tracked vehicle. As a refuge worker cut the twine on a bale and tossed it behind the sled, elk gathered behind the sled to feast on the hay. They were wary of the sled, as if they had been spooked before we got there.

Finally, the biologist fired the dart gun and a cow elk slowly rolled over. Scientists, Drs. Frank and John Craighead quickly placed the experimental collar on the cow elk as she lay immobilized.

We retreated to the sled. She slowly arose and shook herself as if trying to get rid of the tranquilizer's cobwebs. She joined the herd. Again, the scientists received good location data immediately, and also later as she migrated north.

A few years later, Carole and I traveled west, and included Yellowstone Park on our itinerary. Somewhere I have a slide of our old black Pontiac station wagon in a plowed "valley" through a 15-foot high snowdrift. It was in early June!

Carole Walters looks at Elk Antler Arch at Jackson Hole, Wyo. City Park.

We were amazed at the elk antler "gate" to a park in Jackson Hole. We also visited with Frank Craighead at his cabin in Moose, Wyoming, a short distance from Jackson. He recommended we see the Gros Ventre Slide nearby, where a landslide had carromed down a mountainside, across the valley, and halfway up the other mountain. While admiring that view I saw a moose calf and walked closer to take a picture, when I heard the cow snort behind me. Hair stood up on the back of my neck. Moose are not the friendliest critters in the swamp, but they are the biggest at nearly half a ton. I made tracks out of there.

At Frank's house, we had a nice visit and recalled the elk episode. He and his brother had also used the OPLE system and a NASA satellite to get data on a winter-hibernating grizzly bear in its cave. To instrument the bear for body and ambient temperature, respiration rate, etc., they had to drag it out of a cave, attach the instrumentation, then stuff over 500 pounds of bear back into its abode while it was still tranquilized. Unfortunately, the bear tumbled down the hill, and they had to drag it back up the snow-covered slope and into the cave to restore its winter sleep patterns.

Dr. Frank Craighead at Moose, Wyo.

Leaving Frank's house, I noticed his back yard was surrounded by an elk antler fence. The Craighead family are all avid hunters. I remembered Chuck Cote's experience in bringing home a huge pair of elk antlers. As he ran through Chicago's O'Hare airport to catch a connecting flight, carrying his antlers bound together with twine, he rounded a corner and almost gored someone running the other way! What a headline that would have been: "O'Hare passenger gored by elk between flights!"

So, I asked Frank if he could spare a pair of elk antlers. He picked out a pair and apologized that they were slightly truncated since his sons made belt buckles from the thickest part of the antler bases. I tucked the antlers into our old station wagon and carted them home, where I intended to make them into a gun rack for our family room.

When I looked over the antlers more carefully, I found I had two right-hand antlers. Groan!

••••••••••

Years later, I received word that Frank Craighead died at age 85. His cousin is retired physician, Dr. John Thomas Craighead of St. Michaels, Maryland. Tom sent me copies of literature compiled by Frank's widow, Shirley; and Tom's sister, Jean Craighead George. They grew up in the Washington, DC area at a time when

Potomac River water was pure enough to drink. In 1940, after getting their M.S.degrees in wildlife management, they co-authored a National Geographic (Geo) article on falconry that led to an invitation from Indian Prince called "Bapa" for short. The brothers wrote another Geo article about their experiences called "Life with an Indian Primce." After earning their Ph.D.s in 1949 they went their separate ways for a time, but wound up in Moose, Wyoming, building almost identical log cabins side by side with a view of the Grand Teton mountains.

The brothers began a 12-year study of grizzly bears as the request of Yellowstone National Park. I remember some controversy that arose because they recommended the grizzlys be moved away from the garbage dumps and back into the wild, which didn't sit well with the Park Service because the bears were a main tourist attraction.

Frank's contribution to the bear research was in the development of radio transmitters so the bears could be tracked and studied, even when denned up for the winter. Many will remember the Geo footage of the brothers dodging a grizzly after it was radio-collared and released in Yellowstone Park. The radio-collar tracking led to the NASA work in the Antlers story.

Many will also remember the Geo footage of the brothers floating down the Snake River, which led to the protection of the Snake as a Wild and Scenic River. Frank told me that the Geo photographers lost several expensive movie cameras in the river when their raft capsized.

As Frank fought Parkinson's disease near the end, he'd often ask Shirley to help him see his beloved grizzlys again, to hold a fly rod, to look for birds, and to visit friends. He died on October 21, 2001.

Frank and his surviving twin brother, John, led colorful, productive, and eventful lives. Their many accomplishments made the natural world a better place.

● ● ● ● ● ● ● ● ● ● ● ● ● ● ● ● ● ●

CRITTERS HUNTING

Hunting techniques here on Futility Base or "FB" (apologies to NASA, my former employer) have been honed to a fine edge, and recent events have given me more time to watch them. Carole's recent surgery made me the caregiver, and the resulting housework has taken five pounds off my corpulent frame. Housework is to be avoided at all costs, most men feel, and is one of the best reasons for getting married once that glandular thing is out of the way.

Anyway, back to hunting, as our FB critters do it. While fixing breakfast one morning, I watched a great blue heron catch, wash off several times, toss his prey in the air to turn it around, and devour head first, three of the biggest frogs I've ever seen. One must have been 12 inches overall. His, or maybe her, hunting technique is fairly standard for herons. It consists mainly of standing still at the edge of our pond, and watching. This bird can stand stock still for 10 to 20 minutes without moving a muscle, a trial of patience most deer hunters fail. Most of us drink a gallon of coffee, then climb up into a deer stand in cold weather—then, that urgency to relieve hits us. Anyway, five minutes perched on a tree limb ain't gonna get us a deer.

So, after standing in one place for a seeming eternity, the great blue unwinds that serpentine neck in a flash and comes up with a frog. He moves so fast 'Ol Ribbet hasn't had a chance to jump back to safety in the pond. If one were to analyze heron hunting techniques, it might be this: hours of boredom, a nanosecond grab. They seem to do this naturally, without over-analyzing the situation.

Other critters observed from Carole's kitchen window include the pair of red foxes that live and raise kits under our neighbor's shed. They hunt our back field, now overgrown with wild grasses. Red is frequently seen trotting across the yard between the house and field, and it's his odor, I think, that keeps the poodle from going out at night. The foxes live on rodents and anything else they can catch on the ground, like squirrels and rabbits. One morning I saw two squirrels at play behind the shed. The fox was heading for them, full tilt. If they saw him it was not apparent. When he was almost upon them, they split up and ran up nearby trees. The fox went between them. Had he concentrated on one, he might have had squirrel for breakfast. One squirrel under paw is worth two in the trees.

Another morning I watchcd two reds hunting the field. They worked as a team, chasing some unfortunate rodent this way and that. Interesting to me was the way they jumped in the air and came down paws first as if they needed an aerial view before pouncing. They played this game for a long time. I never did see whether they caught their prey.

• • • • • • • • • • • • • • • • •

FAT ALBERT

Its raining grackles and squirrels as I write this story. The bird feeder is empty because we are over-grackled, a fact that hasn't occurred to Fat Albert, our neighborhood terrorist squirrel.

As his buddies watched, he jumped up and grabbed the one-inch copper pipe that supports the feeder, shinnied up to where it meets the four-inch diameter PVC drain field pipe, got up that about two squirrel lengths, then found himself slowly slipping back down the wet pipe, holding on for dear life.

He was one puzzled rodent.

His tactics had always worked before. He ran up the steps leading up to our second-floor deck for an eye-level peek-see at the treacherous feeder. Maybe then, he saw it was empty as Mother Hubbard's cupboard. He left.

• • • • • • • • • •

Feeder's full – Albert's back.

ELEPHANT STALKER

Don Witten was a Public Relations Specialist at NASA Goddard Space Flight Center when I was Photographic Section Chief there. Don had a trip lined up to cover the San Marco (Italian) satellite launch from a platform off Kenya, and took along Applied Physics Lab photographer, Mike Mandella. Don asked me if I wanted to go, but I'd just heard from another NASA traveler to Kenya about finding dead bodies along the road, I politely declined the trip, since I was really needed back at Goddard. Heh, heh.

Don decided that motoring through the Tsavo Game Park would be a pleasant side trip. "The hotel manager advised [us] to carry a gallon of water with a lemon in it, and check out the spare tire," Don said later. "And, wouldn't you know, right in the middle of the park, we had a flat tire."

"After the flat was fixed, I decided to be stupid and stalk a nearby herd of elephants for a close-up with my Nikon. Acting very much like a lion stalking a herd of zebras, I worked my way very close to the bull in charge. In fact I got so close he took several steps toward me, raised his trunk, and bellowed like hell. I quickly captured the scene and ran like hell for the car. (Tsavo rules say sane people should NEVER leave their car).

"When I got back, Mandella informed me that I was nuts. But he had captured it on [movie] film. He said he would have kept the camera rolling even if the bull elephant had tossed me in the air and trampled me." "As a 'Modus de Mort' it would have been much more spectacular than a simple heart attack. And, just think, I would have made the evening news."

"In looking back on this event, I realized the real danger was not from the bull elephant, but more likely the Cape buffalo that could have clipped me from a hiding spot in the nearby bushes. Or, maybe I could have stepped on a deadly Green Mamba snake, the major cause of death in Kenya. I was so busy stalking and shooting that I never once looked to the side of where I was walking."

"NICK"

Nick Sherrill, Warren Clarken, and I sat in our goose blind in Mr. Evans' front yard. No matter that the blind was only 50 feet from the Evans' house, we had some really great hunting there. The blind was staked to the Eastern Bay shoreline at the southeast tip of Maryland's Kent Island.

Three dozen Canada goose water decoys danced in the morning sun. It was one of those "bluebird days" when nothing flew, or was likely to. By midmorning, there was talk of mutiny, of giving up for the day.

To break the monotony, attention was directed to the deplorable state of Nick's 1100 shotgun.

"I never clean it," Nick said, "that's why it always works."

Warren made a face. You could see your reflection in the barrel of Warren's 1100. My 1100 was somewhere in between Warren's sanitary scouring and Nick's total disregard for the laws of corrosion.

Our scientific discussion was interrupted by the clucks of geese coming to our decoys, wings set. Lots of geese. We hunkered down, showing nothing but eyeballs through the brush on our blind. The birds kept coming, like they were on a wire that ended in our dekes.

"Never seen so many @#$@# geese," English teacher Nick stated poetically.

When the birds were in range, we stood to shoot. Safeties clicked off. Wham! Wham! One shot each for Warren and me. hree shots for Nick. Birds fell.

Warren and I looked at our three-shot semiautomatic shotguns in stupefied horror. *Both* were jammed. My problem was caused by oversized brass in my reloads; Warren had a broken shell feed spring. Nick continued blasting away, stuffing more shells into his steaming 1100 with fidgety fingers. He even tried to jam his goose call in the chamber.

Warren and I took quite a ribbing about our shotguns that day. Warren wanted to hunt the following day, but couldn't get a replacement spring that quickly. Nick volunteered to loan Warren his gun—on one condition: "You don't clean it! I'm really serious about that. Clean guns *jam*. You promise?"

"O.K.," Warren agreed, wrinkling his nose like he had just smelled something disgusting. Using a shotgun that harbored enough dirt to grow potatoes was foreign to Warren's nature. (He cleaned it that night).

We were interrupted by a huge cloud of blue smoke that slowly drifted toward our blind. Nearby, the piercing clamor of an engine screaming in anguish filled the air.

"What's that?" I asked, startled.

"Mr. Evans warming up his car," Nick said. The late Winfield Evans, then in his 80s, was a World War I veteran, once a top fighter pilot. That's the way they had warmed up those big radial aircraft engines in WWI. Full throttle. Mr. Evans had simply stayed with the program into the 1970s.

"Bleeping lousy car," Evans complained, smacking the

screaming Cougar's fender with his cane. "Don't make 'em like they used to. Only got 30,000 miles on this @%$# thing (thump with the cane), and it burns a &*$#% quart of oil between here and the #%@#$ Post Office!"

• • • • • • •

Goose blind stories help pass the time between hours of boredom waiting for birds, and several short seconds of panic when the boss goose finally gives his flock the O.K. to plop into the decoys.

Nick told us about his bay leaf. His wife, Jo, had added a small bay leaf to one of her gourmet meals, but forgot to remove it. Nick ate the leaf.

Extreme pain at the very output end of his digestive tract sent Nick off to the local Emergency Room. "It felt like glass in my ass," Nick explained.

The doctor had a peek past Nick's sphincter and found an intact bay leaf. (They don't digest, except in a garbage disposal, maybe). You can imagine the hilarity in that Emergency Room, probably the only humorous thing that happened that day, that week, perhaps that year. They may have even framed the bay leaf and tweezers, the medics enjoyed it so much.

Nick continued his story: "Anyway, my buddy wanted to bow hunt for deer." (We'll call the buddy "Geronimo" here for anonymity, and other reasons later explained). "He bought one of those powerful compound hunting bows and a bunch of arrows, and set up a bale of hay to practice. He pulled the string back— you know it takes some strength. But, instead of turning the arrow and string loose, he released the *bow*. Smack, right in the face! It took several stitches to close the wound, a big, red vertical slice above one eye."

"Next, I took him deer hunting with me. I dropped him off at a tree stand. I went farther into the woods and returned just before lunch. He was flat on the ground. He'd gotten drowsy up in the stand, fell asleep, then fell out of the tree." (You're supposed to yell "Geronimo" when you bail out, but he was asleep). "He had a big split over the *other* eye!"

Nick took his guest to the same Emergency Room for stitches. "He looked funny with those two big red gashes, one over each eye," Nick chuckled.

"The doctor came out to check my buddy," Nick continued. "As soon as he saw me, he hollered loud enough to bring out every doctor and nurse: '**Look who's here!** It's the guy with the **bay leaf!!**' "

We got a pretty good laugh out of Nick's story, but one thing puzzled me.

"Nick," I asked, "you mean the doc recognized your *face*?"

• • • • • • • • • • • • • • • •

BUZZARDS OR GEESE?

The wind blew at 25 knots or so from the front of the goose blind as Warren Clarken and I sat and watched what we thought were 10 buzzards at the far corner of the field, since buzzards had been circling our woods lately.

We had a burlap cover for the blind's opening, so we didn't see the birds walk past the front of the blind. When I lifted the burlap to call to far-off geese, I noticed the "buzzards," basically big, black birds, were nearby, and upon closer examination, turned out to be "wild" turkeys. They fed and ambled off to the left and across the county road with not a care in the world.

Buzzards, by the way, are out of season.

• • • • • • • • • • • • • • • •

GEEZERHOOD

"Happy Birthday," Carole said, as she handed me a nice card and a present. "And, by the way, don't forget to take the trash out." Mentioning my birthday and trash in the same thought string didn't dampen my enthusiasm for the day—at least I was vertical and breathing.

Birthdays come and birthdays go, but when one reaches geezerhood, there are some pluses and minuses that younger folks don't even think they'll have to worry about. Like bad knees, root canals, and hemorrhoids.

My days of having to climb up 15 or 20 feet into a deer stand in pitch-black darkness, while I worry about which of the 2x4 steps have rotted out, or which 16-penny galvanized nail didn't get the full shot of rust protection and therefore is about to give way, are pretty much in the past.

"You're going to hunt deer with us, aren't you?" my friend Stan asked recently.

"I'm too dang old to drag a deer out of the woods," I answered.

"Don't have to drag it any more," he said, pointing to his new 4-wheel-drive all terrain vehicle.

"Yah, sure, you betcha," I thought to myself in my native Minnesotan dialect, "but who is going to drag it to the ATV?"

Which reminds me of the time Sven and Oley were deer hunting and Oley had a heart attack while dragging out a deer. Sven came along and told Oley to lie still, that he would drag the deer to the truck and go get help. While Sven was loading up the deer another hunter came along and helped hoist the heavy animal.

"Yah, sure, you betcha" Sven explained, " I'm going to town and get help for my buddy Oley—he's there in the voots wid de heart attack."

"You mean you're loading up a deer while your buddy is in the woods with a heart attack? Why?"

"Vell," Sven rationalized, "Ain't nobody gonna STEAL Oley!"

One of the benefits of geezerhood is that I can tell that joke to my peers about once a week and get a laugh every time.

So, instead of climbing a tree I can sit on my dove bucket on opening day holding a borrowed muzzleloader and wait for a deer to come up and shake hands with me. Only problem is how am I gonna get up off the bucket.

• • • • • • •

Carole and I recently returned from a meeting of the Southeastern Outdoor Press Association in DeLand, Florida. One thing I noticed about these great outdoors writers was that, man or woman, members under 50 were calling me "Sir." I'm not attempting to belabor the geezer thing here, but it made me wonder how much I'd actually aged since our last meeting.

The last meeting day is Saturday. We usually go to a firing range during the day and attend a coat-and-tie banquet that evening. You may be surprised at what some writers call formal attire. One wore a large leather hat with a dinner-table-sized brim. I doubt he ever takes it off, even to shower. Younger members consider an advertising T-shirt and jeans formal wear.

At the range, I avoided firing a 7mm magnum rifle. No one needs that much power—or kick—unless they want to hunt elephants or Bengal tigers from the next mountain away. My .30-06 or 12-gauge slug shotgun is enough for any deer hunting I would do and a lot of folks consider a .243 good enough, plus it kicks a heckuva lot less.

Sharon Rushton, who started the "Hooked on fishing, not on drugs" program, is now espousing the "Step Outdoors" agenda. Step Outdoors attempts to get one-on-one participation in outdoors activities by having mentors ask their friends to fish, hunt, shoot, or otherwise try new ways to appreciate the outdoors. Sharon had encouraged several of the lady attendees—some are writers who don't do hook and bullet pieces—to shoot various firearms and thereby get a feel for things considered "out of their traditional (writing) box."

Ron Guidice, representing Smith & Wesson, had an assortment of pistols for the writers to sample. He suggested .22 pistols as a starting point for ladies and newbies, but even so, one lady showed off her paper target with a shotgun slug hole dead center.

I tried an "Air Lite" S&W revolver in .357 Magnum caliber, wanting to find out if the lightweight titanium handguns in large calibers would kick you so badly you would flinch on the second shot and miss your target. There was no appreciable difference in the kick in that pistol between the standard .357 round and the practice round you can use in the .357, a .38 Special. I put all of my shots in the black at 25 yards, and my safety instructor said, "An intruder would have been in big trouble."

Next to me, a self-labeled "Tennessee Hillbilly" fired a .44 Magnum pistol with a pretty long barrel and a telescopic sight at a target without feeling the kick. Of course, he stood about 6-foot six and weighed close to 250 muscular pounds. "Shucks, 'twarnt nothin' to it" was his comment. He carries a .44 Magnum revolver while rifle hunting for deer back home. Says his .44 Mag will really discourage a rattlesnake.

• • • • • • • • • • • • • • • • •

HOW TO COUNT GEESE

While hunting with Dr. John "Jack" Scanlon recently, I noted so many birds flying away from us, and I gave a count of "357."

Later, after more birds flew away from us, I said the count was up to "696 birds."

Doc asked me if I "count their feet and divide by two." "No," I said, "I counted their feathers and divided by 1,138."

Don't laugh. It ain't easy. Try it sometime.

BS IN THE BLIND

Farm owner and host Dr. Stanley Minken, huntmaster Alan Faulkner, Tim Michel, Sam Willman, and I entered the commodious 4-foot x 16-foot blind at first light. We loaded our shotguns in anticipation of seeing the many ducks Alan spotted here for several days before our Veteran's Day hunt. Alan and Tim had placed a dozen mallard decoys along the shoreline for our hunt.

"You should have a camera," Doc Minken said, looking at the colorful sunrise across the creek. I did have a digital camera in my duffle, and the sight was something to behold. Low-hanging clouds scattered the morning sun's rays, and thunderheads towered skyward to our left. The spectacular colors of the sky were mirrored in the waters of Caulk's Cove. I'm setting this beautiful scene at great length to make up for the fact that we didn't see any %$%#@ ducks.

So, the BS session began. "Why didn't you put out more decoys?" Doc Minken asked the huntmaster.

"Don't need any more," Alan answered foggily. He had a whale of a cold, so bad he thought he'd have to die to get better.

"I thought more decoys would be better," the Doc said.

"No, I've killed a lot of ducks with only four decoys out," the huntmaster said.

"Sam, what is that shotgun?" Doc asked Willman. "A BP5."

I looked at it sideways trying to guess the shotgun's maker. Sam had installed part of an old high-top boot with its laces on the stock to build up the comb so it would fit his cheek snugly when he brought it up to shoot. Whatever a pro gunsmith might think about this modification, it must work, because Sam sure out-shot me on doves earlier this year.

"It's a Browning," Sam answered my unasked question.

During our bull session, a pair of mallards flew past within range. We were preoccupied with trivia, and missed seeing them until they were out of range. The pair set their wings and drifted downward to light just off the shore near a big tree.

"We should have been hunting THAT blind," Doc said. That under-tree blind, down the shoreline a hundred yards, had never been good, according to past discussions. Doc was putting a lot of pressure on the huntmaster, who built the big blind from which we were now hunting.

One of the neighbors told Minken when he erected that other blind, "Don't be surprised if you wake up some morning and find it burnt down." While that was not a neighborly remark, the Doc withheld a surely scurrilous comeback. Gentlemen dealing with animal-rights people should always keep their cool.

We watched a big buck walk slowly across a field on the other side of the cove. The Doc's property extends quite a distance down both near and far shorelines, and included that field. During the rut, bucks are very busy indeed, and this one looked like he'd barely make it through the breeding season.

"I saw a buck the other day that had his head hanging almost to the ground when he walked," Alan said. "His breath came out in a cloud in front of him. He was really tired."

The entire time we were in the blind, flock after flock of Canada geese flew around us calling to the lone goose on the cove. Several groups of geese landed only 100 yards away, just off the tree by the unoccupied blind where a dozen mallards quacked happily now.

"We shoulda been goose hunting," someone mumbled at a 100 or so geese paddling around the cove.

As the threatening storm clouds advanced from the west and chances of seeing any ducks receded in the east, I decided I'd better leave and accompany Carole to her doc's appointment. "Anybody want a ride back to the barn?" I asked the rest of the crew. They indicated they'd stay and hunt. I walked the 100 yards to my parked SUV and loaded my gear just as a drop of rain hit. Lightning was not too far off, and I had some doubts about standing under a huge oak tree too long. As I drove around the edge of the field the rain came down in sheets.

Alan called me later to report the crew had killed two mallards. Properly divided, each hunter who stayed would have had one breast and one leg. This hunter being a guest writer, had he stayed, would get two parts that went over the decoys last.

NOTHING LIKE A NEW SHOTGUN

Remember that great cartoon of two vultures sitting on a bare tree limb on a devastated hillside? One turns to the other and says, "Patience, hell, I'm gonna KILL something!"

Well, that's the way I felt while hunting Canada geese. Hunting buddy Warren Clarken and I had put out my sad-looking, weather-worn decoys at dawn. Then, we sat in the hedgerow blind for two hours watching the sun rise and listening to shotgun blasts from all over the neighborhood, but my field hadn't seen a goose yet. I fingered my new 20-gauge Remington 11-87 shotgun impatiently. I hadn't fired it yet, and I was itching to test it.

Several flocks flew past so high up they were wearing oxygen bottles. Calling didn't phase them at all. Not that MY calling would, anyway, but I like the sound of my 40-year old Olt 77 goose call. Making some goose racket is part of the hunting ambience, like freezing and getting soaking wet.

About 10:30 a.m., a small group of geese gaggled its way over the tree tops across the way. Even my calling didn't dissuade them from dropping in. Before they did, Warren and I had guns in hand, safeties were off, and he said, "I'll take the one on the right." He was shooting from the right side of the blind. He fired his Beretta 12-gauge once and his target dropped. I fired my new 11-87 once and nothing dropped. I tried to shoot again at a rapidly-departing goose and nothing happened. I was amazed to see the shotgun's action open and a yellow shell hanging on its carrier in the opening. The bolt hadn't closed to pick up the second shell. Now, this was embarrassing. Brand new gun, brand new 3-inch steel shot shells. I hadn't even touched the mechanism, unusual for me, but usually deadly for anything mechanical that I can bend or break.

While Warren picked up his goose, I warned him I was going to test the gun with a new set of shells. I fired the first round safely at an empty part of the field. One round, OK. Second round jammed again. I manually jacked the new shell into the chamber and fired it. OK. Third round went in and I fired again. OK. I was rapidly losing confidence. I loaded three more rounds (waterfowlers must plug their shotguns so they'll only take three shells), and all three shells fired this time without a jam.

I unloaded my 11-87 and cussed at it, as they say on the Eastern Shore, "'Til a fly wouldn't pitch on it." I passed my unloaded gun to Warren, who had his one-goose limit and had to unload anyway. He passed me his Beretta, which we both knew worked. We waited for another gaggle of geese in vain.

Carole and Warren's wife, Lois, drove down the lane about noon and stopped to admire our only goose with some hilarity. I asked Carole to pop the trunk open so we could load our gear and our now empty guns. Carole drove off to the house. Warren and I had walked about 50 feet down the lane when there was a goose explosion from a nearby creek. They came over the treetops in waves, 50 or more at a time, setting their wings and drifting toward our decoys. There were geese in the air everywhere. Carole and Lois, at the house, were enjoying this more than Warren and I. All our shells were in the trunk of Carole's car.

So we stood in the middle of the driveway, looking up at swirling masses of geese, almost low enough to grab with a crab net, and all we could do was smile at them. They continued to pile into the dekes, look around, and when they didn't see anyone they knew, took off again. Didn't matter, another bunch came right behind. Each group that was faked into taking a close look at the decoys, afterward flew low over the house where Carole and Lois were standing chuckling at our discomfort. The birds all landed in Broad Creek. A few flew into my neighbor's yards on both sides.

As we put away our gear and I gave the recalcitrant 11-87 a further dressing down, the creek out front was loaded with cackling Canadas, probably laughing at Warren and me.

Lunch was Carole's delicious Canada Goose Brunswick stew, a tasty blend of goose breast chunks and veggies. Recipe on page 190.

As we munched on stew and cornbread, seven Canada geese marched single file, up the side yard next to the hedgerow, to the pond for a drink of fresh water. The rest of the geese cavorted on the creek and in our front yard. Warren and I vowed revenge—to be extracted the following morning.

Gunsmith Greg Wolf fixed the 20 gauge gun by firing several boxes of shells. It's OK now, just needed a bit of loosening up.

Canada geese rest in Broad Creek after a day of hunting.
●●●●●●●●●●●●●●●●●

THE PIG SLAPPER

One of our NASA Goddard Space Flight Center contractors sent a crew of technicians up from mid-Florida with a satellite package to be tested. Naturally, these boys being from an area rife with outdoors opportunities, brought along some stories about their exploits.

"Y'ever hear of a pig slapper?" one tech asked. No one had.

"Wal, this ol boy down home loves to slap pigs." (Pigs, as he called them, are mean and myopic wild boars. Most of them have a mean disposition and tusks out to here).

"This old boy sneaks up behind a pig and slaps it on the rear end, real hard. Then, he stands real still, doesn't move a muscle. The pigs can't see him unless he moves. They run around in circles mad as hell, looking for their tormentor. When they settle down he slaps another one."....... Don't try this at home.

BLUEBIRD DAY

When I first heard about the muzzleloader and migratory Canada goose season overlap, I thought there might be some conflicts. However, most folks I talked to didn't see a problem.

At Lostock Farm, the patrons hunt deer from a half-hour before sunrise until mid-morning, then climb out of their stands for some goose hunting. Their goose limits (and maybe a duck or two) are often filled by lunch time, when they adjourn the field for some of Babs Minken's venison chili. In mid-afternoon, they return to the deer stands until quitting time.

Here on Futility Base, we hunt (not necessarily shoot) geese from early morning to about noon, then hunt deer from about 3 p.m. to quitting time. No conflict there, and as in most other places, it's working out pretty well.

Geese were behaving strangely here, not flying all morning, then they often come to the decoys as soon as we come in for lunch.

Dr. Bruce Helmly and I sat in my goose blind all morning and watched high flyers. I feel no urgency to kill a limit of geese every day. The ambience is often enough. I felt the doc wasn't upset we didn't do well, either. We talked about the advantages of living in such a beautiful area, and they are many. One may not make as much money in this semi-rural area, but "quality of life" is more important for many people.

One pair of geese looked good, but they were acting really spooky, according to neighbor Sam Willman, who saw them go over his place zigzagging erratically. Sam came over to sit with us for a while, but didn't bring his 10-gauge double-barrel cannon.

Dr. Helmly and I went to lunch, then he was off to go Christmas shopping (he and his wife have three young children). As the doc walked to his vehicle in my driveway, there were geese up next to his car, some close enough to kick his tires.

Later, Sam brought 10 stuffers (taxidermy-mounted Canada geese) to add to my raggedy silhouettes, but still nothing flew over us. No wonder, the geese were happily munching grass on my front lawn. Some days it doesn't pay to get out of bed.

WATCHING SPRING CRITTERS

Deer snacking on sunflower seeds.

As I poured myself an ice tea, something caught my eye at the pond just outside the kitchen window. A spike buck whitetail deer was getting a drink from the pond. In midday! Normally, deer are almost nocturnal, with the highest periods of activity from dusk to 10 p.m. or so. As the buck walked slowly up the lane, he watched a bird fluttering ahead of him. When I looked out the side kitchen window, two deer were under the bird feeder.

This made me think about all the critters we've seen here on our 9 acres of yard, field, and a small wooded copse. The deer are almost tame. If my memory serves, here are some highlights.

As Carole and I returned home at the edge of dark recently we counted 11 deer in our neighbor's field. Coming down our lane, we counted 17 in our field. I went back up the lane to pick up the empty trash cans and a parade of 28 deer crossed the lane in front of me. Perhaps the two groups got together, but it is not unusual to see large herds of deer on our small place, in the 6 acre field, or at the front yard pond, drinking.

Last year we had considerable deer damage here. Not only did bucks in rut tear up newly planted Leyland cypresses getting the moss off their antlers, but they ate tomato plants (before we built a fence), ate daylilies, hosta, English ivy (ground cover around the foundation of the house), lower leaves and small limbs off a once-beautiful Nellie Stevens holly, leaves off the rose bushes, low limbs off the cedar trees, and some late-blooming pansies still in pots on the patio!

One may wonder why I don't hunt them, but my deer-hunting days are over. At my age, field dressing and dragging a deer out of the field appeals to me a bit less than a root canal. And, a neighbor who deer hunts only showed up once. However, he has donated some venison to the cause. Opening the place to others for hunting is out of the question in today's litigious society.

While Carole and I are not expert bird watchers, we did list the varieties of bird life that inhabit our place. There are too many to list here, over 70 different species. But, we do enjoy watching the activity at the bird feeder just outside the kitchen window.

One morning at breakfast, a hawk flashed down from above and grabbed a cardinal as it tried to leave the feeder. Red feathers flew as the hawk hit the hapless bird. Carole was upset and mad at the hawk. My reply was "Everything in nature eats somebody else and your feeder has become a veritable smorgasbord of tasty birds for the hawk." She's "chumming" the birds in with seed, and by concentrating the songbirds, she's made a veritable smorgasbord for hawks and eagles.

When we built our house, large windows were part of the plan. We included five sliding glass doors, plus large awning windows in every room. Watching Broad Creek as we ate lunch one day, we saw an osprey dive toward the lawn and drop a fish, then fly straight into a nearby cedar tree, unusual behavior for a fish hawk. Right behind the osprey was a bald eagle who swooped down, picked up the fish, then flew across Edgar Cove to some tall pines to enjoy his lunch. It occurred to me the eagle could make a pretty good living by simply following the osprey around.

Yesterday, the bald eagle swooped down and picked up a rockfish carcass someone tossed overboard. He (or she, to be PC) carried his lunch to my neighbor's dock where he sat on top of a piling and dodged dive-bombing seagulls while he dined.

Hummingbirds come to our two feeders in the summer, multicolored little critters that burn incredible amounts of calories with their rapid wingbeats.

Goldfinches are a riot when they feed upside down at our "upside down" thistle feeder hung in a crab apple tree outside the kitchen window. House finches haven't figured out how to hang upside down and feed, but the goldfinches must be smarter. Chickadees must be on a par intellectually with the goldfinch—they figured it out.

Crawling critters observed include everything from several types of snakes (didn't get close enough to ask them what kind they were), turtles, toads and frogs, raccoons and foxes, and rodents like rabbits, muskrats, and squirrels. A river otter once fished out our pond, catching every striper hybrid, a very efficient angler, indeed.

Wild turkeys were in evidence for a while last year. They had just been transplanted here, and since they hadn't been subject to hunting pressure, they were pretty naive. They stood flatfooted in the county road and shook their fists at passing cars. The local good 'ol boys must have showed them some manners, because I haven't seen them lately, except for one lone hen turkey drinking from our pond.

A huge squadron of buzzards has been soaring over the neighborhood of late. Something must have piqued their interest, like roadkill deer or turkeys.

The great blue heron and several types of herons and egrets fish our pond regularly, though I think the pickins are pretty slim unless they like frog legs.

Waterfowl in our field and on Broad Creek include several varieties of ducks, swans, sea ducks, plus cormorant and loons. Ducks we've spotted include harlequin, mallard, common merganser, canvasback, pintail, and bufflehead, among others. Whistling swans arrive in winter, but the abominable mute swan is with us all year. Mutes destroy an incredible amount of submerged aquatic vegetation (SAV), and make huge piles of stuff in the yard, which Carole's poodle finds really neat to roll in. Mutes are also aggressive, particularly when accompanied by their cygnets.

We recently heard a lady on a radio talk show tell how her small dog was picked up by a large hawk just outside her front door. Luckily, she had a leash on the dog, and she was able to drag the dog/hawk combination, swing them around and bang the hawk against three walls of her vestibule, sort of a "thump, thump, thump" maneuver. But, the hawk held on until she knocked it out, put her foot on the bird's neck, and pulled the squealing dog loose. The vet closed a six-inch gash in the dog. And animal control picked up the hawk. Both combatants wound up in cages in the vet's office, most likely glaring at each other.

Our veterinarian told us about a bald eagle that has decimated a neighbor's barn cat population, from about 26 down to zero. This got us to thinking that we should watch the poodle a lot closer when she is out in the yard.

Eternal vigilance is the price of pet ownership.

● ● ● ● ● ● ● ● ● ● ● ● ● ● ● ● ●

"It isn't pollution that's harming the environment, it's the impurities in our air and water that are doing it."
—— Al Gore

"How much clean air do we need?"
——Lee Iacocca.

Cindy, the Walters' chocolate Lab retriever.

EASTERN SHORE'S LOVEABLE LABRADORS

If a canine popularity contest was held on Maryland's Eastern Shore, the Labrador retriever would win it, paws down. Although the Chesapeake Bay retriever is the Maryland State Dog, the Labrador retriever would likely pass as Eastern Shore's (Shore) "Official Dog." It is nearly impossible to spend more than a few hours on the Shore without seeing a Lab somewhere: on nearly every piece of waterfowl art—including coffee cups and tea towels, in someone's yard, in the back of a pickup truck or station wagon, or smiling from the right front seat of a Mercedes driven by a blue-haired dowager in Easton or St. Michaels.

Why are Labrador retrievers so popular here? Labs are hard-working, loyal, friendly, obedient, tolerant, eager to please, and very intelligent—in short, all the qualities you'd expect from a Boy Scout—or find in a typical Shoreman. Plus one more: instant relaxation. If Labs are not working, eating, or playing, they take a nap. So does a laid-back Shoreman. If ever two souls east of the Chesapeake Bay were meant to go hand in paw, it was the Lab and the Shoreman.

Labrador retrievers have long been an intrinsic part of waterfowl hunting. With large fields and a multitude of shorelines to attract Canada geese and ducks, Shoremen found a willing helper in the Lab. Not only do Labs find game that might otherwise be lost, but also watching a good dog retrieve waterfowl in field or water adds to the thrill of the hunt—and on dull days everyone in the blind has a Lab story.

One recurring story is about two good 'ol boys in Dorchester County who found their favorite duck marsh frozen over at dawn—no open water to float the decoys. Their black Lab, Arster, (Shore dialect for "oyster") romped along the shoreline. One hunter lit a stick of dynamite and tossed it onto the ice to blast a hole for the decoys. Unfortunately, the hunters didn't stop to think—you can't throw anything away if you have a Labrador retriever; he always brings it back. Arster ran out on the ice, picked up the dynamite and trotted happily back toward the blind. As the dog approached with the burning fuse growing ever shorter, the hunters cringed in the blind, yelling at Arster to go away. What happened? There are at least 100 endings to this story. You have to supply your own.

As newcomers to the Shore 22 years ago, we brought our black Lab with us. Christy, so named because she had christened a square mile of our carpet as a puppy, was my constant companion in the field, goose blind where she loved to rest her head on my knee, shop, and house. She retrieved a double on Canada geese at seven months old. Like the Labs you see on TV sniffing out drugs or bombs, Christy had an incredible nose. She once followed the scent of a low-flying Canada goose for almost a mile and retrieved it when it went to ground.

Christy resting.

Christy adapted well to the Shore. Oyster shells skipped along the water's surface were great fun to retrieve, because they called for a tail-up dive in three feet of water. She spent hours stalking tasty soft crabs in grassy shallows, and was surprised to find that not all crabs were soft enough to eat. Hard crab claws attached to a dog nose can stir up a lot of commotion.

At age 11, in failing health and plagued with arthritis, Christy hunted with me one rainy, cold November day. She retrieved our one goose and carried it back to the house. She died that night. Our last hunt is a treasured memory. For a long time, I saw her sleeping black form out of the corner of my eye.

Our next Lab was Cindy (for Cinnamon of Aerie), an innocent-looking six-week-old chocolate Lab puppy. Being a waterdog, Cindy naturally fell into the pond on her first day home, and slid slowly off the pier into Broad Creek on her second. Cindy was my constant companion at home under my knee hole desk when I was writing or when I was in the field.

Cindy checks out a decoy.

Some Shore Labrador owners have configured home, cars, and clothing around their Labs. Exterior doors are usually painted the color of mud (dog paws). Door screens have been reinforced with chicken wire—or maybe rebar if there is a cat in the neighborhood. Inside, dinner and coffee tables must have enough room underneath for a Lab. Knickknacks at Labrador tail level are moved to high ground. Shore station wagons sport wire cages or grillwork separators, and sedans have an old blanket on the back seat.

Also on the Shore, carpets and clothing usually match the color of dog hair, since Labs seem to shed two pounds of hair annually for each pound of dog. You may notice Shore folks wearing charcoal or black clothing; assume they have black Labs. The same goes for tan clothes (yellow Lab) and dark brown duds (chocolate Lab).

The American Kennel Club (AKC) accepts three colors of Labrador retriever: black, yellow, and chocolate. White Labs are actually very light yellow Labs. But, their owners dress in light clothing, too, like Jane Smith and her late husband, Page, of Crowe Point Farm near Easton. International big game hunters, the Smiths imported their white Labs from England. "White as your shirt," Page said.

As Page and Jane Smith sat at opposite ends of a sofa in their "game room," two white Labs roughhoused under a glass-topped coffee table. Several black Labs (it was too dark to tell how many) snoozed in the brick woodbox under the fireplace.

Watching the Smith's Labs cavort from lap to floor and back to the sofa, I remembered when our Cindy and one of her pups pestered a local waterman: "Ain't you a bit over-dogged?" he asked.

Two of Cindy's Pups–Sammy & Sugar Toes.

Over-dogged or not, the Smith's sent their Labs off to "school." Trainer Jeannette Hutchison walked two white Lab pups around the yard in unison, then told both to "sit" and called them to "come" one at a time. They did as told, and the Smiths smiled at their trainer.

Men and dogs have likely hunted together since we lived in caves, but modern retriever trainers expect perfection. The Talbot Retriever Club (TRC), affiliated with the AKC, gives retriever demonstrations at the Waterfowl Festival® in Easton, Maryland every November. Past President of the TRC, Marion "Butch" Chambers, and his wife Bonnie, regularly host TRC members at their spacious place in Trappe. Butch starts a puppy with obedience training, and later advances to retrieving.

The Chambers' grounds have been reshaped for retriever training with two big ponds and small hillocks where handlers stand so their dogs can see hand signals in the field or on a pond. Butch has several dogs in training at a time; if he sees a dog will not be a potential field trial champion, he sells it. Though not champion material, the dog is still a finished hunting retriever, housebroken and socialized. "I hunt all my dogs, field champions or not," says Butch, "Labs are good at transferring training to field situations. The proving ground for genes is in field trials—the skills are the same for field trial and hunting dogs."

"I never cease to be amazed at what they can learn," said Seth Jewell, Past President of the TRC and a member of the Women's Field Trial Club. The back seat of her station wagon was folded forward to accommodate a dog cage containing a yellow Lab puppy, sprawled on her back, resting. A considerable amount of dog paraphernalia filled every space not occupied by three dog cages. "What is more important?" Seth shrugged, "Having a clean car for your clients or having crates for dogs?"

Mike Callahan provided an interesting insight to Shore philosophy at a TRC training session when asked if his yellow Lab, Zach, always rode in the back of his pickup truck. "Why, shore," he joked in Eastern Shore dialect, "I'm part of the good 'ol boy network—I've gotta do it!"

AKC field trials are interesting to watch, but many good dogs never get top honors because out of the large field of competitors, only four top places are awarded. Book author, the late Richard A. Wolters and several other trainers felt that field trials had left good hunting dogs by the wayside. They started the North American Hunting Retriever Association (NAHRA) to test each dog against a known standard, where nearly every dog could advance to the title of Master Hunting Retriever.

Trainers who run Labs in both AKC and NAHRA say the skills are the same in both groups. Field trials include a "mark" retrieve where the dog sees and remembers several downed birds at a time, and a "blind" retrieve where the dog is sent to get birds it didn't see. The handler relies on whistle and hand signals to communicate.

In response to interest in hunting trials, the AKC now has hunting trials similar to NAHRA's. An advantage to winning AKC titles is that titles go on the dog's AKC pedigree.

Obedience, even in Labs not meant for hunting, is necessary for the dog's safety and sometimes for your own. Once, I heard a car speeding down our street and called to Christy who was near the street, to "**SIT!**" Without thinking, she quickly sat in place as the car zoomed by. Her obedience saved her life.

Obedience training paid off for Malcolm McConnell of Queenstown, too. He owes his life to "Buddy," a big yellow Lab. "Buddy's afraid of thunder and lightning," said McConnell, "and he's gun-shy. I've never been able to break him of that."

McConnell stepped into deep muck as he and Buddy walked the beach near an old goose blind. McConnell had waders on, and slowly sank into the mud. His waders flooded. When he tried to free himself, he sank deeper. He grabbed an overhanging tree branch. It broke off. "I called Buddy, who was on fast ground," McConnell said. "I told him to '**HOLD**' one end of the branch. I held the other end of the branch to keep from sinking more. I freed the belt around my waders, and got out of them. Buddy still held onto the branch. I was able to get to the fast ground by holding the branch." "I owe my life to Buddy," McConnell said, "I'll never complain again about him being gun-shy!"

McConnell's hunting buddy, Col. James S. Hanke (USA Ret.) trained his Lab, too. Hanke's 90-pound chocolate Lab, Chief, did a double retrieve on Canada geese at a ripe old age of eight months—though he had never seen a goose. "I told Chief he had to earn his keep after the hunting season," Hanke said. "I tied a towel around the refrigerator door and he learned to pull the door open. Initially, he brought me ketchup and everything else until we broke the code (military talk). We put beer on the bottom shelf. On his first beer retrieve, he punctured the can. He didn't like it—thank goodness!!"

Chief learned to bring Hanke a beer if he said the code words: *I'm a little thirsty.* Now, Chief meets Hanke at the door with a beer when he comes home from work!

Beer fetcher, family member, field trial competitor, hunter, and loyal companion, perhaps the real reason for the Lab's popularity is its lovability. When your Lab gives you a big slobbery, slurp across the face, all else is forgotten.

No doubt about it; those lovin' Labs are as much a part of Eastern Shore life as Canada geese, crabs, and arsters.

● ● ● ● ● ● ● ● ● ● ● ● ● ● ● ● ●

SUV BASHERS DON'T GET IT!

Mega-liberal SUV-basher Robert F. Kennedy, Jr. allowed conservative Sean Hannity, Fox News Channel, to interview him on the subject of SUVs recently. Bad move for the Kennedy agenda. Hannity let Kennedy unload the whole Democrat-movie-star-liberal talking point outline on the evils of SUVs, and how they used so much gas, their owners were supporting terrorism, etc., etc.

Then, the clincher: Hannity asked how frequently Kennedy traveled by private jet. "That's a cheap shot. I won't answer that question," Kennedy snipped. When pressed further, Kennedy allowed his private jet travel was fairly frequent, but "I'd never buy one," he said. "I only use them when traveling to environmental meetings."

THE TAJ MA BLIND

I met Butch Chambers at a coffee stop in Cambridge, Maryland at 6:30 a.m. as agreed. After tanking up on coffee, I commented about all the mud on his truck. "Got it stuck," he said.

"Got four-wheel-drive?" I asked. "Yes, but that only allows you to get stuck further from help." The guy is an outdoorsy-type philosopher. And an enthusiastic hunter.

Butch introduced me to Jim Michael, another of our hunters for the day. Jim joined Butch in his truck, and I agreed to follow their rig in my Yukon. Butch was towing a landscaper's trailer with plywood sides, loaded with Bigfoot Canada goose decoys. Bigfoot geese are full-bodied, with removable heads and the enormous feet they need for better stability in a strong wind. And, at three for $100, they ain't cheap.

We met Dr. John "Jack" Scanlon at the entrance to his Garyview Farm. He directed Jim to join me and show me where to park. Butch took another road followed by Jack in his Jeep, and they wound up at a blind big enough to accommodate six hunters and a Labrador retriever. But, we were only four, plus a very enthusiastic black Lab belonging to Jack.

What Jack calls his "Taj Ma Blind" is suspended across a ditch between two corn fields, with a door at each end, and a wooden catwalk outside each door. The plywood blind has an open top, and its sides are covered with tall grasses. Its position allows the hunters to shoot either field by simply turning around.

By the time Jim and I got to the blind from a parking place under the trees eleventeen miles away, Butch and Jack had already put out a third of the decoys. Each one could carry six of these unwieldy decoys by sticking each arm through the legs of two decoys and grabbing another with their hands. It took me a while to catch on to this technique—after all, I leave my silhouettes out all season, only taking them up for deer firearms season and at the end of the goose season.

"How many decoys do you have on the trailer?" I asked Butch.

"Ninety-six," he replied, "I believe in a lot of decoys."

Ninety-six dekes for a possible four geese (if we limited out), I was thinking. A lot of work for four folks, even if the Lab retriever did help. I was still doing the math when we had all the dekes out, about half on either side of Taj Ma Blind, with a big hole downwind.

It was then that I discovered my thermos, calls, and goose ammo were safe and warm back in my garage. I mooched three 12-gauge Hevishot BB loads from Jack. "One of these (a white shell casing) was the first one of these out," he said. "Sort of a collector's item," he added.

No sooner than everyone's shotgun was loaded, geese began to fly. This was two days after the full moon, when there was still ample light at night for geese to feed in the fields, and loaf around without flying during the day. This could be a tough hunt.

"They're getting up off the pond," Butch said as he began to make goose music with his Sean Mann call. The longer barrel on this instrument gives the skilled caller a bit more range and the ability to cluck softly if the geese have their wings set, gliding toward the decoys. Jack also activated his Mann magnum call. Jim made some great music with his Falk call. By now, you know where my calls were, and "that's a good thing," as Martha would say. I have been known to "call them away."

The geese formed up in a large vee and headed toward Beckwith Creek across the way, but they were gaining altitude with every wingbeat. I was thinking, "Delaware."

"They've already filed their flight plan," Jack said. It was a remark he was to repeat often as the morning wore on. I've never seen so many flocks of geese fly in similar patterns. Every group that got up from that pond or a distant field flew upwind to some far-off landing strip.

Butch began working flocks that must have been a couple of miles away. His calling was a bit strident at first to get some attention, then he backed off a bit if the birds came closer. Finally, if they were close enough, and had their wings set, he barely clucked. Jack followed suit, and Jim timed his tempo to Butch's. Jim could make a rapid-fire call that sounded like a whole flock feeding.

One flock of a dozen or so finally fell for the caller's blandishments and set up on the dekes.

"Get ready!" Butch whispered. We all put a hand on our shotguns that were positioned butt on the seat with the barrel end resting on the front wall of the blind. This arrangement keeps the guns from falling down with possible dangerous consequences if a Lab gets too frisky and bumps them.

As the geese were suspended over the decoys, Butch called to "Take 'em!"

Four shotguns were jammed out between the reeds and several shots were fired. Three geese were down. I had fired two shots, but when everyone is shooting at the same time and at the same birds, it's hard to tell who shot what.

Jack's black Lab went to work, picking up a bird that wanted to get away. Jack brought the others back to the blind.

"OK," Jack said when we were settled in again, "Keith, you shoot next, and that will be a limit." It's funny how everyone assumed I was the only one who missed on the first volley, but that's not a new experience for me.

It took considerable calling and a lot of "gee, look at how many birds there are in that bunch" type remarks before another small group headed our way. We were so busy watching the incredible numbers of flocks of geese flying, mostly too high for a good clean shot, that all the jokes that were begun never got finished. And, I had my stock of Sven and Oley stories ready, too. Shucks.

Several flocks of geese flew overhead, peeking down into the topless blind as they went over, and kept going. We all kept still with our shining faces obscured, but we could almost hear the smart old lead gander in every bunch laughing at us above the whoosh of pin feathers.

Finally, a small group tolled and flew over the decoys looking for a place to sit, and I fired my last shell (the collectible one). The lead goose fell, making our day. Now, we had our limit, and everyone

could get back to business and do something productive. Butch had a
deer to get back to, and Jim seemed happy to get away. In about ten
minutes, all the decoys were back in Butch's special trailer.

Left to right: *Jack Scanlon, Jim Michael, and Butch Chambers.*

Jack gave me a tour of Garyview Farm, and the home he shares
with his wife, Kathe. The beautiful showplace house was designed by
their architect son. Then, Jack and I headed to Cambridge for some
breakfast. It was 9 a.m., later than the usual finishing time for these
hunters. Who said I couldn't jinx a whole farm? I kept these guys from
their regular breakfast schedule for at least two hours.

RODGER: HOME AT LAST

I called him "Rodger," the lone Canada goose that showed up at our pond one November several years ago, since he immediately fell in love with the plastic goose decoy floating there.

I thought Rodger was a cripple, since he didn't fly when I took Cindy the Lab and Josie the Poodle for their morning walk. Later, I figured he was just devoted to our pond's goose decoy. He didn't limp like a cripple or flee in fear of man—or dog.

Rodger's cousins in our nearby corn field called to him, but he didn't leave the pond. When feeding on pondweed, he strayed a few feet from his decoy. But when he felt threatened, he swam to his deke and hunkered up right next to it.

Rodger stayed on the pond until ice formed. When ice was thickest and he was most vulnerable to predators, I photographed him standing next to his decoy. Perhaps his deke meant security. Maybe he thought it resembled a lost mate.

I had no idea what was in his mind. Who can figure a goose?

The ice prevented him from feeding on pondweed, so he grazed on the lawn grass next to the pond. He never strayed to the field 100 feet away, where many of his Canada goose buddies spent the day, munching corn or winter grasses.

Every morning when we arose, we'd look to the pond for Rodger. He'd often be standing on one foot on the ice, right next to his decoy. We expected to see him at daybreak.

Rodger became our steady hand on the tiller, our anchor to windward, a dependable bird in a sea of unpredictable events.

One morning after a partial thaw, I walked too close to the pond. Rodger nervously swam through the slush to the opposite side. I walked the dogs up the lane. I looked away from him at an angle but ambled closer, the way you can sometimes approach animals. They may think you are not converging on them, that they are unseen. I once got within 20 feet of a bedded pronghorn antelope with this trick.

It must have been Rodger's season to fly north to Canada's Ungava Peninsula; his turn to follow the time-worn migration pattern that millions of Canada geese have flown before him. In spring, north to the nesting grounds. In the fall, he might again fly south to winter here on Maryland's Eastern Shore. Then, in spring he'd return to Ungava to propagate his species.

Rodger took off. I didn't know he could fly so well. He looked back at me, perhaps in farewell, maybe because I'd come too close.

I hope he returns. But not to the field where we hunt—To the pond where we can watch him at dawn, next to his decoy

.... EPILOGUE

The following winter, as I fixed our morning coffee, I glanced at the pond from the kitchen window. Frequently, I see deer getting a drink in the morning mist, or a great blue heron eyeing our pond bluegills with breakfast on his mind. That morning I saw a Canada goose hunkered down in the tall grass that rings the pond.

"Carole," I called down the hall, "Rodger is back!"

"Really?" She came to the window to watch the goose. "Do you think it's Rodger?" "I don't know," I replied.

When we walked the dogs that morning, Rodger (I'm sure it was him) swam across the pond and floated next to the goose decoy I keep there to thrill visiting city folks ("there's a live GOOSE on your pond!" they say about the deke). The dogs paid no attention to Rodger; seen that before.

On our way back, Rodger croaked a "her-onk" at us. The poodle seemed more interested in the ample amount of goose poo that dotted the lawn. She liked to roll in it, happy to be a green-streaked silver poodle.

A few mornings later, Rodger was hunkered down next to the grass at the edge of the field. He didn't move a feather as Carole and I walked past him 30 feet away. The dogs didn't wind or see him, though he was in plain sight. On our return past the pond, Rodger crossed our path from the field edge to the pond. He was moving pretty slowly, dragging both wings on the ground. He looked sick. His neck seemed to be swollen. The next morning, he was not on the pond. I thought he'd left us again.

As we drove past the pond that afternoon on the way to do errands, I saw Rodger, head down on the water, against the far bank. He was dead. That saddened both of us, but there was no time for a decent burial.

It may seem silly to wax nostalgic over one goose when we'll have hundreds of them in our field and on the pond later in the winter, but Rodger was special. Like, when you name a barnyard turkey or chicken, can you have it for dinner?

The next morning I got a shovel out of the shed and carried Rodger up the lane. When I returned, Carole asked, "Did you take Rodger?"

"Yep."

"Where?"

"Up to the end of the field, and into the woods."

Rodger was home at last.

THE MELITOTA HUNT CLUB

"I've got a hunt club on an Eastern Shore farm near Chestertown," NASA engineer Jim Baker told me. "We have geese, deer, and sometimes mallard ducks. Bass in a pond. A house you can stay in. Herman LaGow (a NASA manager) loves it there. He goes over even in the summer. Takes him back to his farm beginnings. Come hunt deer with us and see if you like it. If you do, you can join."

Farm beginnings was an apt description. Sort of like British understated humor. The farmhouse near Melitota was sound, but lacked attention. It had not seen a woman's touch, or a broom, for years.

The porch sagged, maybe from the weight of a cord of firewood handily stacked on it. Paint was not peeling—it was gone! Most of it simply drifted off the wood while no one was watching. A kitchen window's broken pane was weatherproofed with a greasy rag.

Herman LaGow's long-eared beagle was on the porch—sort of a sad-eyed welcome committee. *Tobacco Road* could have been filmed right here, I thought. I liked it right away.

New members never get the "hot" deer stands. Privilege follows longevity. I saw no deer, but heard lots of shots from the surrounding woods. We were on our stands from before dawn to 9 a.m., when all but those with the strongest kidneys had to climb down from their trees and take a walk.

Huntmaster Baker directed a deer drive. As we walked toward a hedgerow that jutted into a field, shots from the road attracted our attention. Several deer ran past the farmhouse and toward us. Guys shooting from the open side door of a van (illegal to shoot from the road) were yelling at us so we'd see the deer.

We were in a line parallel to the deer's escape route. I swung, leading one deer as you lead a clay target, and fired. The deer dropped. Baker looked at me, mouth agape. "Some shot," he said.

Oh, yeah, I thought. Do it all the time. We paced off 135 yards. Pretty good shot for a shotgun slug. Never did tell anyone I was leading the first deer, but killed the third one.

Lunch at the old farmhouse was a rare treat. Tables end-to-end nearly filled the length of the kitchen. Chain saws and gas cans, combined with two or three refrigerators, some old stoves, and the busted window with the rag, gave the place a homey ambience.

We opened our brown bags. Baker opened one fridge and extracted a pot with a spoon in it. He warmed the contents on a stove.

"Whatcha got?" someone asked.

"Muskrat," Baker said, "want some?"

"I'd like to try it," I said. "I hear it's pretty good."

"I like it," Baker said as he dished me up a pile of dark meat. "Pick out the small bones," he added.

"Muskrat" is an unfortunate name for a clean little rodent that lives in the swamp and eats veggies. City rats eat all manner of disgusting things and spread diseases. "Mushrats," as they are called in Dorchester County, eat clean food like marsh plants. Their meat is actually very tasty. It is dark and sweet, much like aged beef. I liked it, but Carole rebels at the idea of serving anything with "rat" in its name here on the Walters Plantation. The muskrat needs a press agent to give him a better image. If he was labeled "marsh rabbit" or "bayou beef" he'd be more accepted in the marketplace.

Baker spooned up some marsh rabbit for himself and several of our adventuresome guest gourmets. He placed the pan and spoon back in the fridge. Either there was no point in washing the pot right away, or there was more meat in it. I dared not ask how many trips in and out of the fridge that pot had made. I did ruminate on the way we men might live if left to our own devices.

Our hunters were at the tooth-picking and belching stage when Baker re-entered the kitchen from outside. He carried a small package wrapped in brown paper.

"Whatcha got?" I asked.

"A new pane of glass," he replied, looking at the broken window with its artistically-stuffed rag. I guess my expression said "why bother with the window?"

Baker smiled and pointed at the window.

"I need the rag," he said.

• • • • • • • • • • • • • • • •

RANDY THE RACOON

Dr. John "Jack" Scanlon had some excitement while turkey hunting at 0600 hours in his copse recently when something grabbed his boot.

Was it "Randy the Rabid Raccoon with a Boot Fetish" that accosted Jack's hunting boot in the dark woods?

Randy's raccoon romance may not have been up to snuff when he pounced on Jack's ravishing Redwings.

TOP NOTCH WATERFOWLING

I thought Rob Jepson was driving his new Ford crew-cab pickup through the back country so far we might be in Virginia, but we were still in Dorchester County, Maryland. We had met at the Cambridge WaWa store, and loaded my hunting gear in his truck for the trek southward. It was the last day of the resident Canada goose season on the Eastern Shore, and teal were in season. As we drove through lowlands that could only be habitable by ducks and muskrats, we'd occasionally come upon a small village of homes on the higher ground.

Rob and Mark Hoke, plus Charlie Smith, had put together a hunting trip for Canada geese and teal, and it was a great shoot. Rob, in addition to being a regional sales manager for Avery Outdoors Products, has a full time job at the largest non-chain outdoors store in Maryland. This was a day to field test some Avery products for Rob. Included were Canada goose shell decoys, Avery Real Grass woven of palm fronds, and everyone had to wear Avery caps – Rob said so.

Mark Hoke has a marble business near Washington, DC, helps Rob in his Avery territory, and has an uncontrollable desire to hunt— deer, waterfowl, turkeys, you name it. So does his hunting buddy, Charlie Smith, and the two have hunted together in some of the best places in the US. And, these two are among the best goose-callers I've ever heard, playing their goose music on Fred Zink "PowerClucker" calls in many different tones and volume, depending on the weather and the way geese were acting.

This day was calm and off-and-on rain. The birds were flying well. We saw incredible numbers of Canada geese, pintails, black ducks, and teal winging their way around the location we were to hunt. Charlie loaded us in and on his pickup truck, and took us to a blind on a freshwater pond where he and Mark had already put the decoys out in the dark. At first light we were comfortably ensconced in the blind, along with Charlie's black Lab, Knight. The dog was as excited as we were, prancing around as if he couldn't wait to hear our shotguns blasting away.

At legal shooting time, Charlie gave that word, and told us to wait until he or Mark called the shot. They saw some geese off in the distance, maybe a mile or more, and started to call, Rob joined them. The Zink calls, though small in length, had a horn-shaped output end, and they put out incredible volume. As thc birds worked closer, they held cupped hands in front of the calls to lower the volume.

A far-off flock of Canadas came for us with wings locked up. I don't think even my calling could have stopped them, but I bring no calls with me when I'm a guest; why embarrass myself in the company of the pros?

As the geese swung over the decoys, Charlie called the shot, and I did, hitting two geese with one shot. "Nice shot, Keith," Mark said. I was somewhat awed at my shot, but said nothing.

More shots were fired and of the 24 geese that came in, seven of them stayed. Knight jumped into the pond and went after the most active goose. Smart dogs seem to do that naturally, I think. I guess it's good training, or native intelligence.

Next flock was four greenwing teals. Mark called them in with his teal whistle. Two birds taken. I was pretty sure I hit one. Here is where seasoned waterfowl hunters use the fine art of "claiming," by hollering "I got that one!" With several shotguns booming at once, it's often hard to tell who shot what, so the first person to "claim" gets the credit.

Mark showed me how he uses his goose calls. He coughs into the call for one type of blandishment, talks into it for another. Sometimes, he gets a nice goose growl by saying, "Ooh, it." Everyone has his own style, Mark says, and his own way of talking into a call.

So many ducks were flying, it made for an interesting morning, even if we had not been hunting. Mallards and pintails would get a "big duck" appellation from the experts. They were out of season.

Teal, "small ducks," which were in season, attracted much more attention from our hunters. Thought to be the creme-de-la-creme of duckdom delicacy, teal rate high marks in waterfowlers' kitchens. But, only small flocks of teal tolled to the decoys all morning, and not many at that.

Geese, however, were another matter. Flock after flock tolled to the dekes, were greeted by mostly accurate fire, then picked up and returned to hand by the Lab. Again, I fired one shot for two geese, and got an immediate accolade from Charlie and Mark. While I was a bit surprised at my marksmanship, I said nothing. Why denigrate something others think I did right, when I knew otherwise?

I had only one goose to go for my personal limit of five. I stopped shooting at geese. If a hunter continues to shoot after taking his legal limit, he can be charged with attempting to take over the limit. In the migratory Canada goose season with a one-goose daily limit, if two hunters are in a blind, and one goose has been taken, one hunter must not shoot at any more geese. In my blind at home, one hunter must unload his gun, because we have no ducks that could be considered secondary targets. Only geese.

About 9 a.m., Charlie asked, "Had enough?" Everyone was happy with the hunt. We had enough ducks and geese for several meals, and we had some of the best waterfowl hunting I've ever experienced.

Left to right: Rob Jepson, Mark Hoke, Lab retriever Knight and Charlie Smith with their geese and ducks.

As we cleaned the geese and ducks, Mark commented on the hunt: "This is what it's all about, friends getting together to hunt."

DUCKS-A-MILLION

"I'll pick you up at 5," Dr. Stanley Minken said on the phone.

"Is that a.m. or p.m.?"

"A.m., we're going duck hunting down on Tilghman Island. Bring waders and prepare for dove hunting in the afternoon."

"Do I need chest waders? Mine leak like a sieve."

"No, knee boots should do it. I'll be wearing chest waders in case we have to put decoys out."

"How are we going to hunt?"

"I don't know, Alan [Faulkner] has something lined up."

When the alarm went off at 4 a.m.,I told Carole "I'm going to give up this %$%#@$ outdoor writing. You have to get up too ^&%$ early!"

"Yeah, right," she mumbled from a nice warm bed. No sympathy there. "And, let the dog out while you're up."

Stan said the hunting would be something different. But we had to find it first. He was fuzzy about the directions. "We go through Tilghman," he said, "Then turn off on Bar Neck Road and go past three driveways on the left. If we pass a brick house, we've gone too far, Alan said."

About the third pass up and down Bar Neck Road, we figured the lane we were looking for might have been on the right. "I saw a brick house," I said.

"Where?"

"Way back there. Coupla miles"

Anyway we found Woody Faulkner's place. Even a blind squirrel will find an acorn sooner or later. It was still as dark as it can get just before dawn.

Alan, Woody's son, was under the dock out front. That takes some explaining. Alan and Tim Michael, his farm manager, were in a skiff that was attached to a tow rope, which was in turn attached to a motorless barge, of which about half was hanging out from under the dock on each side of same. The drill was to pass the guns and duffle down to Chelsea Faulkner in the barge, then lie down on the pier and dangle our legs over the side above a swivel chair, then jump down. Stan and I, ages notwithstanding, made it without killing ourselves or even swearing, which was good since we didn't know it was Alan's daughter, Chelsea, up front until she said, "DUCK!" as Alan put the towboat's outboard in forward gear. Stan and I scrooched down as far as possible to miss being decapitated. "Are we through yet?" Stan asked.

"I am. But if I were you I wouldn't raise my head yet."

The entourage slowly wended its way across Blackwalnut Cove to the far shore. We handed navy-style anchors to Alan and Tim for the bow and stern of our craft, although it's hard to tell which end is which without a motor or steering.

After the barge-blind was anchored, Stan, Chelsea, and I watched Tim and Alan put out almost 100 floating Canada goose and duck decoys in the gently advancing daylight. "Isn't that beautiful?" Stan asked. We agreed the sunrise was spectacular, and I said that it wasn't about killing ducks, it was the ambience. Some grumbling here.

The Canada goose decoys had separate anchors and were more labor-intensive to put out. The duck decoys were strung together about 10 to a piece of cord with an anchor at each end. Alan maneuvered the skiff expertly to lay each string of dekes until we had ducks on the downwind side and geese upwind and close by.

I marveled at the hunting barge-blind. Alan had acquired a 23-foot fiberglass pontoon boat, stripped off about everything from the deck up (except that swivel seat), and built a two-foot high knee wall of 2x4s and plywood around the perimeter of the hull, leaving a two-foot wide part of the deck on the port side. On the top edge of the wall, he mounted two collapsible sides decorated with camouflage that both folded down much like the top of a convertible automobile. Alan secured the skiff on the port side of the barge, covered the white motor with a burlap sack, and came aboard along with Tim.

Once the camouflaged sides were erected, we were pretty much hidden from a duck's sight. When asked how he had picked up all this hunting knowledge, Alan said he'd been taking gunning parties since he was 13. Now, he has a daughter older than that, and Chelsea's an avid hunter, too. So is her boyfriend, Tim.

"Here they come!" Alan cried out. A flock of ducks went whistling past like they were jet-powered. No one was ready. No guns were up. No shots fired. We had to be faster. "Man! Can't they fly fast!" someone said. Flocks of blackheads (actually bluebills, Alan said) and buffleheads whipped past at flank speed.

We were ready, and all fired at one bluebill winging away over the decoys. The duck went down and started swimming. Alan and Tim went to retrieve it in the skiff. I looked down in the water by the barge. Eleven empty shotshells were floating there. One was yellow, from my 20 gauge. I figured a 20 was enough gun for little ducks, and for the doves we were to shoot later. The rest of the empties were all 12 gauge.

Chelsea Faulkner holds "her" duck.

"Wasn't that an embarrassing display of shooting?" I asked rhetorically. "Eleven rounds for one duck!" No one disagreed. I thought Chelsea shot the duck, but with that much ordinance going off at the same time, it's hard to tell.

Some geese flew past, very high. Alan called to them, but they knew where they were going, and kept on toward that unknown destination. I asked Alan what kind of goose call he was using. "It's a Big River Game Call," he said. I'd never heard of that make, but it sure sounded good.

More fast ducks. "Why didn't you call?" Stan asked Alan. "Wasn't nothing but a bufflehead," Alan said.

Another duck came in low. Alan fired. Missed. "Chelsea, why didn't you shoot?," Alan asked.

"Daaad! I didn't want to shoot your decoys!" It's alright if a dad shoots a decoy, but if daughter does, she'd get yelled at. Youngsters get smart about that stuff early.

During the next hiatus, Alan said he feels field silhouettes are just as good as any decoys for Canada geese. He's used Bigfoot and stuffer decoys, and said they're all about as effective. He uses about 200 Canada goose silhouettes at Stan's farm pond. He says Bigfoot dekes are best when the ground is frozen. Silhouette stakes are hard to poke into the hard ground then.

Alan noticed the ducks were flying a pattern about 200 yards out from our position. He said he was going to Centreville and file for a blind permit out there when we quit for the day. It wasn't long before we did. Nothing was flying on this pretty day some call a "bluebird day."

Picking up the decoys went faster with Stan amidships helping to stow the strings of dekes in plastic trash cans.

A hundred decoys, one duck. They said it was better yesterday.

● ● ● ● ● ● ● ● ● ● ● ● ● ● ● ● ●

COOLING IT IN THE BLIND

With a big storm coming, I decided to try my field blind for Canada geese. Goose hunting can be a gentleman's sport. The birds mostly fly later than daybreak, sorta banker's hours. A guy can sleep in a bit, have a nice breakfast, fill a thermos with a hot beverage, and slowly walk to the blind, noting the pleasant day, the wind direction, and thank goodness the decoys are already out. Yawn. No pressure.

"Don't forget," Carole said, "It's garbage day!" So, I load the cans in the back of the Yukon and stuff in a cased shotgun (empty with the bolt open) and some shells, the thermos, and a magazine, and take the cans to the end of the lane. After positioning the cans in their proper spot, I drive back down the lane, drop off the thermos, some kerosene for the heater, and a magazine to read during the slow times. Back at the house, I pull on knee boots, walk up the lane part of the way, load the shotgun, and watch the sky, since birds have been flying this morning. This is the way we should hunt, I think—slowly, enjoying the ambience, no hurry. The Lab retrievers I had in the past liked this part, bouncing on their front paws, tails wagging.

When I hunt alone, I bring a magazine to read. I put up the burlap windbreaker, light the stove, pour a cup of hot tea and relax. All the comforts of home.

Years ago, I wrote a story about hunting for geese at our small place for the now-defunct "Waterfowler's World" magazine. The piece was called "Vest Pocket Goose Hunting" and in it I told about hacking away at the computer or working in the shop until the geese flew, then grabbing gun and dog and walking to the blind with its ever-present decoys for some great hunting. One angry reader (why are some readers always angry?) wrote that I had it too easy, that hunting should be all about freezing in the rain and snow and sleet—or all three, and how putting out decoys with frozen fingers was more fun, and picking them up after the hunt was so much more fun. This guy, from a northern state, was into pain, and was mad at me for being comfortable. Go figure.

Anyway, I called in some geese this morning, missed them (did that twice, or maybe thrice), and blamed it all on a new hunting parka Carole gave me because the old one was so disreputable she wouldn't even let me take out the garbage while wearing it. The new coat has more padding and throws me off my usual great aim. So does the earth's rapidly-shifting magnetic fields (steel shot), a crooked gun barrel (I swear it's a spiral), and a tenth-of-an-inch change in coat material thickness.

So, as I read "Turkey Call" magazine (please, no smart remarks), four geese silently set up on the dekes. I remained silent. Good move. Finally, a limit. I picked up my empty shell casings (OK, several), and cleaned the goose.

Sooner or later, even a, well you know... can hit a goose.

• •

DOG TALES

Friends of our recently lost their pet dog. Dogs are part of the family to most of us, and losing one to old age or other misfortune can be devastating. Our friends' plight brought to mind some old dog stories I had filed away, and I'd like to share them with you.

Outdoors folks often find their open-air experiences enhanced by the companionship of a dog. Hikers, hunters, boaters, anglers, walkers, you name the sport, and a happy, sniffing, curious pup can point out things you might have missed. These stories might amaze and entertain dog lovers—maybe even those folks who never had a dog!

GUNNER

"You won't believe this," our veterinarian, the late Dr. Ed Hahn, of Centreville, MD, told me. That's the usual way he starts a hunting or fishing story, and he knows I always believe anglers because they are always honest, truthful, and reliable—like Boy Scouts.

It seemed that Ed's son Jimmy's old yellow Lab retriever, Gunner, was getting along toward the sunset of his years, and the family knew it was almost time to say goodbye.

Gunner was a constant companion in the boat and blind. He slept with Ed's son, Jimmy since Jimmy was a kid. Ed often called me from his boat as he was reeling in a fish. Gunner, Ed often said, was sleeping up forward, no matter how rough the water. Gunner accompanied Ed and Jimmy in their jon boat as they hunted ducks in various marshes. He was a great retriever, never lost a duck or goose. Never complained about ice or freezing water.

As Gunner neared the end, Jimmy and Ed dug a grave for him on the bank near the creek, and sat with him a while.

As they were saying goodbye, a lone Canada goose flew circles over the trees, honking strangely. "I never heard a goose make that noise before," Ed said.

"The goose landed just out from the shore and just sat there looking at us," Jimmy said. "It was really weird." The bird made noises like no goose they'd ever heard. A strange, sad sound.

Ed hugged Gunner and administered a shot. As soon as the great dog breathed his last, the goose took off and made a few circles over them before flying away. They buried Gunner.

"Eileen was watching from the house," Ed said. "She saw the goose, too. It was the strangest thing. We were all crying."

Any time you think your vet has become calloused and hardened about putting a pet to sleep, belay that thought. Remember Gunner.

BOB DOG

"I said the next dog I got would be called Bob," Paul McCauley of Pasadena said. "So the dog is a female, I called her Bob anyway."

Bob is a four-year-old border collie who wears a black-and-white overcoat. Bob is a little skittish around strangers, but idolizes Paul. He had her trained

Bob Dog

as a pup, and she, like all smart herding dogs, obeys instantly without stopping to think it over, the way other dogs like poodles do.

So, anyway, Bob had only visited Paul's friend's place on Kent Narrows a couple of times, but Bob evidently locked the house's waypoint in her doggie GPS, for the next part of the story is unbelievable.

First, set your cross hairs on a map of the Route 50 Bridge where it crosses Kent Narrows. Assume the "plus sign," or cross hairs has four quadrants, northeast, southeast, southwest, and northwest. The east-west line represents U.S. Route 50, and the channel under Kent Narrows bridge is the north-south line that crosses the first line centered at the bridge. Next, remember that Bob's "vacation kennel" is in the southwest quadrant, and that Paul's friend lives in the northeast quad. OK, now you are oriented

Paul had a trip planned and put Bob in the kennel. Before Paul left, he got a call that Bob climbed a six-foot fence and escaped. The kennel folks were frantic, and sent their employees out to scout for Bob. Paul was upset, too. They got word that a truck hit a black-and-white dog as it crossed route 50.

Paul looked all over the territory Bob might have traversed. He followed every lead. When Paul left for his trip, he had a lump in the pit of his stomach; he thought Bob was a goner.

As soon as Paul returned from the trip, he began to follow up on some of the thoughts that occurred to him while he was away. He waded into the marsh behind the vacant strip mall near the Kent Narrows Bridge, calling and calling for Bob. No answer. Paul saw no buzzards, so he still had hopes that Bob was OK.

A week later to the day of Bob's "escape," Paul's friend heard a faint bark outside. It was Bob! "She was covered with ticks and briars," Paul said, "but otherwise she was in good condition."

The people at the kennel were so concerned they cleaned and preened Bob until she was good as new.

Now, here's the rest of the story. Bob was in the SW quad, remember? Paul's friend lived in the NE quad on our little map. Bob had only visited the home a few times. Bob had to cross route

50 (she must have escaped being hit by that truck), and swim Kent Narrows against a considerable current. Maybe she was smart enough to wait for slack water; border collies are smart like that.

The last time we saw Paul and Bob, the dog (on a leash) was sitting at Paul's feet, looking up at him and smiling. Border collies can do that, you know. Especially smart ones like Bob.

CINDY

Our Cindy, formally known as "Cinnamon of Aerie," came to us as a seven-week-old chocolate Lab puppy. She was wild, wooly, curious, and irrepressible. She took directions well about sitting, heel up, and "fetch." I was always concerned that the dog-trainer's command "back" would simply point out a part of a goose's anatomy to sink dog fangs into when retrieving the bird. See "Happiness is a Warm (Chocolate Lab) Puppy" story on page 191.

As Cindy mellowed, I found that she was sensitive. Yelling upset her. I soon established that the way to train her was to simply explain what I wanted in mellow tones, and give her the reason why she should do a certain task.

By this time, she was so laid-back that the poodle could grab her tail and swing on it, and Cindy would just turn around and smile at the silver-haired little $#@^&%.

Cindy was a so-so retriever, good at bringing back bumpers, making water retrieves, and getting a goose off thin ice. But, in the field, she'd put one paw on a goose and beckon with the other paw to me in the blind. "Come here and get this smelly bird," she seemed to say.

Always the considerate dog, Cindy saved us a heartbreaking decision when she was 11 years old. After one surgery she pranced around like a puppy, and we took long walks again. After a month or so, she got sick again, and we took her back to Ed's office, where she died that night of pneumonia.

I couldn't face getting her collar and ashes from Dr. Hahn for a month or two. Believe me, he knew how I felt.

Later, Carole and I decided to spread Cindy's ashes around our place in her favorite hangouts—the goose blind, around the pond where she loved to take a dip (and couldn't understand why a soppy, wet Lab wasn't welcome in the house), and at the dock where she often advised me about crab pots and fish cleaning.

It is 90 feet from the dock back to the house.

It was the longest walk.

● ● ● ● ● ● ● ● ● ● ● ● ● ● ● ● ●

WATCHING FALL CRITTERS

Finally, some weather that didn't include rain. This anomaly inspired the critters here at Futility Base. The full moon brings 'em all out, I say.

A hen turkey flew into our field of spring onions (the farmer has been plagued by rain, too), and sat down low. I hope she's not sitting on eggs, since the farmer drags some pretty heavy equipment around when he's planting.

Two rabbits were cavorting amidst Carole's freshly-planted flowers. Petals were strewn all about. Carole did not take this lightly. The semi-automatic BB gun came out, but she didn't hit anything, or even scare the romancing rabbits.

At the pond this morning, a great blue heron was trying to stare down a smaller green heron on the opposite shore. A Mexican standoff. Neither one moved a feather. Herons can stand still for what seems like hours, which is what gets them their breakfast. Fish must think they are statues right up until they are snatched up and flipped down a heron-throat. Our stunted bluegills in the pond have been working overtime to feed local herons.

While mowing the lawn last week between rainstorms, I saw a small black snake holding onto the part of a big frog that enters the pond last, if you get my drift. The frog was slowly dragging the snake toward the pond. The snake was wriggling backwards for all it was worth, trying to get a reverse grip on the grass. Neither critter was making much progress, and I felt sorry for the frog, so

I parked the tractor's starboard front tire on the snake. When the snake opened its mouth to swear at me, the frog gave two jumps and splashed into the pond. I backed off the snake, which slithered away unharmed, and still hungry. I don't know how a small snake could swallow that large a frog, anyway. A big frog was later found floating on the pond, dead.

Our local mockingbird has taken over. He or she sits on the roof peak and yells at anyone who would have the temerity to venture outside. It has a nest in a nearby holly tree, so don't go there, he/she says.

Before we installed three chimney caps, we could hear its annoying caterwauling in both fireplaces and the unused flue that terminates in the garage. Sometimes a bird would slip and fall down a flue, but not since the caps were placed.

The bird's latest gig is to chirp like a telephone and make us pick up an instrument and listen to a dial tone.

I'd give him some practice in mocking a shotgun, but I might tear up some roof shingles.

● ● ● ● ● ● ● ● ● ● ● ● ● ● ● ● ●

GOD WRITER MISSES A GREAT HUNT

The dean of Maryland's Geriatric Out Door (GOD) writers, Bill Burton, missed a great Canada goose hunt yesterday, hosted by a nationally-renowned vascular surgeon, guided by the Eastern Shore's top goose master, aided and abetted by a banker and a chef, plus the guide's father and daughter. Together, this awesome group showed an outdoors writer that the proper placement of decoys and the furious application of lung power to a tube of cocobolo wood, could lead Canada geese to the front of the blind, gliding through the cold morning air like they were on a wire.

However, the extreme cold, with its known propensity to shrink steel shot and warp shotgun barrels, plus a sudden and sharp change in the earth's magnetic field, can cause the cold-shrunken shot to penetrate portions of the clear, cold morning sky at exactly those places where goose bodies are not.

So, although Bill Burton missed the great shooting by Dr. Stanley Minken, owner of the 200-acre Lostock Farm in Bozman; huntmaster Alan Faulkner; Alan's father, Woody; and Alan's daughter, Chelsea; plus banker Jonathan Hyde; chef Larry Schwartz; and this writer stood amid the decoys and found a limit of Canada geese. The only thing we could surmise was that the geese were so astonished to be confronted with an armory of blazing guns the likes of the Spanish Armada they fell to the ground and gave up.

"You use too many commas," Burton once told me, "and make your sentences shorter."

"I like commas," I replied, "they give the reader time to take a breath between thoughts."

"So do short sentences."

I told the dean of GOD writers the late Bill Perry once said a lead shouldn't have more then 17 words, and his editor gave him what-for for using big words. An occasional big word is useful, I say—it flatters your friends, and sends your enemies to the dictionary. And, who can't live with a 76-word lead sentence? Is your attention span that short? Humph!

We hunted a new 16-foot blind that was designed to accommodate up to six hunters and a guide. The blind is set on the shoreline. Its top is low enough to allow a hunter to turn around and shoot the field behind the blind by standing on a raised platform. We placed several dozen silhouette decoys in the field behind us and three dozen floating decoys in the creek in front of us.

Alan placed the water dekes from a boat with motor that wouldn't start because someone placed the wrong gas hose in the boat in the pre-dawn darkness. No names need be mentioned here.

It was dawn when we got settled in the blind. Alan had brewed fresh coffee using a small generator. Heat had not yet been installed in the new blind.

The huntmaster issued instructions: "If you have four geese down with six hunters, only two can shoot after that," Alan said. "If more hunters than two shoot, it could be called attempting to take over the limit, and result in a big fine."

Alan's duck call was the first bird-noise we heard. Two black ducks were checking out our dekes, passing back and forth out of range. They went away.

Dr. Stan told about the wedding of a friend whose fiance was large with child. "A formal wedding with a white shotgun?" I asked. "Oh, it was a hunter's wedding, there were shotguns all over the place."

Woody said he caught two rockfish on his way out crabbing last fall, and he called Alan on the radio to tell him where. Alan runs the "Chelsea Lynn" charterboat. "The fish must have been really thick in there," he kidded his dad, meaning "If YOU caught them."

"They'll fly about 9 a.m." I guessed.

There was some heavy shooting across the creek. "I'd sure like to find out who THEIR guide is," Stan said.

"I taught you everything I know about guiding," Alan said, but Stan said he was the teacher and Alan the pupil. "And neither one knows anything," someone replied. "And, if you'd bought a better farm with some birds on it..." Alan concluded.

Alan called in a group of geese. His long call had a deep tone, like the Bubba-Daddy of all geese. Everyone but the writer stood to shoot, an absolute barrage. One goose on the water. The rest flew away. Later we figured they fired about 15 shells for that one goose. Alan, always considerate, was not shooting at that point.

Two geese came into the silhouettes behind the blind. I shot once, one goose down. Jonathan shot once, one goose down. He and I were done for the day, and we unloaded our shotguns.

"Chelsea," Stan said to the pretty teenager during a break in the fireworks, "It's a good thing you look like your mother (sideways glance at her father, Alan), or you'd really have a tough life."

Chelsea fired her 20 gauge and downed a duck. "I think I shot it," she said. "You've learned the fine art of claiming," I said. Where did she learn that?

Several big groups of geese came toward the water decoys. They were so close together we didn't risk shooting. It's too easy in a large flock like that to shoot over an individual's limit of one goose per person. You might hit two geese.

Larry took a goose from a small flock. Five down.

Alan asked Chelsea to hand him his shotgun, a 3-1/2 inch 12-gauge. A "gentleman's fowling piece." He was getting serious, He'd called up to now without shouldering a gun. Now it was time to get his bird.

A flock of geese came in from our right, spread out pretty good. Less risk of shooting over the limit. Alan and Chelsea stood to shoot. Chelsea shot a goose. It was a hard shot for her from the corner, and she is too short to shoulder a shotgun and hold it over the top of the blind's front wall comfortably. Good shooting! Now we had six. One to go.

Alan shot and a bird faltered, then flew away. He looked at us with an amazed expression. "Did you see that goose? He looked like a feather duster, and he flew away!" I almost got the impression that not every goose leaves after Alan shoots.

"So," I said, "Chelsea knocks one down with a teeny 20-gauge, and your goose flew away after you hit it with that howitzer?" On the next flock Alan claimed his bird. It was out in the water and Stan waded out for it.

"Mousse won't retrieve?" I asked to much laughter. Chocolate Mousse is a 11-year-old chocolate Lab. I didn't know it, but he can barely walk. Stan told us that he had a duck down last year and invited Mousse to swim out and retrieve it. Mousse walked to the water's edge, looked around at Stan, and VERY slowly, step-by-step headed back for the house. Stan had to wade out and get the duck, and by the time he was halfway back to the house himself, he passed Mousse, walking slowly step-by-step. "And, he was really a gung-ho retriever when he was young," Stan said.

Well, we had our limits, and there were decoys to pick up. Alan and Woody poled around in the creek to pick up the water decoys, and the rest of us stowed the field silhouettes.

It was 10 a.m. The birds had flown late. Our first flock came along at 10 minutes of 9 (10 minutes before I had predicted), and we were picking up the dekes at 10 a.m. It was a great morning of Canada goose hunting with a great group of friends. It doesn't get any better than that.

Kneeling: Stan Minken and Alan Faulkner
Back row: Johnathan Hyde, Woody Faulkner,
Chelsea Faulkner, Larry Schwartz, and Keith Walters.
Chocolate Mousse in front sniffs a goose.

● ● ● ● ● ● ● ● ● ● ● ● ● ● ● ● ●

The old lab.

THE LAST HUNT

It was a quarter-mile, more or less, down the country lane from the house to the hedgerow blind. The man and his old black Labrador retriever had walked it many times. When they were both younger the young Lab had pranced and spun in circles with the excitement of the hunt. They often rose early and spent mostly gameless days on the marsh, just watching the water decoys dance in the sun.

Now, he owned his own goose field. His blinds were heated. Goose hunting was much easier now. Good thing, too. Waking up at 3 a.m. to freeze all day in the cold rain had lost its appeal.

Man and dog walked slower now. They were older, true, but long hours in this blind at the edge of the field had taught him the birds wouldn't fly for another half-hour. No hurry. They would enjoy the day.

Dreary and overcast. A good day for hunting the Canada goose, the man thought. The wind, laden with misty rain, came from behind the blind. The decoys faced into it. No geese were flying. The Lab snoozed under the seat of the blind.

The aging dog had walked down the lane much more slowly this morning, he thought. Maybe she was sick. She was 11 now, and her muzzle had turned white, contrasting with her shiny coal-black coat.

The white hairs of age cascaded down her chest like a glacier. The man started to daydream, and remembered when she was received into the family as a puppy.

He remembered the Lab pup's habit of curling up and going to sleep in his lowered trousers and drawers as he sat on the throne. He had called his wife to bring a camera. The picture was still around somewhere if he could only find it.

The Lab pup took naturally to water. The man had waded into the muddy creek to show her what great fun it was. The pup was a little hesitant. Finally, he picked her up and carried her out away and lowered her into the water. She never left it. Once a water dog, always a water dog.

The pup soon learned how to swim through decoys to retrieve a goose wing. Labs have a great nose, and can easily detect the difference between live birds and decoys. Once, she even found her lost collar in thick underbrush at his command.

When he worked in his shop, read a book, or watched TV, the black dog lay at his feet—always visible out of the corner of his eye.

The summer the man and his wife built their waterfront retirement home was no picnic for the Lab, then 7 years old. Sleeping under a travel trailer, the dog whined as the mosquitoes took their sacrificial pint of blood each night. The problem was eased when the man sprayed under the trailer, and dosed the dog liberally with insect repellant at bedtime.

The Lab soft crabbed at low tide along the river shore. When a soft crab left the security of its seaweed sloughing place and scurried away the Lab grabbed the soft morsel for lunch. She was greatly surprised to find that every crab was not soft. A hard crab's claws can put a bad hurtin' on dog nose.

As time passed and the dog aged, she was barely able to move around. The vet said she had arthritis in her hips. Weighing possible complications, the vet and the man agreed that a small daily dose of prednisone would improve the dog's quality of life, but in the long run, possibly shorten it.

He was stirred out of his November reverie in the blind by the soft clucks of Canada geese, wings set and gliding toward the outer edge of the field silhouettes. Peeking through the brush of the blind, he saw three birds with feet down about to land. The dog was alert, but made no sound. He clicked the safety off and swung toward the first goose and fired. He missed. The second shot connected, and the bird fell.

He let the Lab out of the blind with the command, "Fetch." She limped slowly out to the edge of the decoys and found the downed goose. When she was younger she ran at top speed, but now she seemed so much slower. He remembered she once grabbed an escaping goose in mid-air by the tailfeathers. We are both too old for that nonsense now, he thought.

"OK," he told the dog, "let's give it up for today." He let her carry the bird back to the house. She dropped way behind him, walking more slowly with each step. He slowed his pace to let her catch up. She was barely moving, but she held that bird up proudly.

The man's wife watched from the kitchen window.

The dog dropped the goose at the garage door, and he let her inside. She lay on her bed and turned her face to the wall.

The Lab hadn't moved by evening. The vet said to bring her in. The man and his wife helped hold the dog for X-rays. She was too sick to care. The vet took blood samples at 11 p.m. and hand carried them to the local hospital to wait in the early hours of predawn for analysis. He told the man and wife to go home, that he would operate later in the morning and call them.

When the phone rang the next morning, neither the man nor his wife wanted to answer it—as if the problem would go away. He picked it up. Bad news, the vet said. The dog's pancreas was badly swollen and blocking her digestive tract. It was possible to save the dog, but the odds were slim, maybe ten percent. She would always be diabetic if she survived. She was now under anesthetic, in no pain. What did we want him to do?

His wife's expression told him she understood what the vet was saying. They had talked about what they would do if the news was really bad. He looked at her. She slowly turned away.

The lump in his throat almost blocked his speech. The vet was not positive about the old dog's chances. He talked to the vet for a moment, the lump in his throat growing.

It was his dog—his decision.

Finally, "Let her go," he said, and hung up.

The wife began to cry.

And so did he.

● ● ● ● ● ● ● ● ● ● ● ● ● ● ● ● ●

"SHARP" SHOOTERS

This is the time of year when the thoughts of young men (old ones too) turn to shooting clay targets to keep wing-shooting talents up to snuff. One needs a clay-target fix or two between hunting seasons to help us remember which end of the shotgun is the business end, and how far to lead something that may be flying, running, jumping, or otherwise trying to avoid being the first invited guest in a pot of stew or chili.

So, Warren Clarken and I hit the sporting clays range a few times between blue-finger bone-chilling cold and the ides of August when mosquitoes can kill your ardor for the outdoors. When we meet at a mid-point equidistant between his home in Annapolis, ours in Bozman, and a sporting clays facility, it is usually what we used to call "The Pottery." This is also a convenient place for our wives, Carole (mine) and Lois (his) to start their shopping trip. After clays and shopping, we all meet up somewhere for lunch.

Warren and I have spent many a day in goose blinds together. We both belonged to a hunting club in the 1960s called the "Sharp Shooters." We had a different, less complimentary, name for the club, but it did have the word "Shooters" in it.

One place we hunted Canada geese was within 50 yards of the owner's house. The blind sat on the shoreline of Eastern Bay. We met a lot of game wardens while hunting there, since the owner's farm lane ended almost at our blind. No trudging through swamp or field to check us out, just leave the warm patrol car, walk 20 feet, and ask to see licenses, check around for corn, etc., then hop back in the warm car and go for coffee somewhere.

One old-time warden had a trainee along, and the fuzzy-cheeked youth dug in the beach sand until he found a corn kernel that must have been there since Lord Baltimore got it from the Indians. He showed it to his tutor, who shook his head, "No," and the kid looked disappointed. He already had his brand-new ticket book out.

There was an inch or so of Eastern Bay water under our blind, and the grizzled veteran officer said that made it an "offshore blind," and did we have a permit for that? No, we didn't. He indicated that the next time he came back (right after coffee), it would be right thoughtful of us to have moved the blind back up on the beach far enough to avoid having tidewater under it, even a drop. We allowed as how that would be a good move, too, and we went to work. The officers left. It was only then that we counted our geese. All I can say is, it's a good thing the old boy didn't count 'em for us.

We met some other officers while hunting a marsh on the Choptank River that was rented by our Sharp Shooters Club. We had a few geese in the blind when we looked across the river to Windy Hill and saw several men launching boats. Turned out they were federal and state game wardens, and they had some questions for the occupants of the seven club blinds along the river front. Like who might have put all that corn around the ponds on the back of the property. It turned out it wasn't us, since we were forbidden to hunt the ponds, but we all got pieces of paper that said we were "hunting on a baited flyway." The federal judge felt sorry for us and halved our fines. Our lawyer took the rest. And, in the deal, we had to build the &*@%$ LAWYER a duck blind.

So, Warren and I have been through some thick and thin together while waterfowl hunting. Oh, I almost forgot the time Morris Hall told Warren to "Get out in back of the blind, they're coming in from the back." Warren jumped out the back door into three feet of water while wearing three-foot-high hip boots, and looked in vain for geese. He heard a lot of shooting from the front of the blind. The geese had swung around to the dekes out front giving Morris, his son, Werner, and I some really great shooting. Warren was not a happy puppy. However, we let him go out in the boat and pick up our geese.

Warren and I ruminated on all the waterfowling fun we had in the past while driving to the sporting clays place. Arriving, we met our trapper, a young college student, Matt Williams. He's studying for an MBA. Matt loves to hunt but missed most of the last seasons while in college.

Warren and I got our gear together. Warren shoots a 12-gauge Beretta automatic. I wanted to see how I'd do shooting the elusive targets with a new Remington 11-87 in 20-gauge. I don't shoot competitively (good thing). I just wanted to get some practice with the 20 gauge. Warren had gifted me with several boxes of Remington High Velocity Game Loads last October for my birthday, but weather and schedules had prevented us from getting in a sporting clays shoot until now.

Warren Clarken

The deal is we shoot 50 rounds total, a few rounds at each of several different stations. The course designer has made it interesting (read, more difficult) by having the clay targets come at, over, or away from us, at all manner of angles.

Matt let us look at sample targets before we shot, since we didn't know where the birds were coming from. After that, we stood in stalls designed to keep your shotgun pointed away from the trapper and your companions, then loaded two shells before calling "Pull." Then, the first clay target is sent on its way by the trapper; upon "report," (your shot), he sends another target remotely, but from a different angle. We did that twice each at each station. Sometimes, if you don't shoot soon enough, the target is doing nasty stuff that makes it more difficult to hit—like dropping, hopping, reaching the trees, or like the "rabbit" target rolling on its side on the ground, it hits a pre-planned bump and leaps skyward just as you pull the trigger. A strong, gusty side wind adds to the fun.

Warren shoots a lot of straight trap, where the targets are lofted in different directions and heights from a single bunker in front of the shooters. After each competitor shoots in turn, the shooters move to another spot in a half-circle. To me, this is more repetitive, and has not as much variety—or fun—as sporting clays with their numerous diversity of positions.

The irony of all Warren's experience in straight trap is that he had trouble hitting the targets that were going straight away, but he hit the tough ones with great regularity.

Warren had a pretty good score, but I only nailed half my normal (lousy) 12-gauge score. We talked about that a lot on the way to my house, where our ladies and a crab meat dinner awaited.

While I didn't expect to whack every target cleanly with my undersize popgun, I talked to a more experienced sporting clays shooter, neighbor Mike Haddaway, about what might have affected my shooting. He recommended I change from the modified choke that came with my shotgun to an improved cylinder one. In the 11-87, choke tubes are interchangeable. No problem. This would give me a slightly wider pattern. My number 8 lead shot was about right. Mike shoots the larger 12-gauge, which has more shot in its shells than my 20. Funny, though, Mike often shoots a 20 while hunting geese. And, I had good luck on the geese last season with my 20-gauge, shooting Hevi-Shot.

This requires more research.

● ● ● ● ● ● ● ● ● ● ● ● ● ● ● ● ● ●

BUNNY BUSTERS

Three members of Bunny Busters met at an undisclosed Dorchester County location at exactly 1100 hours. Precision planning is the hallmark of BB members, since hunting the dangerous long-fang rabbit requires scrupulous attention to detail. Also, we wanted to prevent any demonstrations by bunny huggers who could distract even the most ardent bunny hunters.

Our host Dr. John "Jack" Scanlon told Butch Chambers and this writer, his wife had objected to his bunny hunting just before a landscaper planted about a grand worth of flowers and other plants. The next morning, all the pretty plantings had been mowed off neatly at ground level. That event assured his lifetime permission to bunny hunt.

When the writer arrived at 1059 hours exactly, Butch had five short-legged beagles in tow, three on one lead and two on the other. Daisy, the matron beagle, was in charge. When she went into full hue and cry, all other beagles present took notice and followed her lead.

Huntmaster Jack positioned the writer at one end of a mowed path, indicating that the dogs would move the rabbits back and forth across it. When the dogs were released,

Butch Chambers and the beagles.

Dogmaster Butch said they wouldn't come to a call or whistle. They'd have to be caught, one at a time. Butch walked through the high bushes toward a stand of pine trees to take his position. All hunters wore blaze orange for safety.

Jack's double barrel 20-guage Charles Daly shotgun looked just right to carry around, light, and well-balanced. From Butch's barrel size, his Remington 1100 looked like a .410. The writer carried his 1187, 20-guage. Number 7 lead shot was determined to be about right.

Jack walked down the mowed path, around the corner, and down the edge of the field before entering the low scrub bushes to take a stand. I hollered to him so I could note his position.

Big snowflakes were falling. The temperature was around freezing. A 10-knot wind was at my back in the open area next to a big pond. I put the hood up on my jacket. My hands were tucked into insulated deerskin chopper mittens. No hope of getting them off in time, so every time I heard the dogs coming my way, I dropped the right mitten and gripped the shotgun in a semi-ready position.

When the dogs picked up scent, they began to bray, each making a distinct and different noise. "Errrr-Yip" went one, "Harrrrr" went another, like he was constantly clearing his throat. Some barked, ending with a "Hrrrr" noise. But when Daisy cut loose with her "Hahrrr-yip" they all fell in behind her. She is a no-nonsense bunny-sniffer, has the respect of the rest of the pack, and lets everyone know it. A good part of the fun is listening to the dogs as they course back and forth.

When the dogs head back toward you, get into shooting position because the bunnies are sometimes way ahead of them. Rabbits have a habit of returning many times to the same spots, so the canine chorus can be followed and some, sometimes inaccurate, predictions can be made.

I heard a shot from Butch's position. Jack called to him and asked if he got a rabbit. The response was affirmative. A rabbit ran across the mowed path I watched, so fast I couldn't get my gun up in time. Then, Jack shot and said he had a rabbit.

The dogs ran across the lane and dove into another thicket to my right. A second rabbit followed them across, as if it was trying to catch up with the dogs. I moved to the other end of the lane so I could shoot back that way. There might be more time to get ready. Maybe. Another rabbit ran across just where I had been standing, again, I was too late.

Jack shot another bunny. I hadn't popped a cap. The dogs were rooting around in a corn field, but there was no rabbit anywhere to be seen. We watched the dogs cross the field and race back into the thicket. Jack allowed I might have a better chance if I watched the spot where he'd shot the rabbits. He moved toward the lane. At least I was out of the biting wind. In a half-hour, no bunnies came past me, though Jack yelled one rabbit had just crossed the lane and was headed my way.

When I figured it was about over, I went back to my truck to recover some caloric heat. The dogs were across the driveway, working another thicket. Jack shot again, and missed.

Butch came by and walked down the driveway just when the dogs chased a bunny across it. Bad move for bunny. Butch walked into some high grass and looked around. He picked up a rabbit.

It was long after lunch time, and the fearless bunny busters decided to head to Cambridge in search of vittles. Jack and Butch caught the dogs and put them back in Butch's dog wagon.

At lunch, we relived the morning hunt. I could have crowed that I didn't have to clean my unfired gun, but that's sort of reverse braggadocio, isn't it?

● ● ● ● ● ● ● ● ● ● ● ● ● ● ● ● ●

WATCHING WINTER CRITTERS

Recent snows have brought out the tracker in me. The snow before the "Great Snow of 2003" showed me more than a dozen deer track trails across the lane and into the field the morning after the snow, which was surprising. I haven't seen a deer since the last black powder hunting season. In the extreme cold weather we've had recently, I'm told that deer gather up in deep woods or thickets to share body heat.

Carole just called down to my dungeon to look out by the three tall cedars where Canada geese are trying to snack on grass in a clear spot under the trees. A doe deer was feeding between the geese. Her left front leg was just dangling as if she had been hit by a car or had been shot. We had one such doe here last fall, but she could hobble a bit on the game leg. This one avoided using that leg.

Canada geese have been challenged by the recent storm. In the morning they are rafted up out on the ice in mid-creek. About 9 a.m. they slowly migrate to our yard and walk toward a frozen-over pond. On the way, they stop at the bird feeder outside the kitchen window to snack on a few sunflower seeds we tossed on the snow, or sprayed from the feeder by impatient blue jays. Finding the pond frozen, they peck around under cedar trees for the wintering grass.

There were seven squirrels under the bird feeder this morning, checking out the surplus sunflower seed supply. One had white ears, but I can't remember if that one was Fat Albert, our neighborhood terrorist squirrel. I think I have finally trained the bushytails that climbing up the feeder pole and snacking on sunflower seeds we put there for birds can be a pain. Just inside the side door is a CO_2-powered BB pistol. It makes more racket when fired than it provides pellet pain, and the rascals move too fast to hit, but they stopped climbing the feeder pole. I see squirrel tracks all around the house, as if they're looking for another feeding station.

I haven't seen a rabbit for awhile. Even with our local bald eagles, bunnies are here, but I rabbit hunt elsewhere. However, there are rabbit tracks all around the house. Maybe they frolic at night, or before I get up.

Getting up around here is no problem. Carole's almost-deaf and mostly-blind poodle gets up at 5:30 every morning as if she heard an alarm clock. "Get me outside NOW," she indicates by shaking her tags and flapping her ears. It is a warning not to be taken lightly. Since we have deep snow at every door except the big garage doors, that's where we take turns taking her out. We snap a long rope to her collar in case she gets confused and starts to wander off, which she has done.

One morning on dog duty, Carole noticed a mourning dove banging into the kitchen window, then flapping wings against the aluminum ceiling over the front patio. Then the bird flew past Carole and around the side of the house. It was probably trying to find a warm place out of the cold wind. Winter kill on mourning doves is considerable. I'm told it can be up to 70 percent, maybe higher depending on the severity of the weather. The bird made a repeat performance later, flying down alongside Carole and sitting on the snow. Kind of spooky in the dark, since some people feel it could be an omen of some kind. Maybe doves like women better.

Another set of tracks we see looks like a big dog's pads, or perhaps a very large cat, like a bobcat. We haven't seen any critter like that, and bobcats often scream at night like banshees, something we have not heard. A bobcat scream is hard to forget.

Canada goose tracks litter the snow, and also their copious droppings. Pretty white snow is no longer scenic.

We were finally plowed out. Jimmy Tyler came down our long lane in a big backhoe, pushing mounds of snow ahead of him. He left a few inches of snow pack under him so he wouldn't displace the blue chip stones in the driveway. When Jimmy left, there was an eight-foot-high pile of snow next to the house. Funny, but when I made my first trip down the lane after the plowing, I saw no deer tracks across the lane and into the field. Perhaps the deer are still "yarding up," as I've heard it called.

A group of robins came in, looked at all the snow, and left, most likely for Florida. "You can't trust a robin to predict spring," Carole's mother often said.

Every type of local bird has showed up at the feeder. One bird puzzled Carole, so she looked it up in the bird book. It looked like a mocking bird with a fat gut. "That's what it is," our neighbor, Marilyn Mason said. She also saw it at her feeder. Mockingbirds usually don't go to feeders so I guess the snow made this one desperate. The Masons are more adept at bird identification than we are, so they are often consulted.

● ● ● ● ● ● ● ● ● ● ● ● ● ● ● ● ●

CAMP COOKING

Cooking in the out-of-doors has its benefits, if you enjoy bugs and sand in your food and face. In the last 73 years I have learned what not to do, and one of those things is not to cook outside, but inside where you have electric ranges, dishwashers, and wives to tell you what to do next.

About 57 years ago, I lived in Glen Burnie on the western shore of Maryland which was then a cow town with recently paved roads and about 1000 fine citizens. My buddies from across Oak Lane were the Sears brothers, Calvin and Wesley. We liked to "camp out" at the Sand Caves, which has long since been a housing development on the upper Severn River. The Sears boys had a grandfather who lived in the woods near Herald Harbor, and he had a classic wooden skiff that was ideal for the three of us boys to fish, crab and swim off of.

So, we rode our bikes to gramps' place and walked through the woods to the skiff, then rowed upriver to the Sand Caves for a week or two of hell raising, which 54 years ago, was pretty tame stuff compared to kids these days. The Sears boys were real river rats and I was their avid student. We lived on crabs and fish and canned beans until we ran out, then we went home.

In those days, we poled the skiff from the bow and dipped soft crabs in four to five feet of glass-clear water over grass beds.

The aroma of fried softies wafted across our noses like ambrosia. That was about as close to Heaven as Glen Burnie boys were allowed to get. Slap a fried soft crab between two slices of bread and wash it down with a soda pop. Hot doggies!

Whenever I came home from camping Mom automatically assumed I was dirty and covered with ticks, which was ridiculous since we spent most of our days in the river swimming and trying to sink gramps' rowboat. She made me strip down to bare skin just inside the back door and march straight to the bathtub. She wrinkled up her nose and tossed my clothes down the cellar steps to be dealt with after the bugs had crawled out. What great fun! Makes me all teary-eyed to remember it.

My next experience in outdoors cooking was in Korea in 1952-1953. We were riding in the back of a deuce-and-a-half truck northward toward the front line, or MLR (Main Line of Resistance), when chow time approached. The driver let us put our can of C-Rations on the truck's exhaust manifold to thaw out the grease inside. Since we were traveling light, we all carried "edee-wa" (means "come here" in Japanese) spoons, made by bending the handle of a large spoon around a packsack snap so the utensil would hang on our belts. Since the cooks called "edee-wa" at mealtime, our bent spoons were ever ready. I kept mine in case the Army wants me back.

Keith's "edee-wa" spoon.

I have nothing but praise for our Army cooks. On holidays, we had roast turkey with all the trimmings when we were on the "hill," and we huddled down in a trench to enjoy our repast. The North Koreans, mischievous devils, tossed mortar rounds at us while we ate, really bad form, you know. The exploding ordinance tossed some Korean sand on my turkey which nostalgically took me back to camping at the Sand Caves.

Our company's cook tent was down the back side of a hill we occupied. As I looked down at the tent, which was sandbagged all around about four feet high, a supply truck pulled up and the driver walked into the tent. No sooner than he was inside the sandbags, a mortar round hit the truck's hood and the entire engine disappeared in a shower of parts! Who said the North Koreans had no sense of humor.

I know this story is taking the long way around, but cooking outside doesn't have to be all incoming mortar rounds and sprayed sand. It can be fun, too.

If you want an outdoors ambiance, add or subtract bugs, sand, spices, or incoming artillery to your taste. You're gonna love it!

FORGOTTEN SIGHTS, SOUNDS, & SMELLS

After a recent round of sporting clays, I got out the shotgun cleaning stuff. Ramrod and wire brush, cotton cloth patches, bore cleaner, and RemOil for the final coating of rust proofing.

When I opened the bottle of Hoppe's No. 9 bore cleaner, its distinctive aroma took me back to my youth. Hoppe's has been around a long time, at least 55 years that I know of. The smell of old No. 9 brought back some great memories.

My shirt-tail cousin, the late Cres Bradley of Glen Burnie, Maryland and I often duck hunted behind the Ice House there. Cres and I would sit on a bank overlooking a hairpin turn in Sawmill Branch that supported a freshwater marsh. Mallard ducks would swing past us at eye level as we sat under a tree on the steep bank. After a shot, we had to wade out into the very cold-water stream and pick up our ducks. Who had a Lab retriever back then? In midwinter, that was quite a thrill—we had no hip boots either, only sneakers.

Walking back across the adjacent corn field, Cres asked if I had remembered to get a Federal Duck Stamp. "What's that?" I asked. He said that's what is supposed to be attached to our hunting license. "License?"

Anyway, Cres was a stickler for cleaning the shotguns we used; both were his. I used his dad's old Model 97 Winchester pump with an external hammer. The %$#@& old Model 97 may have killed or wounded more hunters by accident than ducks on purpose. The exposed hammer was always catching on something; twig, weed, clothing, anything, and whether the hammer was cocked or not, you could kiss a leg or foot goodbye.

Cres used a classic old Fox double, which was much more civilized for the time, though it had what today would be called a "hair trigger." The only way to carry it was broken open—but loaded, of course. When we got to Cres' house on Crain Highway, usually soaked to the skin (who had a raincoat?), we'd uncap the Hoppe's No. 9, soak the wire bore brush with it, and work it back and forth through the barrel until no lead deposits showed, then run cloth patches through until it was squeaky clean. Then, a coat of light oil finished the job.

It's funny how little things like sights, sounds, or smells trigger old memories.

The smell of wet Labrador retriever brings instant recall of great waterfowling trips. Most Labs want to get as close as possible to their owners after a swim, but before shaking. Add the aroma of wet Canada goose feathers to that, and total recall is complete.

Days we, as members of the "Sharp" Shooters Club spent in a blind off Morgan Bennett's marsh on the Choptank River, waiting for geese to toll to our decoys, for instance. No dogs on most of those trips, especially after one of our Glen Burnie cop members brought his young Lab one morning. It swam out to get a downed goose and brought back a decoy. Howls of laughter could be heard all the way back to Glen Burnie. He made a house pet out of the mutt, saving him tons of further embarrassment.

When we bought our property in Bozman in 1979, I had a black Lab, Christy. I built a standard 4-foot x 8-foot blind and tied it to a tree along our shore. Before we built a house here, Carole and I—and Christy—hunted that blind with some success. Christy was a great water dog, and brought back many a goose. Every time I get wind of a Lab, wet or dry, it brings back those great hunts. A dry Lab's fur has a pleasant odor, at least to an outdoorsman. It must come from the natural oil on their fur. And, have you ever noticed the sweet, milky smell of a Lab puppy? A wet Lab is something else entirely. When Christy brought a wet goose into the blind and shook, proud of herself, I guess—at least a gallon of saltwater covered everything, including expensive shotguns.

Our Labs are long gone now, but our 13-year-old silver poodle tried to bring in some odors for us to enjoy. She liked to snack on, and roll in, Canada goose droppings, not realizing a bath always follows a roll in what dogs consider perfume—but people don't.

When I walk the poodle on a calm morning, the odor of deer droppings (another great doggie snack) permeates the air. The lawn smells like a barnyard, we have so many deer. This morning, I took the doggy-doo flipper and played lawn golf with deer droppings, flicking them out of the driveway and into the lawn.

While we enjoy watching deer romp and play, the main drawback is deer ticks and Lyme disease. Farmers don't like the way deer munch on emerging soybean plants, either. Hunting season for deer will hopefully thin the local herd a bit.

Sights of fall that increase my pulse include the arrival of Canada geese, leaves changing, striped bass hitting surface plugs as they stoke up on baitfish for the winter, and having a king mackerel jump six feet in the air holding my live bluefish bait like a Lab holds a duck. These are the things of which dreams are made.

Huge vees of Canada geese will call from the sky as they ride cold autumnal winds southward to their Eastern Shore wintering grounds. Their timing is dependable. My friend, the late Bill Perry, outdoors columnist for The Star Democrat, Easton, MD always said Canadas always showed up on September 15. I never kept track of that, but their cries from the heights are a thrill every year.

The sights and smells of saltwater rivers, bays, and the ocean always intrigued me, too. I guess that's why some people follow the water, often hanging on to their favorite harvesting method long after the resource won't provide them a living. They're hooked. Sporties are often "hooked" on declining resources, too. We are happy to fish for stripers, even though we can only keep two a day over 18 inches instead of the 12-inch minimum size and no bag limits we once had.

Ever notice the aroma of live crabs as you lift a trap out of the water at the dock? It's a sort of seaweedy smell. And, notice how some varieties of fish smell different? Menhaden have a pungent odor, which is not always pleasant as they decay in the sun. Most people want to stay upwind of a chum bucket. Those who don't may be hanging over the side shortly. Our vet, the late Dr. Ed Hahn, told me a story about his old Lab, Mack, who kept the boat's deck spotless, even after his daughter was seasick. That's a picture I'm glad I missed.

Rockfish have a different odor, too. It's said to be much like thyme. I don't know about that, but they don't have a fishy smell unless they lay on ice in the store too long. Fish experts sniff a fish's gills to determine freshness, and some say the eyes should be clear and not cloudy. I can say that stripers I've seen in the case on ice never smell like thyme. That's a good reason for catching my own fresh fish.

The smell of pine needles always reminds me of camping out as a kid on the Severn River. The place was called the Sand Caves because the bank was undercut and shallow caves dotted the shoreline. They also caved in regularly, trapping unsuspecting amateur spelunkers.

Other places we camped and hunted (the two were synonymous then) included a place near First Bridge in Glen Burnie when we bailed drinking water out of Sawmill Branch, not realizing a school for delinquent girls dumped raw sewage upstream a few miles away. The stream was clear as a bell there, and people said the gravel and sand bottom purified the water. It had no odor—what did we kids know? But, it always seemed like every place we camped had pine needles on the ground. We'd pile them up and put our blankets on them for a refreshing night's sleep.

An ever-changing scene greets us each morning and evening now across Broad Creek. The light constantly changes and reflects in diverse patterns off the water. Our present view brings back some great memories of our first house on the Little Magothy River in Cape St. Claire across the Bay, where sunrise, a cup of coffee, and a quiet Sunday morning on the porch comprised the ultimate happiness.

Sights, sounds, and smells of the outdoors. They are stored in our own memory banks just waiting for us to recall the good times. Savor them.

The late Os Owings of Jamaica Point Farm in Trappe, Maryland once told me, "The day that makes a memory is never over."

It's true.

Aerie House   **BOOK ORDER FORM**
P. O. Box 279
Bozman, MD 21612-0279
410-745-2236

> AERIE HOUSE WILL PAY FOR SHIPPING TO ONE ADDRESS ON
> PREPAID ORDERS OF 2 OR MORE BOOKS (Any combination).

Author's Signature Only___ Personalized w/names for gift giving?
___yes ___ no. Should we enclose a gift card stating the book is from you?
Yes ___ No ____.

(Please print names)   **Book Title**

_____

_____

_____

CHESAPEAKE OUTDOORS

Number of copies ____ @ $17.95 each $_____

Maryland residents add $.90 sales tax per book $_____

Shipping add $ 2.00 per book $_____

CATCHING STRIPED BASS

Number of copies ___@ 3.95 each $_____

Maryland residents add $.20 sales tax per book $_____

Shipping add $1.10 per book $_____

         TOTAL ENCLOSED $_____

Make Checks or Money Orders Payable to *Aerie House*.

VISA & MC ACCEPTED—CALL OR MAIL ORDER FORM
Send to: Aerie House, P. O. Box 279, Bozman, MD 21612-0279

SHIP BOOKS TO:_____

STREET _____

APT. NO._____ **P. O. BOX NO.**_____

CITY: _____ **STATE:**___ **ZIP:**_____

PHONE #: _____

      (In case we have a ? about your order

VISA or MC NO. _____**EXP. DATE** _____

SIGNATURE:_____

       (Required if using credit card)

Aerie House is a division of Keith Walters LLC
THIS ORDER FORM MAY BE PHOTOCOPIED!